PUNJABI TALIBAN

Driving Extremism in Pakistan

PUNJABI TALIBAN

Driving Extremism in Pakistan

Mujahid Hussain

PENTAGON PRESS

Punjabi Taliban: Driving Extremism in Pakistan / Mujahid Hussain
Translated by Tanvir Afzaal

ISBN 978-81-8274-591-9

First Published in 2012
Reprinted: 2014

Published by
PENTAGON PRESS
206, Peacock Lane, Shahpur Jat,
New Delhi-110049
Phones: 011-64706243, 26491568
Telefax: 011-26490600
email: rajan@pentagonpress.in
website: www.pentagonpress.in

Printed at Avantika Printers Private Limited.

To

The peace loving saints of Punjab
whose land is now under siege by terrorists

Foreword

In the year 2011, it is clear that Pakistan Army will not fight the Taliban and Al-Qaeda the way the world wants it to. The reason is Punjab. Many will find this a strange formulation but the fact is that Al-Qaeda has been rendered impregnable by the shift of allegiance of Punjab's 'non-state actors' from Pakistan Army to Al-Qaeda. The basis of Al-Qaeda's impregnability is in the persistence of Pakistan Army's designation of these 'non-state actors' as state assets and any attack on Al-Qaeda and the Taliban in the Tribal Areas will lead to a backlash in the country's biggest province.

Mujahid Hussain's book tells us how holy warriors using terrorism as their modus operandi have spread out from Punjab to new centres of turmoil in Pakistan's intra-state conflict. The most significant section of the book relates to South Punjab and the rise there of the mother of all terrorists Sipah-e-Sahaba and its various spawn pledged to a war against India, the Shia community, and Iran. The organisation has ruled as coalition partner in Punjab and its leaders have been elected – 'by mistake' – to the federal parliament after the organisation was declared terrorist and banned in the country. The influence of the warriors in Punjab is through intimidation that works both on the people that swell their ranks and the governments at both the federal and provincial levels.

There are factors that persuade Pakistan to fight against the terrorist organisations located on its soil. There are equally a number of factors militating against Pakistan's campaign to fight terrorism. Together, these two contradictory compulsions characterise the current scene. Because of this fault-line of intent, the determination to fight against terror is constantly undermined, leading at times to internal rifts in the institutions that decide and implement anti-terror strategies.

The persuasion to fight terrorism grows out of concern for 'loss of territory' and writ of the state to terrorist organisations that impede exercise of sovereignty. Terrorism undermines the ideology adopted by the state to keep the people of Pakistan united, and therefore terrorism has to be brought under control if not altogether removed. Since 2006, the Planning Commission too has woken up to the fact that two economic functions – investment and exports – are discouraged by Pakistan's lack of 'soft image' which in turn is caused by high levels of violence in society.

The factors militating against the intent to fight terrorism are located within the nature of the state. Pakistan is an 'Islamic state in the making' unlike Iran where a clear status of the Islamic state has been achieved through 'legitimate' use of coercion by the clergy. In so far as terrorists claim to fight for the implementation of the true Islamic system (sharia) they usurp and supersede the function of the Islamic state. The sharia does not accept the modern state that punishes only crime (munkiraat) and is not able to punish lack of piety (marufaat). The Taliban claim to perform both functions and are supported by the network of madrassas and the clergy.

The state has used terrorists in the past through 'non-state actors' in a foreign policy of covert 'proxy war' in Afghanistan and India. It has not abandoned its intent to do so even after these elements have aligned themselves with Al-Qaeda and the Taliban. The use of fully armed non-state actors in deniable wars has tended to create multiple centres of power in Pakistan, meaning that the state has abdicated a large portion of its claim on the 'monopoly of violence' in the Weberian sense. Parts of the state handling these clerically headed non-state organisations have suffered a split from the decision-making apparatus of the state, in this case the military and the intelligence agencies.

The security institutions of the state are indoctrinated to link the survival of Pakistan to conflict with India. This gives rise to an ambivalence that undermines the fight against terrorism. There is a tendency to blame terrorism on India in the face of clear evidence that violence is being perpetrated by the non-state actors trained by the state as jihadi organisations to fight India. Psychologically, this is the most dangerous hurdle in the national effort to overcome terrorism and normalise the state. The conflict with India is embedded in Pakistan's nationalism, based on textbooks and the message from the media, which Pakistan lacks the intellectual suppleness to remove. Anti-Americanism and anti-Westernism radiating from the Islamic world in general and the Middle East in particular muddy the water further.

Who are the terrorists? There is a regular stream of incoming Arab warriors that Pakistan facilitated during the war against the Soviet Union in Afghanistan. This 'replenishing' stream still continues and forms the inner core of Al-Qaeda located inside Pakistan. This foreign 'manpower' injection also includes expatriate Pakistanis who no longer integrate in the Western societies where they live. Both types imbibe terrorism from clerics: expatriate workers in the Middle East are radicalised in sympathy with local populations mostly alienated from their 'pro-West' ruling elites; expatriate Pakistanis from Europe embrace violent worldviews owing to their alienation from the societies where they live.

Money is a major cause behind conversion of normal Pakistanis into terrorists. Even the jihadis whom the state used against India were in most cases attracted to the meagre support offered by the state to help their families back home. (Most jihadi organisations were made self-financing with the passage of time.) Later Al-Qaeda began to pay large sums to the affected families; and its warlord Baitullah Mehsud was allowed to accumulate enough wealth to pay Rs 6 lakhs (600, 000) for each child suicide-bomber supplied mostly from Punjab by businesslike clerics with expertise in 'persuasion'. Reports have now confirmed that children are being forced to become suicide-bombers. Punjab leads in the support to state's India-centrism — the jihadis have come mostly from Punjab where 60 per cent of Pakistan's population lives.

South Punjab is once again in focus with India asking Pakistan to punish the terrorists located on its soil, and Pakistan asking India to make a move on the resolution of the Kashmir issue. The Pakistani challenge is expected to come in the shape of an increased ingress of non-state actors into Kashmir across the Line of Control. Since a large number of the non-state actors have joined Al-Qaeda and the Taliban in the latter's campaign to punish Pakistan through terrorism for cooperating with the US in Afghanistan, getting a fresh crop of non-state actors out of them is going to be difficult. The two jihadi organisations most expected to do the job – Jaish Muhammad and Lashkar Tayba – are located in Punjab. Out of the two, the latter is less involved with the Taliban terrorism against Pakistanis, but its sympathies for the 'Arabs fighting the Americans' are also known.

Maulana Muhammad Azam Tariq, killed on 6 October 2003 along with four bodyguards in a drive-by shooting at a toll plaza near Islamabad, was the charismatic leader of Sipah-e-Sahaba who converted Punjab into the hinterland of terrorist jihad and supplied Sindh and Karachi –his alma mater was in Karachi - with a new strain of sectarian violence. He won the National Assembly constituency in 1990, 1993 and in October 2002. The 1990 election was particularly a big success when Tariq defeated the government-backed candidate Sheikh Yusuf by a big margin. In the 2002 election under Musharraf, he contested the election from jail. The government, first let him contest the elections, then filed a petition in the Lahore High Court challenging the Pakistan Election Commission's decision to allow him to stand despite the cases against him.

Sipah-e-Sahaba succeeded in getting two members inducted into the Punjab cabinet of chief minister Sardar Arif Nakai in 1995, beginning the conversion of a traditionally peaceful Barelvi Punjab to a violent territory bristling with jihadi enthusiasm. Today, it is well set to become the behind-the-scenes ruler of the province with an important nexus with Al-Qaeda. An offshoot of the Sipah called Jaish-e-Muhammad became the Army's favourite fighting arm, led to the despatch of 500,000 jihadis to the disputed Kashmir Valley to fight the Indian soldiers.

The foreign policy of Pakistan is in the hands of the army. The PPP government in power is too involved in its battle with the state judiciary and its rival party Pakistan Muslim (Nawaz) or PMLN to compete with the military for the running of Pakistan's international relations, especially the ties with India. It has therefore joined the 'national consensus' against India and is promoting a revival of the Kashmir issue on the basis of the 'jihad leverage'. In Punjab, the PMLN is securing the electoral ground for a victory in the midterm elections when they come, by aligning themselves with the Deobandi elements dominant in South Punjab. Already many of its local supporters in that region belong to Sipah-e-Sahaba and its sister organisation Jaish, the outfit that fights Pakistan's battles with India.

What is happening in Punjab at the present moment? Jihadi publication daily *Islam* (23 Feb 2010) reported that Punjab Law Minister Rana Sanaullah visited Jhang and paid his respects at the tomb of the founder of the greatest banned sectarian-terrorist Deobandi organisation, Sipah-e-Sahaba: Maulana Haq Nawaz Jhangvi. He led a delegation of the PMLN which also counted parliamentary secretary Iftikhar Baloch and party MPA from Jhang, Sheikh Yaqub. He visited the tombs of other Sipah-e-Sahaba martyr-leaders like Maulana Isarul Qasimi and Allama Azam Tariq. *The News* (27 Feb 2010) in a report titled *PMLN sees no harm in seeking banned outfit's blessing* observed: 'A defunct sectarian organisation, Sipah-e-Sahaba, is rearing its head again and its leaders' participation in an election rally in PP-82 constituency, along with Punjab Law Minister Rana Sanaullah, has sent shivers down the spines of citizens here, who have seen sectarian bloodshed for over a decade before it subsided in 2002'.

Pakistan has become 'path dependent' in its embrace of the doctrines of strategic depth and India-centrism. And most of soldiers to make this strategy operational emanate from Punjab. The public mind mostly located in Punjab is prepared against India on the basis of textbook nationalism inculcated over the past decades; in the case of Afghanistan, the public mind is imbued with an intense anti-Americanism issuing from pan-Islamic sources. In both instances, the state encourages a schizoid national identity that ignores contradiction so that no change in the embraced foreign policy doctrines is allowed. In the coming days, the nexus of terror in Punjab will come to represent the true face of the Pakistani state using non-state actors as its instrument of expansionism. Mujahid Hussain's narrative of Punjab in the following pages will make that perfectly clear.

Khaled Ahmed
Lahore

Preface

The prevalent situation in Punjab resembles the terror-hit areas of Pakistan where the power and authority of the State is practically non-existent. The nation is not in tandem with the State about such a war. According to the opinion makers and influential figures from the right-wing, this is not Pakistan's war and Pakistan is throwing away its precious resources in this war by 'others' and killing its compatriots just to please others. Unfortunately, the people who are considered 'our own' never miss any opportunity of hitting hard on Pakistan's army, its citizens, and its public institutions.

Pakistan's largest province has become the target of terrorists and sectarian elements who are spreading terror every day through their deadly attacks. It is an astonishing fact that these terrorists also enjoy the support of the local cohorts. These terrorists have been trained by the powerful institutions in Pakistan with the purpose of defeating the 'enemy'. According to a careful estimation, the number of such *jihadis* and sectarian elements exceeds 150,000 and they not only have been imparted training but are also being provided financial assistance and safe havens. Now the Pakistani State is at the mercy of such an enemy that has all the characteristics of ancient tribal warriors but who still enjoys social support.

Some very remarkable changes have taken place in Punjab in between the first and the second Urdu edition of this book. Punjabi Taliban has also started targeting the Sufi shrines in various towns of Punjab and most importantly a new series of attacks against minorities has also been unleashed, which is fiercer and more fatal than those in the past. For example, in Lahore two places of worship of the Ahmadiyya community were targeted by suicide bombers wherein approximately 100 people lost their lives. But the federal and provincial governments did not have the courage to show their empathy with the victims and left them utterly helpless. None of the senior government officials turned up to show sympathy with the victims because of the widespread fear of the religious zealots who consider the Ahmadiyya community anti-Islamic hence, anti-Pakistan. An emotionally charged Nawaz Sharif, former Prime Minister of Pakistan, declared the Ahmadis as his brethren but following a huge hue and cry in the media he hurriedly issued an explanation that they were called brethren because they were compatriots and that brotherhood was not based on faith.[1]

After the massacre, the bigots again turned the attention towards their anti-Shiite campaign and there is no letting go of it. There is no doubt that the Punjabi Taliban and their auxiliary outfits are vehemently trying to capture Punjab and they seem to be successful in this campaign. A Barelvi-Deobandi war has started in various parts of Punjab and the frequency of the attacks on shrines has enhanced. The Barelvis allege that the extremist Deobandi *jihadis* and the sectarian elements are targeting the clerics of the Barelvi sect as well as their shrines on the behest of some powerful players of the present government of Punjab. The most criticised person is the Provincial Law Minister Rana Sanaullah who allegedly has close ties with Maulana Muhammad Ahmed Ludhianvi the key leader of Sipah-e-Sahaba who is busy in a fierce war of turf with the famous Barelvi cleric and member of national assembly, Sahibzada Fazal-e-Karim in Faisalabad, the hometown of Rana Sanaullag. It is worthwhile to mention that Rana Sanaullah has claimed to have made some extraordinary efforts to get a piece of land worth, 350 million rupees, allotted by the Government of Punjab to the seminary of Sahibzada Fazil-e-Karim who is still not satisfied and has continued with his campaign against Rana Sanaullah.[2]

There is not the remotest possibility of any crackdown against sectarian forces and religious extremist outfits in Punjab as in almost every bye election the incumbent government of the Pakistan Muslim League (PML) faces defeat and thus favours the strategy of getting help from militant groups to counter the increasing popularity of the

Pakistan People's Party. The close rapport of PML with the banned sectarian organisations and other *jihadi* outfits is increasing which has prompted the Chief of Army Staff to caution the Chief Minister of Punjab about the ever increasing wallop of militants in his province. The government has not shown any interest in controlling the Talibanisation of Punjab. Certain events clearly point towards further deterioration of the situation where violent attacks on various sects, the State, and its administrative institutions are inevitable.

Many extremist killers arrested in Punjab get substantial relief from the courts because the law enforcement agencies (*a*) are unable to provide sufficient evidence against them; (*b*) fear them; and (*c*) have a soft corner for them. For example, provincial government is patronising them with the intention of getting its militant might enhanced in future; a fact played down by the mainstream media as many in the sector have sectarian tendencies or sympathise with extremist religious outfits. If any independent reporter tries to expose this fact then the report does not get published and even if it does, the reporter faces serious threats to his life. The horrific murder of an investigative reporter of an English newspaper in Rawalpindi who was researching in Rawalpindi and Islamabad about Taliban and their supporters, is one such example. After his murder, his newspaper and even his colleagues kept mum on an 'advice' from Taliban and their supporters as well as from some high government officials. Thus the life of an independent and brave journalist was wasted in vain.[3]

Recently an old friend of mine, who is an editor of a national newspaper from Islamabad, called me in London to tell me about the praise he got for one of his columns from the I.G. Police Commissioner as he had written a very forceful and emotional column in favour of the chief of an extremist sectarian organisation. He added that various high-ranking officials in Punjab both covertly and overtly support Taliban as they believe that it is better than the corrupt political leadership and they (Talibans) have the capability to establish a rule of law and justice in Pakistan unlike the civil government.[4]

The beginning of year 2011 in Pakistan was quite shocking as the Governor of Punjab, Salman Taseer, was assassinated by one of his bodyguards. It is worthwhile to note that in the service book of the bodyguard it was clearly stated that he may never be deputed as an escort for any V.I.P. due to his dubious character. Later the assassin, Mumtaz Qadri, held Salman Taseer responsible for this own murder because he had branded the infamous Blasphemy Laws as Black Laws when visiting a jailed Christian woman, Aasia Bibi, in prison. She has been sentenced to death on the charges of blasphemy. After the cold-blooded murder of Salman Taseer, a heated debate among his supporters, extremist religious groups and political parties has sprouted and they, including a great number of Pakistani citizens, believe that his murder was 'justified'. Maulana Fazal-ur-Rehman even launched a campaign of safeguarding the honour of Holy Prophet Muhammad. The Federal Interior Minister, Rahman Malik, has advised the Ex-Federal Information Minister, Sheri Rahman, to leave Pakistan, as her life is also under great threat after the murder of Salman Taseer. It is worthwhile to mention that Ms Rahman had drafted a bill suggesting amendments in the existing Blasphemy Law. Prime Minister Yousaf Raza Gilani did not condemn Salman Taseer's assassination, as he himself is a follower of Barelvi sect and he was afraid of any fatwa against him from Deobandi clerics or from any Deobandi organisation.[5]

Mumtaz Qadri has been hailed as a hero by the Barelvi organisations and the leader of Pakistan Muslim League, Vakeel Niazi, and the local Barelvi clerics garlanded him when he was brought to court for the initial hearing. Mumtaz Qadri who is a follower of Barelvi sect, has also been given the title of 'Ghazi' and more than 5000 people gathered to greet his father at the hearing.. They were chanting slogans in favour of Mumtaz Qadri and they gave him a ride over their shoulders. After observing that Mumtaz Qadri has been 'fostered' by the famous Barelvi leadership, the Deobandi parties are withdraw up their support, while the chief cleric of the renowned Deobandi seminary, Jamia Banoria Karachi, has strongly condemned the campaign where Mumtaz Qadri is presented as a hero. This edict is based more on their sectarian hatred for the Barelvi organisations than on any of their own religious conviction because these outfits are gaining mass support due to Barelvi affiliations of Mumtaz Qadri.[6]

This humble effort to study the existing situation of Punjab would not have been possible without the valuable assistance of many of my friends and I am highly grateful to them. I have always got the love and affection of my friends in Pakistan and whenever I returned there, I have always of the best input from these intellectuals and researchers. Khalid Ahmad, Wajahat Masood, Tanveer Jehan, Amir Rana, Sabir Nazar, Zakriya Khan, Tanvir Afzaal Zaigham Khan and Riaz Danishwar have provided me guidance. The love and affection particularly of Andleeb Haider, Muhammad Ali, Aleena Fatima, Sarah Hussain, Zaki Hussain, Mariyam and Hussain from South Punjab has always proved a valuable support for me. I feel special gratitude for my old buddy, Malik Sarfraz Ahmad, who extended great help in this study. I am also grateful to my Urdu publisher who persistently encouraged me for this research and provided me with books and other relevant material for my research.

September 2011
Islamabad

Mujahid Hussain

Contents

1
Identity of Pakistani State

Finally, the Taliban has selected Punjab for its heinous activities where their suicide attackers are killing dozens of people every day. Although the Taliban were fighting unitedly against the Pakistan army, the police and the Shiite community in the tribal regions as well as settled areas of Khyber-Pakhtunkhwa previously, but after a partially successful military operation in Swat and eventually the start of an offensive in the terrorists' hub of South Waziristan, they have headed towards Punjab and Islamabad. Unfortunately, the current policy adopted by them has proved more effective and fatal and has jolted the very foundation of the Pakistani state. It was reckoned earlier that these hardened fighters and experts of guerilla warfare in hilly areas would not come down to the plain areas. However the perception did not prove to be true and they have been visibly successful in planning and implementation of more effective attacks in urban areas. That these terrorists enjoy the full backing of local extremists and sectarian mindsets of Punjab is the most threatening demonstration of this phenomenon as this beckoning has made their attacks even more deadly and precarious.

On the other hand, it is becoming increasingly hard for the rightwing intellectuals and defence analysts of Pakistani mainstream media to continue their support for their long-time cynosures because at present Taliban are not any more an organisation of terrorists. Mainly Pashtuns from the tribal belt and countless Jihadists and sectarian elements from Punjab have joined their ranks, who are engaged in hitting the local targets and fortifying their centres in different areas of the province. The centre of right Punjab Government lead by Pakistan Muslim League (Nawaz) now finds itself on tenterhooks due to ever increasing pressure by the federal government and the army that it should have a firm control over the emerging local Taliban. The Provincial Law Minister of Punjab has categorically denied the existence of any Taliban in Punjab and that his government does not intend to conduct any operation in the province in near future, particularly in the South of Punjab.[7]

Despite all the said factors the continuous defence and apology for the Taliban militants in Pakistani media is a painful sight, while on the other hand condemnation for these brutal acts of slaughtering innocent civilians by them, is almost non-existent on talk shows as well as in editorial pages. On the other hand after every gruesome incident people are subjugated to the farcical repetition of condolence messages while an equally tiring response by governmental and non-official circles is churned out as a ritual. The clerics are in unison that many outside forces are determined to weaken the Pakistani state and majority of right wing religious politicians hold India, the US and Israel responsible for the current reign of terrorism. The leaders like the newly-elected head of Jamaat Islami Munawar Hassan, their former chief Qazi Hussain Ahmed as well as Imran Khan and Hameed Gul share the same opinion about the present situation, which according to them, is a logical consequence of pursuing American policies. Although the rest of religious leaders are also not willing to go beyond expressing their condolence for such incidents, but if any impartial investigation of the current wave of terrorism in Punjab and the reasons behind them is made, many of these sacrosanct clerics would be found to be culprits themselves.[8]

The present chief of Jamaat-e-Islami publicly owns his predilection for Taliban. It is not simply an expression of the hatred for the west but the underlying motive is to regain the lost political dominance, for example in Karachi, and it is only possible to achieve this with the help of Taliban. For the moment they do not seem to care how high a price the whole nation would have to bear. Moreover the present chief of Jamaat-e-Islami is also negating the idea of 'unity among different Muslims sect' put forward by his predecessor, Qazi Hussain Ahmed while he seems well aware of whom to rely upon for future political and military dominance. We must not ignore the fact that the new head of Jamaat-e-Islami is yearning to take back his party in the heyday of Afghan Jihad, besides getting full support of ex-khakis, the torch bearers of the fundamentalist Islamic revolution in Pakistan who had been patronising the Jamaat-e-Islami to get undue political benefits in the past as well.

The elements engaged in crippling Punjab have been declared local jihadis by the federal government and they intend to capture the state by weakening the security institutions. However the religious political parties are adamant about the involvement of local jihadis and they are in the habit of pointing fingers at India. According to them it is not only desirable to even the account of Mumbai attacks but to punish Pakistan for its role in Kashmir as well. But the claim instead of being based on facts, is much like some 'ritualistic belief'. Otherwise it would have provided best prospects to Pakistan to do away with the insult faced at the international level because of the Mumbai attacks. As Pakistan does not have any proof of India's connection in such attacks, the wishful thinking of religious parties and militants remain unfulfilled whereas the attack on Army's General Head Quarter (GHQ) has proven an all-out support of jihadis and sectarian outfits of Punjab for terrorist elements. The members of banned militant organisations of Punjab are not only fighting along Al-Qaeda and Taliban but are collaborators in suicide bombing and other acts of terrorism in Islamabad and Punjab as well.[9]

The international community has grave concerns over the security of Pakistan and there is increasingly a perception that it would sooner or later be declared a dangerous an unstable country like Iraq and Afghanistan. Pakistan has almost been completely deprived of foreign investment after the deadly attacks at Marriott Hotel and presently the flow of capital to Pakistan is non-existent except for relief funds during natural calamities. After the utter failure of state machinery in blocking the Taliban and their supporters, responsible for launching deadly attacks against the state institutions and the followers of other sects, the future affairs in Pakistan bear highly gloomy features.

It is difficult to predict whether political parties of Pakistan or its civil society could ever be able to launch any worthwhile movement that would have the capacity to weaken or let alone to single out the extremists at public level. The presence of some very powerful supporters of the militants in political parties and the country's media, who strive very hard to block the secular persons or parties from coming into power, could be the main reason behind it. These elements have the greatest desire to expel the incumbent government from the corridors of power and they allegedly enjoy the support of some strong political forces as well. Essentially this war is one of the most decisive ones among all the battles being fought for the survival of the state, and it would also determine the features and the future of the state. On a media dominated by rightists, it is almost impossible to kick-start any debate regarding the root causes for the present state of affairs in Pakistan as the majority of the intellectuals has already held a lop-sided but determined opinion that the hatred for Islam by the US, India and Israeli; their intolerant attitude towards the nuclear assets of Pakistan; and the desire of the 'Veteran Satan' i.e. the U.S. to pitch the 'Islamic Army' of Pakistan against the devout mujahideens and to capture its nuclear assets, are the major reasons of the problems confronting the integrity of Pakistan. The orthodox and retrogressive forces have a great clout in almost every institution of the state and they are trying hard to make violence and hostility a second nature for the states institutions and its people. Viewed in historical perspective, it is not a new phenomenon at all as our state has been facing such attitudes and mindsets from the onset and these very ideologues had been 'blessing' the newly established state with their distorted narratives and staggered directions.

Historically, it would be highly difficult to prove whether any clear intent to the true nature of the intended Muslim state existed or not, when a separate homeland for Muslims of South Asia was being demanded. The current insistence on the religious identity of the state of Pakistan is the result of the later occurrence of incidents apart from the strenuous efforts by the "religious architects" for laying some self-styled "ideological foundations" of Pakistan. Essentially the present insistence on such an identity seem to be part of the process of establishing an Islamic state, started when a draft named Objective Resolution was prepared by a cleric who was not an elected member of parliament. However the bill was presented in the constituent assembly on 12th March 1949 as a part of framing the constitution for the new state. Neither did this kind of perception, exist earlier, nor did the ideas and actions of the founder of Pakistan hardly give any impression that he intended to establish a theocratic state where the followers of the majority religion would be given a free hand to exclude the people of minority beliefs and creeds from the decision-making process on the key issues, in utter disregard of democratic norms.[10]

If one conducts a thorough study on the earlier days of independence of Pakistan, he/she would come to know that although the shape of an ideological state was given to Pakistan on the bases of sectarian observations and experiences of the Muslims in undivided India, unfortunately the same people were engaged in laying the "ideological foundations" of the newly born country, who, during the last violent days of the Independence movement, had gone through traumatic situations in Hindu majority areas and had to face loss of life and property by the Hindu and Sikh extremists during migration towards the newly-found country. No doubt, a vast majority of such people had to go through a tormenting situation before they reached the promised land of Pakistan. That their Muslim identity is the fundamental cause behind these hardships and difficulties; this belief took deep root in their mind due to the circumstances they had to go through. No wonder then that Hafiz Muhammad Saeed, chief of Lashkar-e-Tayyba (L-e-T) declares today that his jihadi outfit would bleed every part of India and after conquering it, would bring back the golden era of Muslim rule in India. In the backdrop of the massacre of 36 family members of Hafiz Muhammad Saeed by Hindu and Sikh marauders during the migration process, such kind of revengeful thoughts should easily be comprehensible.[11]

Shortly after the partition, the religious outfits with a lower level influence in the urban areas started challenging the ambiguous bases of the newly found state whereas it was very easy for famous religious scholars and intellectuals to compare the difficulties and hardships of newly established state with the features of the state of Medina and the situations faced by the followers of Prophet Muhammad during the earlier days of Islam. The vague and outdated ideas in the Muslim history regarding the basis of a state further fortified this notion. Thus the process of transforming Pakistan into a theocratic state soon after the adoption of the Objective Resolution in 1949, elevated the clergy in the role of self-proclaimed custodians of the fundamental principles of the state. It was the starting point for the clergy towards gaining power along with other retrogressive forces whereas the weak political leadership finally gave in and the army started ruling the country directly 1958 onwards. The Pakistani state neither has been able to get rid of the clutches of the orthodox forces since then, nor has it ever managed to free itself of the grip of the unholy alliance of the religious-military elements. The civilian leadership continues to be weak and a 'suspect' in the eyes of military and mullahs (clerics).[12]

Led by a so-called pious (but in fact) a hardliner sectarian chief named General Zia-ul-Haq, the Pakistan army once again staged a coup d'état; and this time the army had the support of some power-hungry politicians, the staunch supporter of a fundamentalist Islamic revolution in Pakistan i.e. Jamaat-e-Islami and right-wing traders who had already heavily financed the movement of anti-Bhutto protests. By declaring the ideology as its base, the army deviated from its erstwhile professional identity of secular traditions, resulting in gradual Islamisation of the army and the business and industrial elites at the same time. After the complete Islamisation of the society, the democratic institutions set up by General Zia provided an opportunity of turning the state laws into Shariah laws. The 'ideological state' of Pakistan was among the third world countries that were on the verge of economic failure. The ideological precedents set in Pakistan were directly associated with extremism. These precedents were unfamiliar for the modern world, whereas countries like Iran had already set an example for it. Pakistani ideologues were of the view that they were busy transforming Pakistan into a state that is not only capable of leading the Islamic world, but also it would be hard for the developed world to ignore it economically due to its 'geo-political' significance.[13]

However the state of Pakistan, rapidly moving away from modern world views had to face severe economic crisis before the very eyes of these ideologues and prior to the USSR invasion of Afghanistan, the economic situation of Pakistan started deteriorating at a quicker pace. Through participating in the Afghan war that continued for around 10 years and getting some financial relief from the United States and Saudi Arabia, the Pakistan army managed to halt this economic crisis temporarily in the decade of 80's. In the meantime, the religious outfits of the country had weilded immense power and an elevated status in the society due to army's inclination toward the process of religious purification as well as the Jihad in Afghanistan. The efforts of giving an Islamic hue to the society and implementation of Shariah, laws had blessed these outfits with more power as compared to the other groups having vested interests. The process of Islamisation within the army diminished the distinction between the religious segments of society and the army officers that were being recruited from the middle class.

Under the patronage of the Pakistan army, the religious outfits were permitted to recruit their own militia. Inter-Services Intelligence (ISI) was especially assigned with this 'pious duty' and within no time, local militia brigades a la Afghanistan, led by religious leaders, started to emerge. The services of student wing of Jamaat-e-Islami were specifically utilised for this purpose and the youth of the educational institutions from all over Pakistan were put to support the Afghan warlords of their choice. The national media of Pakistan portrayed the militant leaders such as Gulbadin Hikmatyar as saviours of Afghanistan whereas thousands of new recruits, after giving a proper militant training, were handed over to him. Meanwhile, the army of Pakistan and its powerful intelligence agencies had clearly defined the fronts where these 'religious militias' prepared by them would fight their battle.

When the Jihadist scenario changed after the Soviet retreat from Afghanistan in 1989 and as such there was no utilisation of those mercenaries in Pakistan, the 'Kashmir Wing' of I.S.I. was established, that would use the armed brigades of religious parties of Pakistan to continue a low intensity war in the Indian occupied Kashmir. The clergy of Pakistan became stronger with every passing day, due to the direct patronage of the defence establishment and the state. At the same time, the concept of Jihad by non-state actors was introduced at the expense of the internal solidarity of the country. The jihadists, chiefs of armed private militias as well as the warlords became much more important and influential than the elected political leadership. Though the idea of state presented by these powerful religious leaders was altogether utopian, they still succeeded in discrediting democracy as a foreign ideology, that could only help the corrupt people thrive. Renowned journalist Khaled Ahmad writes:

> "For them the democracy was acceptable under the shariah only. Most of the religious leaders did not agree with the shariah laws implemented by General Zia-ul-Haq either. On the other hand, the elected representatives indulged in pilferage of state resources and misuse of their offices, because a situation of uncertainty always prevailed about their tenure, moreover they were practically deprived of any real power. However the material corruption on a far bigger scale by the clergy was such a thing that has never been and might never be challenged at any forum. The country was declared a state heading towards a fast deterioration or such a failed state that could collapse anytime under the burden of its foreign debts"[14]

Khaled Ahmed further writes that after the partition of the sub-continent, the state of Pakistan started progress towards implementation of shariah considering it an important tool of nation building. It had realised at a very early stage, that the target of Islamic legislation would not be possible to achieve in the circumstance of some sentimental and low church affiliations of the people about religion, so the clergy would have to be taken on board in order to legitimise the state institutions. So the Council of Islamic Ideology (CII) was set up pretty soon, especially comprising some experts of Islamic jurisprudence that had the majority of clerics from the Deobandi minority sect (believing and practising a high church religion). However the Sufism could not be relied upon as the fundamentals of an ideological state. In the C.I.I., comparatively enlightened scholars like Dr. Fazal-ur-Rehman were not tolerated for a longer period of time and the dominance by the clerics from the seminaries reached at its peak when the founder of Jamia Banoria Karachi Maulana Yousaf Banori was appointed the chairman of C.I.I.[15]

The state of Pakistan kept on ceding space for the religious bigots and the powerful institutes of state continued pushing forward their ill-famed doctrine of 'strategic depth' by dint of their power and clout. Pakistan had a renewed interest in Afghanistan and the process of providing reinforcement to the hardliner religious force started under the name of Taliban. The rise of Taliban in Afghanistan and inclusion of jihad in the Kashmir in Pakistan, shunned the people of Barelvi sect out of the battlefields of jihad arranged by Pakistan. No Barelvi was eligible for jihad in Afghanistan as their Islam was not considered 'authentic' by the sponsors of Jihad. So a considerable number of Barelvi students started getting admission in Deobandi and Wahhabi madrassas before going to Afghanistan. The people of Shiite sect were intentionally kept away from Jihadi centres as well as other institutions of religious dominance, because a cold war between the biggest Muslim sponsors of jihad i.e. Saudi Arabia and the Shiite Iran was on its peak and keeping away the Shiite of Pakistan was considered the best option under the circumstances.

Saudi Arabia provided the initial capital for the Zakat fund established by General Zia-ul-Haq on the condition that an important Wahhabi seminary in Faisalabad would also be given a major chunk of it as a grant. It is worthwhile to mention that later in 2002, an important operative of Al-Qaeda named Abu-Zubaida, was captured from the same city. The former Chief of Army Staff General Aslam Baig was the first person to allow the Deobandi seminaries to establish the armed wings of their youth in Bahawalpur and Rahim Yar Khan. These youth were supposed to be utilised as 'second defence line' in case of any possible Indian attack via Rajasthan. The Arab Sheikhs were enjoying a regal status in the areas. They used to come here for hunting of some rare species of birds and a practice of financial support to religious seminaries also started after a rapport was developed between the Arabs and the local seminaries. The same financial support gave rise to militant outfit Sipah-e-Sahaba under the leadership of Haq Nawaz Jhangvi who was considered an utter enemy of Shiites and the Islamic Republic of Iran. Anti-Shiite sentiments as well as the dominance of Deobandi sect, was the prominent feature of jihadi outfits during the heydays of jihad in Pakistan. These jihadists were also used in target killing of important Shiite personalities and for this purpose the Sipah-e-Sahaba normally selected the youth that either had experience of jihad in Kashmir or were ready to join any possible jihadi caravan. In these circumstances they also enjoyed the 'support' of some powerful institutions of the state and in case they were found involved in any sectarian crime the local police never risked to arrest them and dare to confront strong institutions like I.S.I. A host of examples of how these sectarian killers, after assassinating members of opponent sects managed to safely enter into Kashmir or Afghanistan under the protected shields of I.S.I. could be cited the police was unable to arrest them despite all the knowledge about them.[16]

After the withdrawal of Soviet forces from Afghanistan, there was a time when jihadis of Afghanistan were still not pitched against each other; a large number of jihadis from Pakistan and the tribal areas were "dedicated" for Kashmir through the endeavors by the I.S.I. The parties like Jamaat-e-Islami and other militant outfits that were considered main beneficiaries of jihad, quickly shifted their focus towards Kashmir along with their previous stores of arms and ammunitions. The centre of jihad gradually started shifting towards Rawalpindi instead of Peshawar and various religious parties of Pakistan started establishing their Jihadi wings, the majority of whom belonged to the Deobandi sect. It is interesting to note that Sheikh Rasheed Ahmed, a famous political leader of the country who had also served as Federal Minister many times, also used to operate a jihadi camp to help the mujahideens from Kashmir where he got the opportunity to establish some close contacts with I.S.I. and other secret agencies of the army. Sheikh Rasheed has never denied it, rather Indian authorities also cited his help for mujahideen from Kashmir as the main reason to refuse granting him visa to India while he was a sitting federal minister of Pakistan.

The extremist Deobandi organisations also quickened the pace of their 'jihad' against Shiites as soon as the holy war in Kashmir formally began and the contents of sectarian curriculum in Deobandi seminaries were fortified as well. The Shiites of Pakistan, on the other hand, were under the influence of the overemotional leadership of Tehreek-e-Nafaz-e-Fiqah-e-Jafria and were busy targeting their opponents with the support of Iran. The I.S.I. and other influential secret agencies continued their support for Taliban in Pakistan and helped the Deobandi militants from Karachi to Peshawar because they were not only fighting the war of I.S.I. in Kashmir but were also becoming a part of various warring factions in Afghanistan under the signals from Pakistani establishment. The seminary of Jamia Islamia at Banori Town, Karachi that was engaged in the "training" of Taliban militants could be named the main seminary indulged in extremism and religious terrorism because not only was the support of Taliban in Afghanistan at full swing but the Jihad in Kashmir and at the "internal" fronts of Pakistan against the opponent sects, was also in full swing while this seminary was playing a principal role in all these affairs.

Apart from the patronage by the state to the seminaries and the clergy of Deobandi sect, the Wahhabi groups and outfits were also provided with full logistic support through Saudi connections to create a specific jihadi atmosphere and to prepare the jihadis against the "enemies" of Pakistan. At present there are 17 Wahhabi organisations in Pakistan, six of them are active in politics whereas three have the honour of participating in Jihad as well. All of them have vast differences of opinion on the strategy of jihad in Pakistan as well as on general dogmatic issues which at times take a serious shape of condemnation as well as mud slinging on each other, as we have observed in the case of Markazi Jamiat Ahle Hadith and Lashkar-e-Tayyba (LeT) of Hafiz Muhammad Saeed.[17]

Another Salfi (Wahhabi) organisation Jamiat Ghurba-e-Ahle-Hadith is of the view that its supporter should continue to covertly oppose the existing political system till the majority of population converts to Wahhabi sect; after that Pakistan would automatically transform itself into an Islamic state. The Jamaat-ul-mujahdeen thinks that the current political arrangement would remain illegitimate until the system of Caliphate is not restored, so we would not participate in the politics. However we would continue to strive for the establishment of an Islamic state. The organisation of Hafiz Muhammad Saeed holds similar views. In fact, only Jamaat-ud-Dawa wields the clout of the scale that has ability to get the attention of the powers to be in Islamabad. The influence of the said outfit can be judged by the fact that no government in Pakistan has the guts to put the chief of this organisation behind the bars. When Lashkar-e-Tayyba (LeT) the armed wing of that organisation wreaked havoc in Mumbai, everyone in Pakistan was afraid of the harsh reaction by India and while Pakistani Ministry of Foreign Affairs was begging the international community to control the enraged India from any possible operation, Jamaat-ud-Dawa was busy receiving felicitation messages from its supporters and it training camps still involved in militant training of thousands of youths.[18]

At the moment Lashkar-e-Tayyba, the armed wing of Jamaat-ud-dawa, is the most powerful jihadist outfit of Pakistan with the greatest number of militants. Although the organisation is facing some hardships in getting donations or other financial resources, due to successive international restrictions as well as some half-hearted steps against it at the national level. However, it is next to impossible to stop the affluent traders and industrialist, especially from Punjab to extend financial support to the organisation. The big donors to the organisation include expatriate Pakistanis, apart from some oil-rich sheikhs of the gulf region. For example, an Ahle-hadith (Wahhabi) Pakistani living in Brescia, Italy remitted hundreds of thousands of rupees to Karachi through Western Union for purchase of arms and other equipment for Mumbai attacks. After he was apprehended by the Italian police, he confessed to having remitted big amounts to the members of Lashkar-e-Tayyba (LeT) but he seemed ignorant of the fact that the LeT would spend the money on purchase of arms for Mumbai attacks.[19]

After the withdrawal of Soviet troops from Afghanistan in 1989, an Afghan government in exile was established in Peshawar but Shiite Mujahedeen, that had take refuge in Iran were excluded from the set-up because of pressure from Saudi Arabia. The Saudi government paid 23 million dollars weekly to this summit of Mujahedeen Shura, comprising of 519 members, as bribe so that exclusion of Shiite groups would be assured. Peshawar turned into a haven of veteran Afghan Mujahedeen and the warlords from all over the Afghanistan were assembled at Peshawar through financial aid from Saudi Arabia and the "expertise" from I.S.I. A series of making and breaking of alliances from different warring factions in Afghanistan commenced, while Islamabad started a campaign of recruitment from seminaries all over Pakistan in its pursuit of the policy of "strategic depth."[20]

There are hundreds of thousands of people in Pakistan who support Jamaat-ud-Dawa (J-u-D), Lashkar-e-Tayyba (L-e-T) and love their "jihadi performance" and who firmly trust that India would disintegrate sooner or later if these organisations continue their present activities and not only will the Kashmiris but the Muslims of India well also get "real freedom". They firmly believe that by dint of a Jihadi spirit like that of L-e-T, Islam can rule all over the world but the Muslims unfortunately, still lack the true spirit of the bygone, golden days of Islam. It is pertinent to mention here that when L-e-T had started its Jihadi activities in the Philippines, in addition to Kashmir and Bosnia, a poem was repeatedly published in "Mujala-tu-Dawa" the magazine of L-e-T, the first verse of which said:

When the Mujahid would return from Washington with a sack full of 'spirit'.

The atmosphere in Pakistan was ripe for sectarian pogrom and thanks to "special" actions by General Zia-ul-Haq the Deobandi seminaries and centres were fully engaged in intensifying sectarian tensions in society. The Shiites of Pakistan were also "ready" as after the Iranian revolution, they were also getting full support and financial aid from the clergy of Iran. General Zia-ul-Haq was also getting ready to promulgate Shariah laws in the country and first by issuing the Ordinance for Prohibition of Riba (usury) and then the Zakat Ordinance, he pushed the Pakistani society towards a clear sectarian divide. Both the Shariah laws, initially introduced by General Zia-ul-Haq turned out to be a complete failure. On the first Ordinance regarding Prohibition of the Riba, the religious scholars were not capable enough to reinterpret the Islamic laws according to contemporary circumstances; whereas there were a host of lacunae about the interpretations of the Ordinance concerning Zakat.[21]

In 1980, the people of Shiite sect staged a protest rally under the leadership of Mufti Jaffer Hussain and by staging a sit-in at Islamabad, forced General Zia-ul-Haq to announce that the Shiite community is exempted from the mandatory deduction of Zakat. The system of Usher (a deduction of 1/10 of the agricultural income meant for the poor) prescribed in Hanfia jurisprudence, was also rejected by the Shiite. The criticism of General Zia-ul-Haq by Ayatollah Khomeini further complicated matters. Maulana Haq Nawaz Jhangvi, a local cleric and orator in the city of Jhang, Central Punjab, declared the Shiite as non-Muslims due to some dogmatic differences. In fact it was a reaction against influential Shiite feudal lords of the area. Although there is a history of "fatwa" (religious edicts) in the Indian sub-continent by the Deobandis and Ahle-hadiths against the Shiite even other sects are also engaged in such fatwa however no tradition of sectarian killing in the bases of these edicts existed before. The rhetoric by Haq Nawaz Jhangvi resulted in a serious wave of sectarian violence in Jhang and people from both sides were killed indiscriminately.[22]

There are some solid evidences that General Zia was properly warned of the anti-Shiite and anti-Iran movement of the Jhangvi group. But he ignored the warnings and gave it all possible opportunities to flourish and turn into a full scale religious-political party under the title of Anjuman Sapah-e-Sahaba Pakistan. There was a new and vigorous resonance of the age-old Sunni-Shiite debate. The dogmatic and theological literature brought out by each sect was extremely provocative and inflammatory. In the meantime, General Zia gave a free hand to the local Sunni population in the town of Parachinar (an area already torn apart on sectarian grounds) to "teach a lesson" to the Toori Shiite community with the help of the Sunni Afghan mujahideen.

The town of Parachinar served as the base for the attacks of mujahideens as well as the smuggling of heavy arms across the Pak-Afghan border. The Toori tribes living there were not willing to co-operate with the I.S.I. and the Jihadis of the Deobandi sect, so they were crushed through a military action on the orders of General Zia-ul-Haq. After the demise of Mufti Jaffer Hussain, the leadership of Tehrik-Nafaz-e-Fiqah-e-Jafria was transferred to Toori Shiite cleric Allama Arif-ul-Hussaini who had also accompanied Ayatollah Khomeini while in exile at Najaf, Iraq (he is considered a martyr in Iran and Iran had also issued a memorial postage stamp in his honour). Arif-ul-Hussaini tried to transform the Imamia Student Organisation (I.S.O.), the student wing of Tehrik-Nafaz-e-Fiqah-e-Jafria into a militant outfit as revenge for the crackdown against Toori tribes and it was not before long that the I.S.O. was up against Sipah-e-Sahaba and other anti-Shiite outfits.[23]

Sunni-Shiite conflicts started all over Pakistan and fatal attacks were launched against important personalities of each sect. On August 5th 1988, Allama Arif-ul-Hussaini was murdered in his seminary of the outskirts of Peshawar. Tehrik-Nafaz-e-Fiqah-e-Jafria and the Toori tribe of Allama Hussaini held General Zia responsible for this murder and also blamed General (retired) Fazal-e-Haq, one of his close aides as an important actor of the murder conspiracy. Fazal-e-Haq was, governor of NWFP (renamed Khyber-Pakhtunkhwa) and considered a key figure for I.S.I.[24]

About two weeks after the incident, General Zia-ul-Haq was also killed in a plane crash at Bahawalpur and there were rumors of the involvement of the Shiite in this accident although no solid evidence has been brought forward till now. On the other hand, governor Fazl-e-Haq was also murdered in an ambush in 1991.[25]

The sectarian war was at its peak in Pakistan and the killing spree prolonged. In Jhang, the sectarian conflicts intensified after the murder of Maulana Haq Nawaz Jhangvi, the head of Sipah-e-Sahaba. The killing spree among the Shiite feudal lords and Sunni tenants in Jhang gradually started to engulf the entire country. Afterwards Sipah-e-Sahaba got some electoral victories in Jhang whereas one of its elected member of parliament Maulana Aisar-ul-Haq Qasmi was murdered during an election campaign. Sipah-e-Sahaba took revenge by targeting local influential personalities. It is worthwhile to mention that when Iranian diplomat Sadiq Ganji was murdered in Lahore, the assassins were apprehended by the police and one of them turned out to be an operative of I.S.I. A strong reaction was seen from Iran's side after the murder of Sadiq Ganji and the Iranian government started providing material support to Sipah-e-Muhammad, a newly formed Shiite militant outfit. Hundreds of youth from Sipah-e-Muhammad were provided with proper training by the Iranian revolutionary guards 'Pasdaran-e-Inqilab'. This also helped intensify sectarian tensions in Punjab and other parts of Pakistan.[26]

Some Iranian cadets were murdered by Sipah-e-Sahaba near Rawalpindi. The investigation of the incident also proved the might of those officials of intelligence agencies who had strong affiliations with sectarian outfits, because it was known that Iranian cadets were murdered on the tips by some 'insiders'. In Karachi, the Lashkar-e-Jhangvi opted for the strategy of "target killing" that is peculiar with the city and more than one hundred Shiite doctors and engineers were killed just because of sectarian identities of their names.[27]

Almost every government in Pakistan has announced its desire to control the mushrooming growth of seminaries under certain regulations but none has succeeded to achieve any concrete result. The "real" utilisation of the aid of millions of rupees during Musharraf era for registration and reforms in madrassas could not be ascertained while none of the targets for which the grants were received were achieved. According to a report by the Institute of Policy Studies Islamabad there are 6,761 madrassas in Pakistan where more than a million students are getting religious education. The Ministry of religious affairs, in its report, has also published similar statistics but the monthly, Herald (November 2001) has reported:

"According to Ministry of Interior Affairs there are around 20 thousand seminaries in the country with more than three million students. In 1947 the number of mardarsas in West Pakistan was only 245, which reached to 2,861 in 1988. The rate of increase in their number between 1988 to 2000 was 136 percent. With 64 per cent of the total number the Deobandi seminaries are on the top of the list, with 25 per cent the Barelvis madrassas are on the second rank, whereas the Wahhabi seminaries are only six per cent of the total number. However the rate of increase in Wahhabi madrassas has been quite fast and with an increment rate of 131 per cent it reached to 310 in 2000 from only 134 in 1988. The ratio of foreign students is 15 per cent. As mentioned earlier there are 17 organisations of Wahhabi sect currently active in Pakistan that manage many madrassas of their own. Six of them have been active in national politics; three have participated in Jihad whereas three were only busy in preaching for their sect. They strictly follow the tenets of their sect, most of them follow the instructions by Saudi Arabia and get financial assistance from well-off Saudi citizens."[28]

The overall picture obtained is that of a Pakistan with an abundance of bigot religious parties, jihadi outfits, sectarian killers and extremist groups as some of its salient features. The army of Pakistan is pitched in a fierce battle with militants of Taliban and Al-Qaeda in tribal areas as well as settled districts of Khyber-Pakhtunkhwa, while supporters of Taliban are being churned out in every area of the country. The number of Taliban was on the rise in Karachi and the local extremists have developed a rapport with Taliban and Al-Qaeda combatants in Afghanistan besides gathering their forces in various parts of Punjab. The deterioration of the internal situation of Pakistan could be guessed by the fact that at present the state of Pakistan is forced to launch a fierce battle against extremist elements that were nurtured by its own powerful functionaries and are now suffering heavy casualities and every town and city is under suicide attacks. Extremists are target killing the high ranking army officers and hundreds of soldiers have lost their lives.

There is a lot of confusion and several misgivings about the Pakistan Army and its mighty intelligence agencies, both in the country and the outside world. Vague as well as contradictory statements issued by Pakistan after the publication of every research based report in American newspapers and journals about the alleged nexus between the army's powerful agency I.S.I. and Taliban have further intensified the perception that the civilian government does not have the capacity to control this powerful secret agency. As international pressure mounts in the coming days, it is by all means possible that any functionary of the Ministry of Foreign Affairs would read out an explanation by Inter Services Public Relations in front of the media and would make a "decisive declaration" that it may be deemed to be the principled stand of the government of Pakistan as well. The major portion of Pakistani media in its stereotype manner would categorise the reports as 'foreign conspiracies' and ex-army generals, enjoying the status of national heroes, would accentuate the populist sentiment by repeatedly rebuking the U.S., Israel and India. But nobody would ever bother to think why fingers are always pointed at the I.S.I. by the global community and why there are claims of its assistance as well as involvement whenever any impartial investigation regarding incidents of ever increasing extremism and terrorism is conducted?

When some investigative reports were published in the American press, senior Pakistani officials also confirmed that they do have "contacts" with the Taliban militants currently active in tribal areas.

However these connections could not be termed as assistance to them. This is neither the real picture nor something that could be called an 'inside story'. Essentially the image of I.S.I. inside the country is totally different from international perceptions where it is seen as an agency operating under a complicated system and a dubious jurisdiction and that it is not only active for destabilisation of their non-favourite civil governments and 'hot pursuit' of its disliked neighbouring countries but it also controls the armed religious outfits and extremists in the region.

It has little significance whether the civilian and military governments of Pakistan agree with this international perception about I.S.I. or not, but we have endeavoured for decades to exaggerate the expeditions and exploits by the I.S.I. in order to prove that the Afghan war was a sacred jihad and all the personalities heading the I.S.I. during the Afghan war are usually presented as heroes and invincible generals at public level.

Certain custom-made books and tales were written to pay tribute to the "successful missions" of the chiefs of I.S.I. in such a way that all exploits by tatar conqueror Tamerlane are dwarfed in front of them. As the sole purpose of these concocted stories was to appease the masses and to even the score of humiliating defeats in the previous scuffles with India, all such achievements by the chiefs of this professional institution or of its different wings were especially highlighted where the eternal enemies like India and Israel, the invader of Afghanistan Soviet army and its secret agencies were shown suffering a humiliating defeat and all their anti-Pakistan evil designs were tarnished. As the local intellectuals and journalists were afraid to challenge the credibility of these tales and were so isolated and unable to point out paradoxes existing in them, these tales were largely accepted without much doubt. Their impact on peoples' minds could be assessed by the fact that the major portion of the Urdu titles sold in Pakistan comprise of the books brought out by big publishing houses of Lahore that present imaginary encounters with Indian secret agencies, Israel, the U.S. and the erstwhile Soviet Union in novel or stories form. Essentially our patriot commandos and spies are found crushing the enemies of Pakistan in every sector in these "spy stories".

For more than three decades our state has been engaged in a process of indoctrination of its citizens and it has instilled certain hardliner and jingoistic characteristics in them, which are not only clearly visible in the mindset of the majority but their impacts are also apparent in most of the powerful institutions of the state. Although all the secret agencies of other countries perform the same tasks as ours but the global perception of our agencies is so different that the international community seems afraid of us. On one hand our security institutions are committed to a fierce struggle against extremists and terrorists in tribal areas and other parts of the country, on the other the image is gaining strength that certain wings of the security establishment are engaged in material and military assistance to extremists.[29]

Observed on the basis of present facts it is quite obvious that some former senior officials of certain powerful secret agencies, due to their specific mindset, are not only desirous of cleansing the state of Pakistan, but also want to capture it with the help of some like-minded parties and groups. We have also observed certain incidents where some senior officers of the state tried to stage a coup d'état in order to run the country according to their specific religious inclinations. Although they had to go through a court martial after their attempts failed, they became very active again after their jail terms were completed. Although such elements have not been successful in their objectives so far but they are still esteem in religious and political circles held in high.

Many of the ex-senior officials in Islamabad are without any doubt still busy in their former 'assignments'; they are helping not only the sectarian outfits of the country but also the Taliban and their supporters. The foreign secret agencies are afraid of the powers of these ex-officers and at the same time they are highly suspicious of their present contacts. One such powerful personage of the past is actively helping the religious zealots of tribal areas while sitting in Islamabad and no civilian government dare take any action against him. Generally it is assumed that he still has access to and wields full support by some very potent institutions of the defence establishment. Moreover, there are suspicions on the international level that many senior officials of Pakistani secret agencies are given a great measure of respect in the Pakistan army apart from enjoying the support of religious bigots.

Under the circumstances, the governments in Pakistan should always be prepared to face the allegations by the international community like that leveled along with some evidential proofs by some renowned newspapers and journals of the U.S. against I.S.I. The situation is quite delicate that could plunge Pakistan into further problems already vulnerable economically and administratively, whereas the civilian governments seem helpless to control the internal situation of the country due to their traditional short comings. It is because of the image that we have created ourselves over the decades concerning our institutions. We had created these images to terrorize our external enemies and to please our people but contrary to that it is now pleasing our enemies and terrorizing our people.

The number of those people has drastically increased in Pakistan who hold the Islamic identity of Pakistan as the main reason for the plethora of its problems and that many of the powerful countries including India are bent to disintegrate the state of Pakistan. In every era the establishments as well as the opinion makers of the state have brain washed its people that Hindus can never be the sympathetic to Pakistan and India is continuously striving to disintegrate our country in order to turn its dream of united India into a reality and there is always room to enhance the colors and glamour of these tales. It would not be unjustified to claim that the activities of provoking the "anti-India" sentiments have turned into a profession in its own right and like many other income yielding professions it also has certain assertive rules of games. Moreover there are certain persons and institutions that have enthroned themselves on the high podium of issuing the "certificates of patriotism" that are acceptable all over the society. Equally in India there is no dearth of institutes and the personalities now who have their sustenance on invoking sentiments of such patriotism that is intertwined with enmity of Pakistan.

There is lot of mental proximity among all these hate mongers of South Asia. The people having this sort of mindset do not believe in democracy and have a yearning for establishing a new state structure based on the religious mythology woven into hate and revenge. They think that the state structure armored with the religious dogmas would turn out to be a mean for their salvation in hereinafter and that would also help crush their enemies forever. Though an outdated concept, it still haunts the imaginations of general public. The political parties of every genre of in both countries have exploited the hollow sloganeering of patriotism in order to divert attention from prevailing serious issues and tried to instill into their people a love and all times preparedness for war.

This business of mutual innihilation and promoting a self-styled patriotism is at its peak in both the countries. In India these duties are performed by its retrogressive religious and political leaders whereas in Pakistan these "responsibilities" are monitored by the potent state institutions who deem themselves more capable of running the affairs of state than entire political leadership. The "patriots" of the both sides have grievances against the opponent groups of their respective countries of not being patriotic like them. In the presence of such powerful groups and factions it is hard to predict whether there is any end to the animosity between the two countries, rather with the passage of time the strategy of cross border infiltrations as well as the support of terrorist groups is gaining strength.

Ideally the state of Pakistan should have prospered at a quicker pace under the people with aforementioned concepts of 'patriotism' but contrary to that Pakistan has rapidly turning into a country with weakest capabilities of administrative skills where the collusion of opportunism and adventurisms has resulted in complete melt down of its economy. Although weak but it is still considered a proper state despite the fact it is unable to fulfill some of its very essential needs. Its energy sector is going through a complete collapse and there is no possibility of improvement in it in the foreseeable future. Its cities and towns are pushed into darkness and ordinary people are at the mercy of harsh climatic conditions. A considerable area of the country is caught up in one or other type of insurgency and its army is busy controlling it. Innumerable people have been slain in suicide attacks that occur every other day and the security agencies so far have not been able to assure the wellbeing of people.

Almost all the administrative sectors of the state face deterioration; mismanagement and corruption are rife. A considerable number of people desirous of a certain measure of cleansing the state of 'undiserable elements' are busy augmenting sectarian tensions while the misery of religious minorities needs no comments. The extremity of religious intolerance could be judged by the fact that numerous people have been murdered just because they belonged to 'different sect' and scores of people are languishing in the jails merely because of their religious beliefs.[30]

The differences and the tensions between various provinces are at their peak and these tensions have changed into a serious rivalry in absence of any formula of equitable distribution of national resources. The governments in Islamabad generally under the influence of powerful institutions of the state take the steps that enhance sentiments of resentment in smaller provinces. Baluchistan, the largest province by area has a long history of bitter experiences of the neglect and constantly unfavorable attitude from the center and insurgencies in its vast areas often take violent forms. Sindh, that is considered the economic back bone of the country, is nearly lifeless due to ethnic and linguistic riots while the law and order situation in its big cities is always perched at a delicate balanced. For a past decade or so, different ethnic and religious groups are pitched against each other in Karachi and the circumstances have left the whole city at the mercy of criminal gangs or extremist religious outfits.

The image of the state at the outside world is that of a weaker and quite shaky state shrouded in thick shades of trust deficit. Due to Afghan wars as well as numerous scuffles with India, Pakistan at international level has emerged as a state that frightens the western world due to various concerns. The nuclear ambitions of a country with a vulnerable economy further highlight these fears. Most of the countries traditionally siding with Pakistan on various issues have withdrawn their support and at international level Pakistan is standing isolated.

The international wave of terrorism as well as the support by Pakistan to former Taliban regime in Afghanistan has further tarnished its global image. There is a general perception in western world now that every act of terrorism anywhere in the world has some how or other its links with Pakistan. Incidents like terrorist acts in the U.K. and Mumbai attacks are proofs enough to strengthen this reflection.

An international sketch about the state of Pakistan that emerges on the bases of a long trail of such incidents is quite discouraging.

Despite these facts the majority of powerful people; the ones having the capacity to influence the policy making is neither ready nor willing to improve the internal as well as external image of the country. They desire to wage a war against the whole world and want total destruction of their 'enemy' neighbours. They are reluctant to adopt a realistic point of view on the internal conflicts of the country and do not agree with the present policy of crackdown against the religious zealots, the real enemies of the state. Under the situation it would be very hard to predict whether that Pakistan would succeed to ameliorate its international image in the near future because the number of people having extremist point of views is also growing rapidly.

At present the "danger" has crossed the border of Punjab and the Army's General Headquarters (GHQ) is not out of reach for terrorist outfits anymore. A number of senior army officers fell victim in that gruesome terrorist attack. The initial investigations revealed that majority of the attackers belonged to those groups of Punjab that have been striving to implement their bigot views in the region with the support from Al-Qaeda and Taliban. Previously the planning of various suicide attacks in different cities of Punjab including the fatal attacks at Marriot Hotel Islamabad was also made in Punjab. For this suicide attack a truck laden with explosives was made ready at central Punjab district of Jhang and all the attackers headed towards Islamabad, from there. Moreover the attackers on security forces at Lahore and Sargodha also came from the southern districts of Punjab. The presence of local Taliban in the towns and cities of South Punjab is very much a serious reality. These elements have started proving their existence by dispatching precautionary letters for elimination of "immodest and anti-Shariah" customs, traditions and beliefs.[31]

2

The Changing Patterns of Society and the State

A fter the gruesome incident of Gojra in 2009, two more persons were brutally murdered through justice vigilante in Muridke as well under the allegations of desecration of Holy Koran. Whereas in a village of district Sialkot a Christian youth was alleged of pestering a Muslim girl was also murdered. According to reports the girl was coming back after a lesson of Koran in local mosque and a part of Koran fell from her hands while resisting the move. Later the mob set ablaze the local church whereas the next day accused Christian boy was found dead in lock up of a police station in Sialkot. Police claimed that he had committed suicide by strangulating himself in prison's cell.[32]

The angry people in Punjab seem to have found an easy formula to eliminate their opponents and having a crackdown on religious minorities while these fuming mobs have started to even the scores against their opponents as well under the similar pretexts. Ultimately the same angry mobs would siege the courts when legal process against the accused would get under way and virtually it would become impossible for judges to continue the court proceeding in any transparent and credible manner. Even though in Pakistani law there is a penalty of life imprisonment for sacrilege of the holy Koran, religious zealots are prosecuting their opponents by mercilessly killing the accused for crimes which are yet to be proved. Increasingly, there is an impression that the state of Pakistan has fallen apart and its laws have become irrelevant. Fundamentalists frame allegations and condemn undertrails to death without a proper trial. According to the evidence collected so far many defunct religious organisations are involved in such activities and their highly trained workers take the liberty of doing away with the accessed and ransackcy his property.

Due to the highly controversial blasphemy laws several people have been persecuted without a proper trial and killed in cold blood. Assassinated persons include a judge of a higher court, government functionaries and members of minority sects. But there is no evidence that any of these mercenaries has ever been punished because of these brutal acts. The number of people murdered under allegations of blasphemy in Pakistan is the highest among all Muslim countries. The fact is also worth contemplation that non-Muslim minorities of Pakistan are socially and economically considered inferior and weak in comparison to the religious minorities in other Muslim countries. They are also subjected to severe restrictions and hardships even in the performance of their religious rites. Even the lives and properties of minority Muslim sects of Pakistan are not safe and they are not only obliged to live under the shadow of real threats but hundreds of them lost their lives in the recent decades.[33]

After every gruesome incident of terrorism the same ridiculous claim is repeated so blatantly that state would retain its writ at every cost. The fact is that the state has lost its writ a long time ago but there is nobody to make the state functionaries realise that the number of the people who have any belief in the writ of state diminishing rapidly. Now instead of leading their lives under the state protection, the vulnerable sections of society and the holder of religious beliefs other than the majority are forced to live under the hegemony of majority sects. Many of the apologists and intellectuals as well as the political leaders tried to absolve the extremist organisations and groups of the carnage at Gojra by calling it a foreign conspiracy but it was very hard to contradict the so apparent reality. The incident at Gojra is a tragic continuation of similar episodes at Shanti Nagar and Sangla Hill where sectarian groups and jihadis of the neighbourhood were involved, who also enjoyed full support of the local administration.[34]

Many of the simpletons still hold a prejudice against the religious minorities is but the result of a few zealots' thoughts and majority of the people do not agree with their view point. This thought is utterly unrealistic and misleading as always a large number of people involved in all the anti-minorities riots in Pakistan comprised of ordinary people who were in the forefront of arson and carnage. These included young students, labourers, peasants and other ordinary workers who resolutely believed that killing the non-Muslims or the Muslims who have gone 'astray' and looting their properties is a sacred deed. Be it the anti-Ahmadiyya riots, incidents of killings during movement of Pakistan National Alliance or sectarian violence against Shiites in Jhang and Kurram Agency, majority of the participants could not be called regular members of any extremist outfit or religious organisation despite the fact that instigators of such incidents were some holy people of the cloak read sectarian hate mongers. Same was the case in the gloomy incidents of Gojra and Muridke where extremist elements simply incited the ordinary people who accomplished the rest of the job in search of eternal bliss in the life hereafter.

The targets of these sacred custodians of the dogmas are pretty clear and cleansing the country of the religious minorities is on the top of the list. These religious zealots are confident enough that whenever and wherever they want, they could exploit the sentiments of ordinary Muslims to crush the dissident Muslims and minorities. The office bearers of local administration seem totally helpless in controlling such incidents simply for the fear of their own lives. They are also aware of the fact that the state does not have the capability of safeguarding them. The staff of the local administration especially the police officials are witness to dozens of the incidents where sectarian elements and religious militant targeted killed their senior officers so nobody is willing to risk his/ her life. In addition, the functionaries of administration are not oblivious of the verity that such incidents only take place with the full consent of local politicians and there is a strong presence of militants' supporters in the powerful institutes of state, who are always willing to help the sectarian elements and the religious extremists in any odd situation.

Efforts are always made to mitigate the gravity of such incidents by declaring them the result of instantaneous provocation but the matter is not so simple as claimed. The ever-increasing violent attitudes in Pakistani society as well as religious and sectarian intolerance could easily be found to have been nurtured for a long time. The fiery speakers and hate mongers from mosques or seminaries have a strong grip, rather a complete control over the minds of ordinary Muslims. This is the main reason behind the fact that whenever any provoking announcement is made from any mosque or madrassa, no verification is deemed necessary and people gather their arms and head for a deadly attack towards the site where any incident of blasphemy had allegedly taken place. From Shanti Nagar to Gojra, every tragic incident took a monstrous dimension only when people were provoked through the loudspeaker of the mosque or madrassa to launch a deadly strike.

In Gojra, people were informed that the agents of Western Jew and Christian forces (read local Christian community) have committed an act of profanity with copies of the Holy Koran. After such infuriating announcements, activists of extremist religious outfits gathered the local youth and the townships of local minority communities were set ablaze under a pre-arranged plan. The incident of Gojra was the second one where the planned and gruesome pattern of Shanti Nagar was repeated by rabble-rousing the local people and attacking the pre-marked Christian population. The Shiite population of the Kurram agency remained the victim of similar attitude where clerics from the opponent sects of Shiite belief spitted fire against them and kept waiting for the chances when they can directly hit the opponent sect. Whereas the "endeavours" by the powerful agencies of state could be counted as the main reason for nurturing hatred in the minds of ordinary people, in fact these were the extremist outfits and zealot groups that have also contributed significantly towards this end.[35]

In 1996, the brother of the chief of a notorious extremist sectarian party in the town of Samandri in Faisalabad alleged that a Christian sweeper, Aslam Massey had committed blasphemy of the holy prophet Muhammad merely for the reason that Aslam Massey had sold a buffalo to the said cleric who was adamant to make the payment on the stipulated time. On one occasion Aslam Massey came for recovery of his amount and the cleric swore on the name of Prophet Muhammad to make the payment on a certain date. Aslam Massey returned on the promised day only to see reluctance on the part of the sacred cleric. Aslam Massey declared that you should fulfill your commitment as you had sworn on the honour of Holy Prophet Muhammad. If I had done so on the name of Prophet Jesus I would have carried out my pledge at any cost. Upon hearing that the cleric realised that he had nothing to answer so he started shouting that Aslam Massey had committed blasphemy of Prophet Muhammad.[36]

Soon the house of Aslam Massey came under violent attack, his aged parents were subjugated to brutal assault and the local police registered a case of criminal offence against Aslam Massey under article 295-C of Pakistan Penal Code (the article that suggest death penalty for the perpetrators of blasphemy). The cleric arranged many rallies with the help of local students and made life miserable for the local Christian community. Aslam was fired from his job and his entire family was shattered. It is almost certain that any zealot would surely assassinate Aslam Massey when he would come back after completion of his jail term but nobody would ever dare ask that sacred man why he had ruined the life of an innocent person and his whole family merely to conceal his dishonesty. Apparently the cleric was a powerful and influential personality of his area with a force of hundreds of armed youth at his disposal.[37]

During the course of previous decade there have been hundreds of such incidents in Punjab alone where minorities or members of dissident religious sects were targeted. A large number of Hindu Pakistani citizens residing in the villages of Harrpal, Aanola, Beeni Salehrian, Saleem, Bajra Garhi and Joyian of district Sialkot alone have been forced to migrate to India by the hands of armed members of a jihadi organisation. These Hindu families had been living in these villages for centuries and they had been forced to leave their land and properties. The groups of mujahideen threatened them with death if they did not leave Pakistan and take refuge in India. The vulnerable and frightened Hindu families obtained visas for India on emergency basis and fled from Pakistan.

As a Hindu farmer, Babu Ram Bhagat failed to get an Indian visa for some reason and his young grand-daughters were kidnapped. The kidnappers, who have previously participated in jihad of Kashmir, announced next day that one of the girls had converted to Islam and she had married one of the mujahids. It is worth-mentioning that the second one who was not willing to marry any mujahid committed suicide by strangulating herself. Terrified, Babu Ram somehow managed to obtain an Indian visa and hurriedly migrated to Jalandhar (Indian Punjab). After some time his son Krishan Das wrote a letter to the villagers informing them of the plight of his father who had not been able to get sound sleep even for a single night after leaving his ancestral village. After sometime he died of cardiac arrest. The villagers still get letters from India from time to time containing news of the predicament of the Hindus who had migrated to India and how they miss their native land. But they are reluctant to come back because of the threats to their lives.[38]

The radical change in the composition of Pakistani society is the fruit of the policies adopted by General Zia-ul-Haq. But the successive governments either have not done anything concrete to restrain these deteriorations and not only made the religious extremists more powerful with the backing of state institutions but more often than not, also used them for their own short-term political goals. In order to get their support and to gain numerical strength in the parliament, the members of sectarian as well as religious extremist parties were given clear opportunities to strengthen their clout and to arm themselves. At present there is hardly any city or town in Pakistan that could be declared free of control by armed religious groups. Even Islamabad that should have been different from other cities because of the composition of its population, is a city with seminaries of jihadist fame where most of the mosques are controlled by zealots. It is also mentioning here that Islamabad is the only capital city of the world sans (any functional) any cinema, whereas there are a number of mosques in this city that are built on land illegally grabbed, and originally owned by government or private institutions or individuals.

There are countless mosques and seminaries in every major town and city of Pakistan that have a control over local communities far more effective than the law enforcement agencies whereas these agencies can never dare enter into the boundaries of these seminaries and mosques.

The imams of these mosques and the administrators of these madrassas not only exert their influence over local government institutions but also resolve the rows and issues of local people including land disputes. The local people do not resort to local mosques and seminaries only in the hope of getting justice and an impartial and just decision but to pressurise their opponents and to harass them as much as they can.

The organisation declared defunct in various periods due to their terrorist activities and sectarian killings are only curtailed to the extent that they cannot use their previous titles in their propaganda literature. It would not be justified to claim that their terrorist and sectarian activities have been totally controlled. Although the pressure from the outside world has caused several operations against them but so far these outfits could not be de-weaponised. Their activists, arrested during these operations, were charged on vague offences that are very difficult to prove in any court of law. There are hundreds of jailed extremists who are the real culprits of terrorism and sectarian violence in the country but they are going to be released sooner than later because nobody is willing to bear witness against them nor does the police have solid evidence that could make the court issue any verdict. A majority of banned outfits and groups are still fully operational and they not only have established close contacts with political parties but also have managed to find their staunch supporters in the ranks of local administration and the police.

That also explains the monopolised control of powerful religious extremist organisations in many cities and towns of Punjab and even the local criminal gangs and individuals have also established links with them in some way or the other. For example, in the city of Gujranwala, where the spoilt youth of famous wrestler families used to engage in looting or other illicit activities by joining some criminal gangs previously, now a jihadi organisation is the chief patron of these criminal gangs and the local administration is afraid to have any action against the said militant outfit. Ordinary people take their disputes to the central office of that organisation where they can solicit "speedy justice". Same is the situation in Faisalabad which is under complete control of a banned jihadi outfit and its jailed chief issues his orders from a prison cell. We are not aware of any single occasion where any business enterprise or political figure of the city ever dared disobey any order or challenge or any decision by the said imprisoned leader. Districts of Sheikhupura, Sargodha, Jhang and Khanewal are faced with similar circumstances where activists of extremist religious outfits are so powerful that they not only hold non-state courts for dispensation of "speedy justice" but also exert considerable pressure on senior government officials in order to have a strict control over the local administration. The people holding the traditional views that powerful political elites and the influential feudal classes remain engaged in extra-judicial and extra-state activities should be better informed that the role assumed by extremist religious and sectarian organisations and everybody seems vulnerable in front of them.[39]

In our society we have often observed that after a crackdown against any criminal gang or individual there was a great type about their real or alleged assets but nothing was ever was brought to the limelight after a ban on any extremist outfit or the arrest of its mighty activists. The main reason is the fear that chills the spines of "impartial and dauntless media" before breaking any news about these groups. Presently, there are countless zealot religious organisations with thousands of acres of land, hundreds of commercial buildings and plazas as well as other valuable assets but none of the "undaunted journalists" dare mention their name as there is no dearth of staunch supporters of these outfits in Pakistani, in particular the vernacular media. Moreover such an effort could also take a heavy toll. The powerful and mighty institutions of the state provide full protection to such organisations and in case of any pressure from the outside world they are not only given an "internal" immunity but these institutions also manage to have a vigilant eye on all the aspects that are considered vital to keep the influence as well as the nuisance value of these organisations intact.

Many of the naïve optimists still think it is possible that Pakistan will also get onto the track to development and forceful impacts of rapidly changing world are the main reasons for it. They are either unaware of the actual state of affairs in the society or they lack the ability to reckon the changes that are taking place in Pakistani society. For example, now it has become very easy to guess the religion and sect of the people simply by hearing the ringtone of their mobile phones. Innumerable people could be found in public places, offices, homes, educational institutions or elsewhere whose cell phones play the ringtones comprising Na'ats (hymns for Prophet Muhammad), verses from Koran, jihadi songs, Nohas, Qaseedas, Azans or other tunes revealing the religious and sectarian inclinations of the owner of the cell phone. They do not forget to have a conscious effort to make the caller aware of their sectarian inclination even if they do not use such ringtones. The caller has no choice but to hear such kind of stuff on his/her called number until it is attended by someone.

It would not be wrong to claim that drastic changes are taking place in the social patterns of Pakistan as it has ceded the way for bigot forces in such a manner that it has virtually become impossible to find traditional components that shaped the erstwhile values of society. The lifestyle in rural areas has totally changed and its makeover is quite weird for the older generations. We can also say that our villages are now deprived of the traditional rustic life of the sub-continent and their inhabitants have not only changed their apparent style but their living as well as every day's custom also resemble "foreign" components. It was not very long ago when we could find such community-based organisations in town and big villages that could show by their names that they were formed for welfare of general public. There existed thousands of such registered organisations all over the country that were established for providing help and relief in floods or other natural calamities but such organisations have become extinct in the span of last decade or so and they have been replaced by other type of outfits. For example, welfare organisations have been replaced by from jihadist to Matami (Shiite ritual of mourning for Imam Hussein) but purely sectarian outfits. Nowadays no community of urban areas is free of organisations "announcing" the religious and sectarian affiliations of then inhabitants.

On January 28th 2009, four youth and a middle-aged person from Ahmadiyya community were arrested from a village of Liyyah, a district in south Punjab on blasphemy charges. The youth from Ahmadiyya community, aged 14 to 16 years were arrested and a criminal case was registered against them under Section 295-C of the Pakistan Penal Code. According to police sources, one Liaqat Ali of village Chak number 172 T.D.A. lodged a complaint that the boys had written a blasphemous word in the toilet of mosque Gulzar-e-Madina of the village. However nobody had seen the nominated boys committing that act and the police had registered the case merely on the basis of doubt and speculation. The plaintiff Liaqat Ali had claimed that he had objected to the said member of Ahmadiyya community saying his prayers in the mosques of Muslims and possibly the accused person had committed blasphemy to take revenge for this restriction. The Ahmadiyya Jammat termed it a case of religious discrimination.[40]

According to the spokesperson of Jamaat Ahmadiyya they are a peace-loving community but its members are being subjugated to discriminatory actions since 1974. A large number of blasphemy cases are registered against the members of their community but nothing has been proved against them till today. The registration of this case is also another example of the vilest religious discrimination. According to him, 94 persons from the ahmadiyya community have been murdered since 1984 and attempts at life are made against 104 whereas thousands of cases are registered including 79 cases of blasphemy. Twenty one mosques of Ahmadiyya community were demolished whereas eleven were burned; moreover government officials also sealed twenty six of their places of worship. According to Saleem Ahmed one hundred and twenty eight dead bodies of Ahmadis were dug out of their graves and they were shifted out of the cemeteries for Muslim community. According to the laws of the land, exhuming any dead body sans court orders and without the due process of law is a serious crime with a specific punishment. But incidents of disinterring the dead bodies of Ahmadiyya sect after being buried in graveyards of Muslims, are increasing in number nowadays and so far nobody has been taken to task for this heinous crime.[41]

As a result of press reports and the investigations made by independent media as well as human rights organisations on the incident of village 172 T.D.A., Layyah it has been found that some members of the defunct Lashkar-e-Tayyba added fuel to the fire and leveled the charges of blasphemy against the Ahmadi youths without any solid evidence, called local media representatives and took photographs of the accused boys and also made inflammatory speeches.

Initially, one Shahbaz Qasim, son of Noor Muhammad Kolachi, having strong connections with Jamaat-ud-Dawa inhibited Ahmadi youths to say their prayers in mosque Gulzar-e-Madina, the only mosque in the village belonging to the Barelvi sect. He was of the view that in the mosque, the boys were preaching their religion among the peer Muslim youth and this was totally unacceptable; despite the fact that Qari Saeed, the imam of Barelvi mosque and other members of the mosque committee had allowed Ahmadi youth to have their prayer in their mosque. On this objection, the Ahmadi boys stopped coming to the mosque but still they had to face a false charge of blasphemy. The possibility cannot be ruled out that the local jihadi outfits would take oath from their activists to assassinate these Ahmadi youths after they are released on bail as it would be a blessed deed and would make them entitled to paradise. The Society in Punjab has rapidly changed itself and sectarian and jihadist organisations are targeting their sectarian opponents as well as the religious minorities with a full force.[42]

3

Changing Scenario of Punjab

In and around last the three decades, Punjab has rapidly changed itself and adopted traits that are utterly incompatible with its previous traditions and norms. It is quite heart-breaking to notice that the demeanour as well as the friendly rural and urban cultures peculiar to the past and deep-rooted secular traditions no longer exist. Almost every beautiful tradition of the Punjabi society has been discarded in favour of ugly habits and intolerant and extremist tendencies have replaced the culture of tolerance and harmony. Unluckily, emergence of this phenomenon was not a result of some natural evolutionary processes but was artificially thrust upon society, whereas the state and its powerful institutions have played a midwife like role in this unnatural nativity. Although this peculiar change was nurtured under the umbrella of an artificial and unnatural Puritanism, pioneered in the urban centres, but still it has flourished under the tacit approval of the rural society. The Puritanism as well as the extremism flourishing in the urban centres seems sullied with a specific kind of corruption and political influence, whereas the bigotry and sectarian hatred apparent in the rural society is linked with the traditional poverty and educational backwardness of rural Punjab.

So far the majority of the experts of social sciences, particularly the intellectuals focusing their research on Punjab have not been able to seriously grasp these rapid and new changes. So we rarely find any note of caution on culture and tradition emerging in the course of the last two decades or so. Although most of our intellectuals delve deep into the religious extremism as well as growth of the jihadist culture in Punjab but they rarely contemplate on the nuances that serve as a stern reminder to the presence of a new culture that is responsible for the promotion of jihadi notions in the region. This could also be attributed to the lack of knowledge among the intellectuals living in urban centres about the minute details of rural culture, who consider everyday media reports as a sufficient source of their awareness. The real knowledge about the rural areas of Punjab fails to reach the people living in urban areas as the elements affiliated with specific political and religious lobbies have strong tendencies to exert their influence upon local representatives of media outlets and majority of these local correspondents never take the risk of bringing "real" information to the limelight for the sake of their own safety.

If we consult the researchers, they generally seem to agree on the point that the situation in Afghanistan has helped promote a new but totally different culture in Khyber-Pakhtunkhwa and the tribal areas. They simply link the violence and religious extremism in these areas to neighbouring Afghanistan and those claiming to have a rather broader perspective hold the Pak army and its secret agencies equally responsible for these disastrous circumstances. But what is happening in Punjab and rapidly changing situation there is neither seen nor presented in an objective manner. The personal bent of mind of these intellectuals and researchers is the main reason for these tendencies who have a natural inclination towards big urban centres and who totally ignore the rural areas, whereas the mainstream media of Pakistan are also reluctant to present the fast deteriorating situation of Punjab as they do not want to portray themselves as critiques of the powerful right wing establishment and the army comprising the majority of Punjabis.

It would not be imprudent to claim that the Punjab presented in the old time paintings or classic Punjabi movies of the 1960's and 1970's does not exist anymore. These old traditions have been engulfed by the new but drastic culture. Those who wish to enter in the imaginary scenery of rural areas are not lucky enough to listen to the sweet melodies of the flute. Instead they have to hear the crackling noise of the bullets of the AK-47 fired or the sound of loudspeakers from those mosques and seminaries that are being constructed at a very rapid pace. If one is reluctant to admit the facts, it is his/her choice but that does not change the ground realities as the scenario of the rural areas of Punjab is signaling the impending dangers and announces the arrival of the monster that has already clutched the tribal areas in its claws and the state of Pakistan has virtually surrendered to the misadventures it had once started on its own.

The main ingredients of the new composition of Punjab have been introduced after the coup against the elected government of Prime Minister Zulfiqar Ali Bhutto and more specifically since the Soviet invasion of Afghanistan and the revolution in Iran by the Shiite hardliners. Although the impact of these three important developments can be seen all over the country but the damage done to Punjab and Khyber Pakhtunkhwa is more tragically visible. Although the actions and policies of military dictator General Zia-ul-Haq and the war in Afghanistan have played a pivotal role in intoxicating Pakistani society with religious extremism but the Shiite revolution in Iran as well as the retrogressive regime of Saudi Arabia highly fearful of the impacts of Iranian revolution has pushed the Muslim countries into a sanguine war. Today the intensity of Sunni-Shiite conflicts could be felt in almost every city and town in Punjab. There is hardly any district in Punjab where Imam Bargahs, mosques or cemeteries are not targeted.[43]

The Afghan jihad on the other hand had infused a "new life" into the clerics and leaders of some sects of Sunni Muslims in the rural areas and had ended their dependence on the local landlord and feudallords. Apart from amassing wealth and ammunitions they were able to get armed and train youth militants for a physical demonstration of their clout. The imam of the local mosque, who was dependent on the alms from the local community (especially in the shape of weekly food on Thursdays) only two decades ago is now a multi-millionaire and has become a symbol of power. Ordinary people are afraid of him not only due to his influence and physical power but also because he has the strong force of the youth always ready to eliminate their ideological opponents. Punjab has now turned into a centre of bigot jihadists and sectarian outfits that have been declared a great danger for the integrity of the state. If the "aid" as well as the supply of manpower from the Punjab is blocked to sectarian killers and extremist groups and individuals active in every part of country including Khyber Pakhtunkhwa, the Tribal Areas and Kashmir and Afghanistan, the intensity of the wars and conflicts in these areas will surely diminish.

Today the greatest number of the organisations and groups indulging in extremist, sectarian and jihadi activities in the region are located in different cities and towns of Punjab. Except for certain militant groups that are active in Khyber Pakhtunkhwa and the Tribal Belt, the centres of all jihadist and sectarian outfits are situated in Punjab. It is also worth mentioning here that the greatest supply of cannon fodder of the militants to Khyber Pakhtunkhwa and the Tribal areas comes from Punjab. According to a conservative estimate, more than fifty percent of the militants active in these areas, hail from Punjab. After the U.S. invasion in Afghanistan the majority of the terrorists of Al-Qaeda and Taliban had taken refuge in Punjab. The prominent operatives of Al-Qaeda like Khaled Sheikh Muhammad, Abu-Zubaida and Abu Khalfan were all arrested from big urban centres of Punjab like Rawalpindi, Faisalabad and Gujrat whereas hundreds of other terrorists were also captured from different cities of province.[44]

A study of various divisions (administrative units) of Punjab has been conducted in order to have a cursory idea of the influence of the extremist and hardliner religious outfits on the otherwise peaceful and tolerant atmosphere of Punjab. This brief but interesting case study highlights the rise of extremism and sectarian hatred in these administrative units of the province. For example we get some shocking details if we study the extremism and the sectarian sentiments being nurtured in the villages and towns of provincial capital Lahore.

LAHORE DIVISION

The Lahore Division has the unique 'honour' that the headquarter of 'Lashkar-e-Tayyba' the largest jihadist outfit of the region is located here and there are hundreds of points in Lahore alone that serve as recruitment centres and provide financial support by collecting donations for the organisation. The headquarters are located at Muridke around 30 km from Lahore, where two townships are also developed under the title of Mecca and 'Medina' colonies for the followers of Salafi (Wahhabi) sect from all over the country in order to provide them with a 'pure atmosphere', strictly in accordance with the shariah law. All the plots of these townships are owned by the followers of the Wahhabi sect and special efforts have been made that the inhabitants of these housing societies remain free of all the pollution of 'anti-shariah' vices of the outside world. For example, the resident of these areas do have the right to read daily newspapers and cannot see the photographs, as seeing photographs is against the tenets of Islam. For this purpose the armed youth of L-e-T remain present at the entry gates of these colonies with ink-markers in their hands to perform the duty of 'self-censorship' of every photograph published in the newspapers. After a hard work of about two hours these 'purged' newspaper are then provided to the inhabitants of Mecca and Medina colonies however they are not allowed to have TV sets in their households. They are only permitted to have transistor radios so that they can listen to the news or programmes based on religious education but not the 'vulgar music or satanic and worldly talks' and anyone found guilty of not obeying these restrictions could also run the risk of eviction from these 'blessed' housing schemes.[45]

There is a vast construction of modern buildings at the L-e-T headquarters where jihadists are imparted education and militant training. Since the time L-e-T has been declared a terrorist organisation by the UNO and the western world, the access to the information about the activities at these headquarters has remained quite restricted. The people of Salfi sect from all over Pakistan have tried to migrate to the nearest city of Muridke so the appearance of that city has also been transformed into a model of shariah laws. Once considered a relatively calm town, comprising staunch followers of the Pakistan Peoples' Party, it is now under control of the political parties that enjoy full support by the powerful agencies of Islamabad. Pakistan Muslim League (Nawaz) and Pakistan Muslim League (Quaid) wield electoral support here and any candidate can easily win the election provided he has the patronage and support of the local Jihadists. L-e-T also has a dominating position in Lahore because its administrative headquarters are located here. These headquarters, and the administrative centres of

L-e-T are located in the old city as well as at the busy commercial area of Chauburji.[46]

The religious parties responsible for infusing elements of militancy and extremism in a rather tolerant culture of the Lahore Division include Jamaat-e-Islami Pakistan, Jamaat-ud-Dawa, Sipah-e-Sahaba Pakistan, Tehreek-e-Nafaz-e-Fiqah-e-Jaffria, Jamiat Ahle Hadith and a host of other smaller organisations that have a forceful presence in their respective strongholds. The city of Lahore also has a prominent place as far as incidents of sectarian violence are concerned and many of the prominent personalities from both Sunni and Shiite sects have been assassinated here. Many of the political leaders, businessmen, poets, intellectuals and bureaucrats have been murdered here merely due to their sectarian backgrounds. The defunct Sipah-e-Sahaba established a large seminary under the title of Jamia Farooqia in the area of Shahdara as its provincial headquarter that served as the base camp for the sectarian killers as well, who after executing their targets returned to that safe haven. The local administration and the police at several times informed their superiors about the presence of sectarian killers in this seminary but no grand scale operation has ever been performed there. Similarly, the biggest seminary of the Shiite sect "Jamia Al-muntazir" is located in Model Town Lahore where Shiite sectarian elements enjoy full protection. Many of the prominent authors of sectarian and hate mongering literature have served here as teachers, most prominent of them was Allama Ghulam Hussain Najafi who was murdered sometime ago while he was coming out of the seminary.

Moreover Jamia Asharfia the seminary named after one iconic scholar of the Deobandi sect is also located in the heart of the city at Ferozpur Road where groups and individuals related with Afghan jihad took training. Some sources have claimed the presence of trained militants of Sipah-e-Sahaba and Lashkar-e-Jhangvi in the seminary but successive governments in Punjab have been reluctant to impose any restriction on the said seminary. Rather the leadership of Punjab has been relying on the "services" of Jamia Asharfia. Mansoora, the headquarters of Jamaat-e-Islami are also located in Lahore and it had been a significant place during the heydays of Afghan Jihad. Jamaat-e-Islami launches all of its political and religious movements from

Mansoora whereas the residence of its Ameer (chief) and the other central office-bearers are also constructed in its large housing complex. Presently, apart from serving as the headquarters of political activities of Jamaat-e-Islami, hundreds of foreign students are also getting education in the seminaries in Mansoora.[47]

Two other centres at the outskirts of Lahore are also worth mentioning here and both are under the control of the influential and armed groups of the Shiite sect. One centre is situated in the village of Thokar Niaz Beg in the south of Lahore whereas the other is located in the north. It is the centre in Begum Kot for the Shiites of an emotive group. An influential saint Bawa Sada Hussain lives here and it is claimed that among others, the current president of Pakistan Asif Ali Zardari is also one of his followers. Bawa Sada Hussain has always been on the hit-list of Sipah-e-Sahaba and Lashkar-e-Jhangvi whereas some of his personal connections include political elite of Pakistan, wealthy ex-patriots and some influential circles of Iran. He is considered the head of Malang (Dervish) group among the Shiite population of Pakistan who is always surrounded by dozens of armed persons. His opponents claim that he is the pioneer of the tradition of Tabbara (an abusive language against the first three Caliphs of Islam and their families) at a louder voice in the congregations of Muharram and instead of accepting the prime importance of the basic tenets of Shiite jurisprudence he gives a central place to the rituals of Matam and Tabbara. A lion who always accompanies Bawa Sada Hussain is one of the distinct features of his center. Many researchers on sectarianism in Pakistan agree to the fact that the centre of Begum Kot has played a key role in escalating sectarian tensions in Pakistan because the preachers of opposing sects, by quoting inflammatory speeches and Tabbaras of Bawa Sada Hussain, provoke their youthful followers towards sectarian killings.

Similarly, the second centre of the Shiite sect located at the village Thokar Niaz Beg, also carries a long history of sectarian tensions. It came to light for the first time when the supreme commander of Sipah-e-Muhammad Ghulam Raza Naqvi turned this village into his headquarters. Originally hailing from the city of Jhang, Ghulam Raza Naqvi had transformed this village into a heavily guarded hamlet for a long time along with hundreds of armed youth and had played a prominent role in the sectarian killings in Punjab. In the meantime Ghulam Raza Naqvi and his companions were branded as bank robbers and dacoits, whereas the inhabitants of this centre also murdered some very important leaders of Sipah-e-Sahaba. Several attempts of a police operation at Thokar Niaz Beg were made but a siege of the village by militant youths has always failed.[48]

The nearby town of Raiwind also enjoys a pivotal place among the jihadist and sectarian circles of Pakistan. Raiwind is the world-renowned headquarter of "Tableeghi Jamaat" of Deobandi Sect. Tableeghi Jamaat arranges an annual congregation that is attended by hundreds of thousands of people from all over the world. Some circles have claimed that the chief of Taliban, Mullah Omar has, several times also participated in this convention whereas the leaders of sectarian parities like Sipah-e-Sahaba and Lashkar-e-Jhangvi have had close ties with the Tableeghi Jamaat. The era of General Zia-ul-Haq gave birth to the tradition of participation in the annual congregation by the presidents and prime ministers of the country as well. Some of the high ranking army personnel are also known for their close ties with Tableeghi Jamaat including Lieutenant General (r) Hameed Gul and Lieutenant General (r) Javed Nasir, the ex-bosses of I.S.I. Moreover the districts of Okara and Sheikhupura are also infamous for sectarian violence as well as being important centres of Lashkar-e-Tayyba. The only surviving operative of Mumbai attacks, Ajmal Kasav who became known all over the world after these terrorist attacks also hails from Fareed Kot, a village of district Okara. Many of the leading commanders as well as "martyrs" of Lashkar-e-Tayyba, Sipah-e-Sahaba and Lashkar-e-Jhangvi come from districts of Okara and Sheikhupura whereas there are thousands of activists and supporters in these districts. In general, the Lahore division could be declared the most important among the divisions of Punjab rife with jihadi and sectarian elements.

On the 1st of July 2009, about 35 households of the Christian community in district Kasur of Lahore division were ransacked and around 15 persons were injured in these attacks. These Christian families were charged with blasphemy. According to police sources there was a row between a motorcyclist Muhammad Riaz and the tractor driver Sardar Massey of the Christian majority village Bahmani Wala on the rights of passage. In order to take revenge Muhammad Riaz, along with his armed companions, reached Bahmani Wala where he was beaten up by the Christian community. A leader of a religious outfit Qari Lateef tried to give a religious twist to the row and it was announced over loudspeakers of the local mosque the next day that the Christian community had committed an act of blasphemy to the Holy Prophet Muhammad. No sooner had the announcement been made than the situation became very tense and a large number of people from the Muslim community attacked the Christian village. According to police sources, no charges of blasphemy could be proved during the inquest.[49]

On September 28th 2009, a local woman Shahnaz Bibi and two of her female companions were paraded naked in the village by Intisar-ul-Haq Muaviya, a former activist of defunct Sipah-e-Sahaba and the present leader of the Pakistan Muslim League (N), accompanied by more than 50 armed accomplices in the town of Phool Nagar (Bhai Pheru) near Lahore. The houses of these women were looted and their young girl, Asma Mushtaq was abducted. Shahnaz Bibi alleged that Nazim (head) of the Local Union Council was giving instructions to the accomplices after which the hair of these unfortunate women was cut their faces were blackened and they were garlanded with shoes. Shahnaz Bibi has also been a former councillor of the area and a litigation case of her house was underway in the local court. According to her, she and two of her female guests were subjugated to this inhuman treatment just because of that conflict. She called the local police, who colluded with the calprits in that heinous plot as it did not take any action despite arriving at the spot. Three of the miserable women were not only taken to the nearby police post and then to the police station in that semi-naked condition but a false case of prostitution was registered against them as well. Later on they also filed a petition in the Lahore High Court and presented to the media the snaps of their public humiliation shot through a mobile phone camera. Shahnaz Bibi removed her headgear and showed her shaven head. She was much concerned about her adopted daughter Asma Mushtaq, aged 13, who was still missing after four days of the incident and was very worried about her well-being. The three women were not willing to go back to their houses due to the terror perpetrated by the local hooligans. It is worthwhile to mention that the local extremist leader of Sipah-e-Shaba Intisarul Haq Muavia claimed that women belonged to the Shiite sect were involved in prostitution. However he could not prove his allegations and later on it was known that he is the local head of Phool Nagar for the political party currently ruling the Punjab province. In the Pakistan Penal Code, death penalty is prescribed for removing the clothes of any women for her public humiliation but there is a strong possibility that nobody would dare become a witness against these influential people and ultimately these women would be obliged to withdraw their case.[50]

BAHAWALPUR DIVISION

Bahawalpur, Rahimyar Khan and Bahawalnagar districts of Bahawalpur Division could be branded the most dangerous areas with regard to jihadist activities and sectarian tensions. In these districts, banned organisations like Jaish-e-Muhammad, Lashkar-e-Jhangvi and Sipah-e-Sahaba enjoy the support of thousands of 'fidayeen'. Jaish-e-Muhammad is a powerful armed wing of the Taliban movement and even today, more than five thousand of its militants are engaged in fierce battles against Pakistani security forces in Swat and Waziristan and against US and NATO forces in Afghanistan. The Bahawalpur division could also be called the most dangerous area of Pakistan where several centres of terrorist outfits still exist and the U.S. and several other countries declare it a region of Al-Qaeda and Taliban's supporters.

The seminary Madrassa Makhzan-ul-Uloom, that is situated in the middle of the Tehsil Headquarter Offices complex in tehsil Khan Pur of district Rahim Yar Khan, was established in 1944. It is a central place for anti-Shiite activities, under the patronage of Jamiat Ulmae-Islam (Fazal-ur-Rahman group). It was founded by renowned cleric Maulana Abdullah Darkhwasti who was highly inspired by Maulana Ubaid Ullah Sindhi, a famous leader of Indian National Congress during 1920s. Maulana Sindhi had been a secret activist of Silk the Scarf Movement that was started by the Muslims of the Indian sub-continent in the beginning of the 20th century in a bid to overthrow the British Raj. Maulana Darkhwasti expired in 1994 and he remained the central Ameer (chief) of Jamiat Ulmae Islam (F) till his death. Now the seminary of Madrassa Makhzan-ul-Uloom is being run by his son Ata-ur-Rahman. The grandson of Abdullah Darkhwasti, who had been a famous leader of Jamaat Ulmae Islam (S) till his death in 2007 had established another seminary in Khanpur under the title of Madrassa Abdullah Bin Masood. One Abdul Sattar Taunsvi used to come to this seminary frequently for many years. He hailed from town of Taunsa in district Dera Ghazi Khan and he was appointed supreme commander of Sipah-e-Sahaba in later years. He also got fame for his anti-Shiite speeches during the 1970s and 1980s. It is worth-mentioning here that the son of Abdul Sattar Taunsvi also got his education from the same seminary of Dar-ul-Uloom Eidgah in Kabeer Wala where Haq Nawaz Jhangvi, the founder of Sipah-e-Sahaba Pakistan had also been a student. Khanpur is also a markaz (centre) of Tableeghi Jamaat in district Raheem Yar Khan and the administrator of this markaz is an ex-student of the same seminary of Dar-ul-Uloom Eidgah.[51]

Some circles claim that Jaish-e-Muhammad still holds some very close ties with the powerful secret agencies of the Pak army and its chief Maulana Masood Azhar is set to establish a huge training centre in the area of Chaulistan in district Bahawalpur. The financial resources for this center are said to be provided by Al-Qaeda whereas I.S.I. is also providing him with 'technical assistance'. Jaish-e-Muhammad has also been allotted five acres of land in city centre of Bahawalpur, where the outfit is busy constructing its headquarters. Currently thousands of militants of Jaish-e-Muhammad are living in Bahawalpur and Maulana Masood Azhar, declared as the main accused by the Indian government after the Mumbai attacks, is also residing here while the government of Pakistan claims that his whereabouts are not known. Certain jihadi resources confide that Maulana Masood Azhar frequently visits the Al-Qaeda militants at Pak-Afghan borders and he spends most of his time in these frequent travels.[52]

Bahawalpur, Rahimyar Khan and Bahawalnagar are considered the strongholds of Jaish-e-Muhammad, Sipah-e-Sahaba and Lashkar-e-Taiyba as thousands of youth are recruited from these districts not only for jihad in Kashmir and for Al-Qaeda and Taliban's resistance in Afghanistan but also for the sectarian killing sprees within the country. The commander of Lashkar-e-Jhangvi Malik Ishaq also hails from Rahim Yar Khan. The group of Malik Ishaq is alleged to have killed hundreds of Shiite. Presently he is in jail but most of the cases against him are either terminated or he has been granted bail in several. According to the latest information he could be released at any time as nobody is willing to give evidence against him. Everyone who ever dared present himself against him in any court has been assassinated and several of the judges have also been threatened with dire consequences by Malik Ishaq and his cohorts.

When Osama Nazir, hailing from Bahawalpur, was arrested from a seminary of Faisalabad in 2004, there was an immediate demand from the US authorities that he should be handed over to them. It is worth mentioning here that he was alleged to have killed one female American diplomat among other people. The name of Osama Nazir was not unknown to the law enforcement agencies of Pakistan. Nazir Ahmen aka Aadil aka Osama Nazir had been working as a vital link among jihadist organisations, Taliban, Mullah Omar, Osama Bin Laden and the financial sponsors of jihad. The criminal charges levelled against him by the investigation authorities are as follows:

He attacked a protestant church in Islamabad on 17th March 2002. The lady diplomat of the US along with her daughter died on the spot whereas forty people including ten American citizens were critically injured.

Attacked a Christian School Murree on 5th August 2002 where six Christian Pakistani citizens were killed.

He also attacked a Christian Hospital Taxila on 9th August 2002.[53]

Investigation as well as the forensic evidence collected from these sites of terrorist attacks brought the name of Osama Nazir to the limelight as he had played a vital role in all of them. The names of Saif ur Rahman Saifi, Rehan Babar, Muhammad Ayaz aka Waqar, Muhammad Izhar aka Muhammad Kashif, Muhammad Asif Raza aka Babu, Abdul Qadeer aka Javaid Iqbal, Muhammad Ata, Muhammad Naeem, Aziz Ullah, Muhammad Ali and Tanveer Iqbal were among some of his cohorts. Osama Nazir got his education from seminaries of Faisalabad and Multan and his links with some leading jihadist outfits from Punjab were established during the period of his education. Afterwards, he joined the Taliban movement as he was inspired by their jihadist philosophy. Soon he left the education incomplete and went to Afghanistan alongwith some of his companions. At that time, the Taliban were ruling over Afghanistan and hundreds of youth from Pakistan were joining them. According to the report by secret agencies, Osama Nazir was initially sent to Kandahar where he got militant training and learnt the use of the latest arms and ammunition and he sided with Taliban in the fight against Northern Alliance.

After the US attack on Afghanistan, Osama Nazir also came back to Pakistan like many of his companions and according to some sources he remained under investigation by several secret agencies. He was also alleged to have married the daughter of one of the important Taliban commanders and according to some information he entered into Pakistan along with his family after the American attack but nothing is known about his wife. Not much information about him has been available since his arrest.[54]

The district of Bahawalnagar, due to its poverty and backwardness has also proved a breeding ground of jihadists and sectarian killers. The murder case of the father of Riaz Hussain Pirzada, many times elected MP of the area, was registered against Maulana Azam Tariq the chief of Sipah-e-Sahaba. Although Maulana Azam Tariq was arrested in this case, he was released on bail later on. Raiz Hussain Pirzada has received so many threats to his life from Sipah-e-Sahaba and Lashkar-e-Jhangvi. He is so scared of the present situation of his constituency that a statement by him was published in the *Daily Jang* on 13th January 2009 where he has declared that no action against the chief of the defunct Jaish-e-Muhammad would be allowed. He also declared that any attack against Maulana Masood Azhar would be deemed a direct attack against the Saraiki ethnicity. The B.B.C. expressed its surprise on this statement by Riaz Hussain Pirzada in favour of Jaish-e-Muhammad chief Maulana Masood Azhar because Jaish-e-Muhammad and Lashkar-e-Jhangvi are jointly involved in sectarian pogrom all over the country especially in the Bahawalpur division. This also explains the enormity of the public fear as well as the reign of terror unleashed by the jihadists and the sectarian hate mongers.[55]

The alleged mastermind of the Mumbai attacks, Hammad Amin turned out to be a resident of Amant Colony of district Rahim Yar Khan where he lived at 1 B 602, Bajwa Street. According to the investigation report by Express News, Hammad Amin who was born in Rahim Yar Khan on 19th September 1971, had completed four-year course in homeopathy after passing his secondary school examination. Afterwards he started a drugstore in Rahim Yar Khan but migrated to Karachi after getting married in 2000 and he fathered two children.[56]

In Karachi, he also worked at a pathology lab for two years. The house from where he was arrested by the special team of Federal Investigation Agency, he had rented only three days before. According to his college teachers Hammad Amin was a mediocre student.

Hammad and his family developed relations with Lashkar-e-Tayyba and he also got a proper training from Jihadi centres of the Lashkar-e-Tayyba. Hammad was given special training for the Mumbai attacks by Zaki-ur-Rahman and other jihadist leaders and also provided financial assistance to his family.[57]

Madrassa Usman-o-Ali is the biggest seminary of jihadists in Baahawalpur that was established by Maulana Masood Azhar. The seminary situated in Model Town, a modern township in Bahawalpur, lays special emphasis on the importance of jihad and there are reports that a considerable number of its students, along with the Taliban, are engaged in battles in Afghanistan and Tribal Areas of Pakistan.

Armed guards remain on duty for twenty four hours at the main entrance of the seminary and nobody is allowed in without prior permission. Allah Bakhsh Sabir, the father of Maulana Masood Azhar and an ex-headmaster or principal of a teachers' training school is serving as an imam in the seminary. To keep them always ready for jihad, the students are imparted physical training as well besides the religious education.

A large number of Pashtun students are residing in the mosque adjacent to the seminary and they have to follow a specific strict discipline. Nobody is allowed to utter a single word about Maulana

Masood Azhar or his father. A large number of jihadists have graduated from the seminary. There is a special accentuation on the significance of jihad in the speeches on Friday prayers or other congregations.[58]

FAISALABAD DIVISION

When we talk about the sectarian conflicts as well as ever-increasing violence by the terrorist outfits, Faisalabad is considered one of the most important divisions of Punjab that has nurtured thousands of jihadists and hard-core sectarian elements. The might of jihadists and sectarian hate-mongers could be judged by the fact that Abu-Zubaida, the infamous terrorist of Al-Qaeda, was captured from the city of Faisalabad. Lashkar Jhangvi, Sipah-e-Sahaba and Lashkar-e-Tayyba give a peculiar 'honour' and 'identity' to this city. In Faisalabad the militants of Sipah-e-Sahaba and Lashakar-e-Jhangvi operate scores of seminaries and other centres that not only serve as shelters for them but according to some reliable information they also make fresh recruitment through these 'base camps'.

The District of Jhang is probably the most dangerous district of Faisalabad division that gave birth to the present fatal tradition of sectarian massacre in Pakistan. Jhang is considered a district of big landholders and feudal lords of Shiite sect. The landless and socially weak peasant communities of Sunnis challenged the supremacy of privileged Shiites minority. Haq Nawaz Jhangvi, a Sunni orator of poor background and mediocre education played a prominent role in changing the culture of the district on sectarian basis. In his sermons, he intensely criticised the Shiite literature produced under deep Iranian influence and projected the Iranian views about the personalities of the divided and more often than not feuding tribal society of ancient Arabia, so that local perceptions as well as the traditional reverence for these sacred personalities could be exploited to provoke hatred against Shiite sect. Later the other fiery heirs to Haq Nawaz very "skilfully" carried on this tradition and an ample fuel was added to fire of sectarian killings.[59]

It would not be wrong to call the district of Jhang an axis of sectarian tug-of-war and carnage. Till today Jhang is like the headquarters for extremist and sectarian killers and all the extremist elements from Lashkar-e-Jhangvi to Sipah-e-Sahaba contact the sectarian leadership present in Jhang for "guidance" in all their activities.

Despite the ban, the above mentioned outfits of essentially sectarian identity have continued their activities in Pakistan under other names but "real" names and leaders are still very much active in Jhang with all their vigour. Maulana Muhammad Ahmed Ludhianvi is still the most forceful personality of Jhang and recently when some terrorists attacked the Army's General Headquarters (GHQ) and kept some high ranking officers as hostages for many hours, army commanders contacted Maulana Ludhianvi, the chief of defunct Sipah-e-Sahaba to negotiate with the attackers, thus his 'guidance' to terrorist helped resolve this serious issue.

On the other hand, the Shiite seminary "Jamia Ale-Muhammad has also been playing an important role in the sectarian pogrom. Allama Muhammad Ismail Deobandi the founder of the said seminary is considered to be an architect of sectarian animosity in Pakistan. As his name indicates he had been a Deobandi before converting to the Shiite sect. He had been a very famous Deobandi doctrinaire and a scintillating orator who could do 'wonders' with his fiery rhetoric. When he left Deobandis and converted to the Shiite sect, he focused his cannons towards Sunni dogmas. He was given a high protocol in Shiite circles and in their congregations he used to start his address with these apologetic phrases like "I've eventually reverted to the true religion and sincerely regret that I had been quite insensitive to your sentiments in my "days of ignorance" and could not recognise the worth of the real personalities of Islam".

His seminary "Jamia Ale Muhammad is often held responsible for sowing the seeds of sectarian hatred. Similarly, after Ismail Deobandi, his son-in-law Allama Fazil Musavi had a knack for "throwing fireballs" to his audience. He was highly satirical in criticising the beliefs and sacred personalities of opponent sects and his hate speeches provided sipah-e-Sahaba and Lashkar-e-Jhangvi the justification to target kill the Shiite community. Eventually Alama Fazil Musavi also became a victim of his own fiery rhetoric and he was murdered in cold blood. It is said that the murderers incinerated his dead body. His goading speeches are still available in video recordings or uploaded on different sites by Sunnis for a better "comprehension" of Shiite beliefs and their younger generation is "full use" of them.

In November 2005, one Yousaf Massey won a substantial amount in gambling while playing with two Muslims. The very next day, one of the losers brought a damaged copy of the Holy Koran to a local book binder and claimed that Yousaf Massey had desecrated the Holy Book. There were immediate announcements from the mosques and an angry mob of more than fifteen hundred people destroyed one dozen houses, five churches, three schools, one convent and one dispensary within no time. After three months, Yousaf Massey was acquitted by the anti-terrorist court for lack of evidence whereas the hooligans arrested for ransacking the Christian properties were also set free on the same grounds.[60]

In Pakistan, the law suggests death penalty for blasphemy of the sacred personalities or the holy books. So far, more than one thousand people have been arrested under these charges and a vast majority of them are Christians. In most cases the real motives comprise so called 'honour', personal or political grudges, property disputes or religious hatred but the issue is so sensitive that merely levelling an allegation is considered sufficient, then vigilante justice take its course as people take the law into their own hands and prosecute the accused. The police are also reluctant to take any action in such incidents and generally arrive very late when all the killing, arson and pillage are over and the mob has satiated its thirst of mad revenge and temper is no more running in high zones. Although the allegations of blasphemy rarely proved true but the plaintiffs who were instigators of these of false allegations were never taken to task either; on the other hand the persons framed in these false allegations were often forced to leave the town or in utter disregard of the principles of justice. Many of them were assassinated in compounds of courts, jails or even in the presence of the police force. Sectarian organisations always played a central role in every incident of pillage and massacre after these baseless accusations against the religious minorities were made. These outfits are not only responsible for the killing of citizens from minority sects or religions they have also been involved in looting their valuables and properties.

None of the accused in heinous crimes has ever been convicted in any court of law as nobody has the guts to appear for evidence for the fear of high-handedness of extremist religious outfits.[61]

In tehsil Gojra of district Faisalabad the terrorists of Sipah-e-Sahaba and Lashkar-e-Jhangvi not only targeted the townships of religious minorities once again but also burned the Christians alive and plundered their properties. After the rumours of firing on the rally against alleged desecration of the Holy Koran, a frenzied mob attacked the township of Christians and set ablaze more than two dozen houses. According to initial information eight persons including three women were burned alive and their houses were pillaged.[62]

Subsequent investigations revealed that all together 35 houses were burnt while the police remained silent spectators. Qadeer Awan, the president of Muslim League (N) Gojra was the real culprit behind that horrific incident and he also happened to be an important leader of the banned sectarian outfit Sipah-e-Sahaba and he targeted the Christians just because of some old grudges of an election campaign and used the false allegation of desecration of the Holy Koran as a pretext to take revenge.

The National Assembly's Standing Committee on Human Rights declared that the gory incident of burning alive of Christian citizens of Gojra in Faisalabad division was an utter failure of the local administration and recommended the inclusion in the investigation all the officers of police and local administration, who had been suspended from the duties after the incident. It was also decided by the committee that the investigation would be conducted by an officer of the rank no lesser than a Deputy Inspector General (D.I.G.) Police and the standing committee would be informed about the findings of investigation. In the committee, meeting the Regional Police Officer Faisalabad Ahmed Raza presented a detailed report which stated that militants of different banned organisation including Sipah-e-Sahaba were involved in the incident and four of the accused, named Fakir Hussein Jatt, Aijaz Goga, Abid Farooqi and Khalid Hussein Khaldi have been arrested whereas an accomplice Maulana Nafees-ur-Rahman was still at large.

At this meeting, the provincial minister for minorities affairs, Kamran Michael informed that one Talib Massey of local village Korian worked as a waste paper merchant while the marriage of his son was to take place on 25th July with the daughter of one Mukhtar Massey, for which both the families were busy in the ceremony of Mehndi (the ceremonial singing and dance one night before the wedding festival). Some of the children took his stock of waste paper and cut it in the size of currency notes to playfully shower them over the guests during the Mehndi ceremony. However the inhabitants of the village found scraps of paper in the street next day with Koranic verses printed on them. The R.P.O. told the committee that there were not only some heated announcement through loudspeakers of mosques but also there were demands to hang Talib Massey publicly. Upon this, some criminal elements threw kerosene oil on the houses of Christians, including Talib Massey and set them on fire. Twelve houses burnt to ashes whereas eighteen were damaged by the fire.[63]

He said that on 1st August there was a rally at Malkanwala Chowk and around one hundred people from different banned jihadist and sectarian organisations, armed with batons, arrived there. As soon as the rally concluded, the angry mob threw stones at the Christians and then started beating them. Some felonious elements exploited the situation and opened gunfire first on Christians and then on Muslims and one Hameed Massey died on the spot. The police officer claimed that the local administration and police encircled the members of the Christian community and took them out to a church whereas the heirs of the assassinated Hameed Massey refused to leave the place. He said some felons sprinkled kerosene oil on the house of Hameed Massey and set it on fire and seven persons in the house were burnt alive. The minister of Punjab for Minorities Affairs Kamran Michael told the Committee that it was not kerosene oil but a dangerous chemical that instantly melted all the metal items in the house.[64]

Faisalabad is also a safe haven for terrorists and most wanted criminals as a great number of terrorists were apprehended here in various operations during the global war on terror. On 26th March 2002, when U.S. officials informed the Pakistani intelligence officers about the presence of an important Al-Qaeda operative in Faisalabad, most of the Pakistani officers were not fully aware of the significance of that 'important personality' of Al-Qaeda, but the officials of the Pakistani F.I.A. as well as American F.B.I. knew fully well about the high value of the target that was hiding in Faisalabad.

When the joint team of C.I.A., F.B.I. and I.S.I. was planning to raid the house where that leader of Al-Qaeda was hiding, they were expecting a high resistance from the other side. Thus very special arrangements were made to prevent any expected flight from the militants of Al-Qaeda in case of a tough encounter.

On 27th March 2002, when the teams from three raiding parties arrived at Faisalabad, except for some important personalities, very few people knew what was going to happen there. The house that served as the shelter for the militants of Al-Qaeda was under siege till dusk, and due to the rapid movement and some announcements by the law enforcement agencies, the people hiding in the house also came to know that they have already been surrounded.

The militants taking refuge in the house had taken retaliatory positions and an exchange of firing ensued. On the same evening of March 2002, the headquarters of C.I.A. in Langley, U.S.A. thousands of kilometres away from Faisalabad was presenting an entirely different scenario. George Tenet the chief of C.I.A. and members of the Abu-Zubaida task force were present in the conference room on the ground floor. Through the latest communication technology they were in contact with operatives of C.I.A., F.B.I. and the officials of Pakistani intelligence officials, the members of raiding teams. There was an extraordinary excitement at Langley when an agent of C.I.A. informed that after a tough encounter, Abu-Zubaida the operational chief of Al-Qaeda had been apprehended while he was wounded in the process.

The arrest of Abu-Zubaida was a great achievement for the U.S. and Pakistan in the war against terror and a severe blow for the Al-Qaeda as the arrest of its operational chief meant that the backbone of this international terrorist organisation had been broken. In a few moments there was breaking news in the international media that Abu-Zubaida has been captured in Faisalabad, an important industrial and commercial hub of Pakistan. Such an easy capture of Abu-Zubaida was quite astonishing, who was a high value target and also a key operative in the attacks of 9/11 and who had been in-charge of all operation and activities of terrorism by Al-Qaeda.[65]

Just after the terrorist attacks of 9/11, the counter terrorism force had set up a special Abu-Zubaida task committee in the headquarters of C.I.A. with a single point agenda of hunting down for Abu-Zubaida. The task force comprised about 100 members including special agents of C.I.A., analysts, technicians and I.T. experts. With the help of thousands of reports by the special agents, satellite images and intercepted telephonic conversations, the task force finally managed to find out that Abu-Zubaida was presently residing in a house at Faisalabad. It took only 12 hours to apprehend him after he had been traced by said task force.

Abu-Zubaida was not an easy target. He was promoted as an operational chief after the elimination of Muhammad Atif, the death of whom in the U.S. attacks at Afghanistan, was in itself a great blow for the Al-Qaeda. He somehow managed to fill the gap created by the death of Muhammad Atif. Born in Saudi Arabia in 1973, with Palestinian parents he was able to establish close ties with jihadist organisations of Palestine and Lebanon. He became an activist of Islamic Jihad at the young age of 18 and came to Pakistan during the heydays of Afghan jihad. Here he had the chance to meet Osama Bin Laden who was residing in Peshawar at that time. His links with O.B.L. continued till his arrest on 27th March 2002.

Abu-Zabaida was known by many pseudonyms like Ziyan-Ul-Badin, Muhammad Hussein, Abul Halai Al Wahab in different circles. It was Abu-Zubaida who formed various cells for anti-America activities when O.B.L. declared a secret war against the U.S., among his close circles. The investigation authorities claimed that he was involved in recruitment and training of jihadist volunteers in Pakistan. According to the investigation team, he was in-charge of Khalidain training camp in Afghanistan, where a large number of European militants of Arab origin were trained.

The U.S authorities assert that he has also been the mastermind behind the 1998 bombing of the U.S. embassy in South Africa. The joint investigation team comprising expert personnel of the C.I.A. and F.B.I., held 40 sessions of investigation with Abu-Zubaida. Although he informed them about a great number of Al-Qaeda operatives a majority of them had been either arrested or killed already. He disclosed that the plans to launch a series of attack on various commercial centres in the U.S. were also prepared but somehow could not be implemented.[66]

At the end of 1999 a military court in Lebanon convicted Abu-Zubaida of bomb attacks on tourist spots and decreed a death sentence against him. According to the investigation team he also planned an attack on the Los Angeles airport in December 1999. Ahmed Waseem from Algeria, an accomplice in that plan, revealed to the military court that Abu-Zubaida issued instructions for these attacks from a training camp in Afghanistan and recruited militants for Al-Qaeda. Ahmed Wassem was also a trainee in the same camp and according to him they were also instructed to get a Canadian passport in order to launch these attacks on the U.S.

The documents captured from Abu-Zubaida's house at the time of his arrest included a letter with signature OBL's, stating that he was alive and well. The evidences and the handwritten notes gathered from the house revealed that Abu-Zubaida was planning attacks on American oil tankers and the U.S. vessels in the open seas.

The investigations from Abu-Zubaida also reveal that he had very close relations with Zakria Musavi, the twentieth hijacker of the planes that hit World Trade Centre and it is also claimed that French-born Zakria Musavi was also a trainee at Khalidain Camp. Abu-Zubaida also told the investigation team that Al-Qaeda had started preparations for dirty radioactive bombs to be used against the U.S. and its allies and that Al-Qaeda was well aware of the secret routes for smuggling this ammunition into the U.S. However, the investigation team refused to accept these claims as they were contradictory to the details provided by him later on.[67]

A narrow road leads to village number 687/27GB of tehsil Kamalia in district Toba Tek Singh in the Faisalabad Division. Mud-thatched houses, heaps of filth, ponds of stinking water and broken roads, with rising waves of dusty air reflect the deprivation and backwardness of the area. It is an everyday scene for the residents of the village, one house of which is the abode of Manzoor Ahmed who is around 70.

The other members of the family include his wife, three sons Javaid Iqbal, Amir Farooqi and Fida Farooqi. Javaid Iqbal is the only married son. Mazoor Ahmed also had a fourth son named Amjad Farooqi. Nobody in his family had ever imagined that Amjad, brought up in this backward and poverty-ridden village, would be known all over the world as the murderer of American journalist Daniel Pearl and responsible for the attacks on General Pervez Musharraf. It is a long story as to why Amjad Farooqi opted for this life. When the government of Pakistan announced a reward on his head for him the list of allegations against him was already very long, for example:

- Attack on the U.S. consulate, Karachi in January 2002
- Attempt to hit Jacobabad airport in February 2002
- A attack on a church at Islamabad on 17th March 2002
- Attack on a church at Bahawalpur in May 2002
- Murder of American journalist Daniel Pearle in 2002
- The attempts on the life of General Pervez Musharraf in December 2003

Amjad Farooqi, a close associate of Naeem Bukhari, Asif Ramzi, Akram Lahori and Riaz Basra, the people wanted in heinous sectarian crimes, had close ties with some very important leaders of Al-Qaeda and it was on their behest that he was engaged in serious acts of terrorism. During the partition of the Indian sub-continent, his family migrated from district Hoshiarpur of East Punjab to Village 687/27GB of tehsil Kamalia. Amjad Farooqi was brought up by his uncle Muhammad Sharif who later became his father-in-law. During his education at college he came into close contact with certain people that brought about drastic changes in his thinking way of life. He also disappeared in the same period. He left his college and none of his family members was aware of his whereabouts. Then reappeared after a considerable period of time as a totally changed Amjad Farooqi. A young man, once afraid of influential people of the area, was a devout preacher of jihad now and also trying to motivate his brothers to join him in jihad. His father once tried to make him aware of the manifesto of Tableeghi Jamaat and advised that him the message of Allah and his Holy Prophet Muhammad could be disseminated through peace and love for mankind but he opted for an utterly different way of life.

In the meantime he became an activist of a jihadist outfit 'Harkat-Ul-Ansar' and took to a life of 'mujahidin'.[68]

During the 1980s, he used to visit the areas of Toba Tek Singh, Faisalabad, Samandri, Kamalia and Multan and collected substantial amounts as part of fund-raising campaigns for 'Harkat-ul-Ansar'. In 1986, he headed for jihad in Afghanistan and made repeated visits there after the circle of his acquaintances expanded. According to credible sources, he also visited India occupied Kashmir several time on behalf of his jihadist organisation. He got training in different camps in Afghanistan and eventually he also became a jihadist chief after the death of previous commander. Once he joined a pesticide firm in Multan but that job was not for him and he was back to Afghanistan pretty soon. According to his brother, he got all the jewellry of his wife a day before he was to proceed for his 'holy journey' declaring that the valuables would be spent in the way of jihad.

Intelligence agencies claim that along with 'Harkat-ul-Ansar', Amjad Farooqi had affiliation with the 'Lashkar-e-Jhangvi'. He was also alleged to have launched innumerable sectarian attacks in small cities and towns of South Punjab on the orders of Shakeel Ahmed aka Mustafa, the commander of 'Lashkar-e-Jhangvi'. Shakeel Ahmed aka Mustafa hailed from Fort Abbas district Bahawalnagar had allegedly eliminated so many members of opponent sects that there was a head-money of 1.3 million for him. After the killing of Shakeel Ahmed aka Mustafa in a police encounter Amjad Farooqi stepped into his shoes. This was also the starting point of his reign of terror and he was more open and confident in his terrorist activities. For the first time his name came into the limelight in the abduction and murder of American journalist Daniel Pearl. Many of the accomplice in this heinous crime had already been apprehended but Amjad Farooqi managed to escape the law enforcement agencies for a considerable period of time. The police resorted to its traditional tactics by abducting several members of his family and kept them under investigation for about a month. After one and a half years Muhammad Akhlaq, Muhammad Hanif, Mazhar, Akhlaq Ahmed, Attar Muazzam and some women were arrested again from the village of the in-laws of Amjad Farooqi but that also did not help to find any clue about him. The women were released after a few days whereas the males were kept under investigation for a month. The relatives and in-laws of Amjad Farooqi were quite fed up with these repeated raids and abductions by the police.[69]

His name was again in media focus after the assassination attempts against General Pervez Musharraf and that triggered a new round of raids on an extended scale for the hunt of Amjad Farooqi. He was last seen by his family in January 2002, when he made a surprise visit to his village. The family came to know about all his adventures, from the murder of Daniel Pearl to life attempts on General Musharraf, through the media. He was well aware of his continuous pursuit by the secret agencies and the F.B.I. so he always avoided visits to his village. Later on he went underground when he was chargesheeted in the Daniel Pearl murder and General Musharraf assassination attempts cases.[70]

In the circle of intelligence agencies, Amjad Farooqi was considered quite a sharp and wicked character and his cunning could be judged by the fact that even his close companion were not aware of his real name. All the persons apprehended in the Musharraf life attempt case used to call him "doctor". The people arrested in the Daniel Pearl case, knew him as Imtiaz Farooqi while the hijackers of Indian Airliners in 1999 used to call him Mansoor Hussein. Abuzar Ghaffari, Haider Ali, Mansoor Sani and Hussein Al-Kareem are some of his other pseudonyms.

The fact that the intelligence agencies till 11th January 2004 raided for his hunt at more than 50 places but never succeeded to get hold of him, is proof of how successful he had been in dodging the intelligence apparatus. The sources claim that he attempted to target many other important personalities of the country including Lieutenant General Ahsan Saleem Hayat the Corps Commander Karachi for several times.

On 26th September 2004, the house of the local commander of the banned outfit Jaish-e-Muhammad was sieged in Ghulam Haider Colony of Nawabshah Sindh there were clues that Amjad Farooqi was residing here. According to some eyewitnesses, he raised his arms in the air and declared "I have made good my promise to Allah; I prefer the death of a martyr than life". At that point a rifle-burst hit him and he died on the spot.[71]

On his death, the intelligence agencies heaved a sigh of relief as the important personalities of the country were in real danger of further assassination attempts as long as he was living. Certain quarters in intelligence as well as jihadist circles claim that he was already in custody and was killed in a fake encounter so that the investigations on General Musharraf's life attempts case could be closed and his links with some high-ranking army officers remained a mystery. The sources also claim that he was arrested in the middle of 2004 and last time he was seen in Tariq Hotel, in Quaidabad area of Karachi. It is worthwhile to mention that the renowned cleric of Jamia Banoria, Mufti Nizam-Ud-Din Shamazai was murdered the same day. The death of Amjad Farooqi also closed for good the chapter of his links with high ranking army officers, politicians, business tycoons and jihadist outfits. A proper investigation in his lifetime could have revealed who had been supporting him from the inner circles of the army in the conspiracy of the assassination attempts on General Pervez Musharraf.[72]

At present Faisalabad has a 'prominent' place due to serious sectarian conflicts and its jihadist culture. The now defunct Lashkar-e-Tayyba claims that a majority of their 'martyrs' hailed from Faisalabad. There are cemeteries specially meant for the 'martyrs' of Lashkar-e-Tayyba in certain towns and villages of Faisalabad whereas the district is considered the second biggest stronghold of Lashkar-e-Tayyba. Faisalabad is an attractive place for Jaish-e-Muhammad as well and it is safely estimated that there are more than three thousand militants who have their affiliations with Jaish-e-Muhammad. Rich industrialists and traders are the third distinct characteristic of Faisalabad and one in the habit of giving heavy donations to jihadist and sectarian outfits. The biggest financial assistance to outfits like Lashkar-e-Tayyba, Sipah-e-Sahaba, Lashkar-e-Jhangvi and Jaish-e-Muhammad comes from Faisalabad.

Currently, Faisalabad is declared a centre of Barelvi-Deobandi and Deobandi-Shiite sectarian tensions as at quite a faster pace the city has not only nurtured the groups preparing themselves for a perpetual war of sects but Faisalabad has also got the distinction of being the centre of Deobandi-Barelvi clashes in Pakistan. Sahibazada Fazil-e-Karim a member of national assembly belonging to Pakistan Muslim League

(N) has the claim of representing the Barelvis whereas Rana Sanaullah boasts of close ties with Deobandis. He is provincial law minister and considered very close to central leadership of Pakistan Muslim League. Once a member of Pakistan People's Party, Rana Sanaullah also represents the Rajput caste of Faisalabad and plays a noticeable role in the traditional Jatt-Rajput tug-of-war. He also has been quite prominent in the protest rallies after the government of Nawaz Sharif was overthrown by General Pervez Musharraf and he was abducted by secret agencies and had gone through severe torture during Musharraf regime but it could not change his political loyalties. This strong affiliation with Pakistan Muslim League (N) brought him closer to the party leadership and his role was extended to re-organisation of the party.

The sectarian outfits and groups of Punjab were developing rapprochements with the Muslim League (N) because due to certain steps by Musharraf government, the activists of sectarian and jihadist outfits were facing great difficulties in carrying on their 'work' after an apparent ban was imposed on them, while because of their specific structure and mindset they could not afford to come closer to the Pakistan People's Party whereas centre to right Pakistan Muslim League (N) was like a natural ally for them. At the same time Muslim League (N) was working under the guidance of leaders like Rana Sanaullah from Faisalabad and Sardar Zulfiqar Khosa from Dera Ghazi Khan having a clear inclination towards sectarian and jihadist organisations. The above mentioned leaders as well as their followers welcomed Deobandi sectarian outfits and jihadist groups into their party, initially in the opposition to Musharraf and eventually to give a tough time to the Pakistan People's Party as well. Thus thousands of supporters of defunct organisations like Sipah-e-Sahaba, Lashkar-e-Jhangvi and Jaish-e-Muhammad etc. joined the cadre of Pakistan Muslim League (N).[73]

The Pakistan Muslim League (N) did not rank as a favourite for the sectarian and jihadist outfits earlier but it drew their attention due to its enmity of Musharraf and its opposition to the war against terrorism waged during Musharraf era. The leadership of Muslim League (N) decided to include the armed sectarian elements and jihadist in their ranks in order to regain their lost strength and influence, and the process was started from Faisalabad where Rana Sanaullah was already following that policy and had gained support from militant from Sipah-e-Sahaba and Lashkar-e-Jhangvi in order to pressurise his political opponents. He did not have to face any difficulty in developing relations with Maulana Zahid Qasmi the son of Maulana Zia-Ul-Qasmi, the deceased patron of Sipah-e-Sahaba as maulana Zahid Qasmi had locked horns with famous Barelvi leader Sahibzada Fazal-e-Karim in sectarian feuds of Faisalabad. On the other hand, Sahibzada was challenging the political supremacy of Rana Sanaullah by getting himself elected on the ticket of Pakistan Muslim League (N). Maulana Zahid Qasmi could bring Rana Sanaullah dual benefits as he was not only helpful in attracting the leadership and thousands of youth from Sipah-e-Sahaba towards the Pakistan Muslim League (N) but could also challenge the political authority of Sahibzada Fazal-e-Karim in Faisalabad city. This year sectarian riots started in the city at the time of Eid-Melad-Un-Nabi (The festival on the birthday of Holy Prophet Muhammad) and allegations of firing on the procession of Eid Milad were made against the followers of Maulana Zahid Qasmi. The situation in the city got severely tense and centres of each sect came under attack by the other. Sahibzada Fazal Karim levelled allegations against Rana Sanaullah that he was extending undue support to the armed activists of Sipah-e-Sahaba and lashkar-e-Jhangvi. When pressure against Rana Sanaullah become intense he in turn levelled some serious charges against that member national assembly of his own party (Sahibzada Fazal Karim) and disclosed that he had allotted a plot of government land worth 350 million rupees to keep him quiet but he is not happy yet. This terrible confession by Rana Sanaullah is sufficient to judge that the sectarian militants of Faisalabad are how resourceful and how the political parties waste public funds just to appease these militants and use them for their ulterior motives.[74]

In Faisalabad, the Deobandi-Barelvi tensions are at their peak and there is a real threat of serious clashes between these two armed sects and these clashes to spread to that extent all over Punjab that it would be very difficult to control. After the suicide attacks at Data Darbar shrine in Lahore, tensions were very high in Faisalabad and other districts. However, timely intervention by the Federal Government helped defuse the situation. The clerics of Barelvi sect in Punjab see a sure involvement of Deobandi sectarian outfits as well as their patronage by the provincial government in the series of attacks unleashed at various shrines in the province. After the attacks on Data Darbar, the organisations of the Barelvi sect demanded the removal of the Provincial Law Minister as he was patronising the terrorists and sectarian elements in Punjab.[75]

Although Rana Sanaullah denies these allegations, he has not been able to establish that he has no links with sectarian as well as the banned jihadi outfits of Punjab, whereas many a times he has issued statements that his interaction with these outfits is of 'political nature' and they are 'pro-democracy' organisations. The details of these linkages of Rana Sanaullah became public for the first time when Maulana Jalandhry an important leader of Sipah-e-Sahaba was accompanying him in the campaign of bye-elections in district Jhang guarded by scores of his armed men, the majority of whom fall into the category of 'most wanted' by the police. After a hue and cry in the media Maulana Jhalandry participated in a TV talk show and presented a list of the assembly members who in the general elections of 2008 had been elected to the assemblies with the 'armed help' by Sipah-e-Sahaba and Lashkar-e-Jhangvi. The strangest fact is that none of assembly members dared contradict the list and indirectly accepted the fact that their electoral victory was not possible without the help of sectarian and extremist religious outfits.[76]

GUJRANWALA DIVISION

Gujranwala is one of the most important divisions of Punjab that is under siege by jihadist and sectarian outfits. Gujranwala also has the "honour" of providing the greatest number of martyrs for the Lashkar-e-Tayyba. The alliance of religious parties, Mutahida Majlis-e-Amal (M.M.A.) had its members of national and provincial assemblies elected from Gujranwala and Sialkot (the only places except for N.W.F.P. where M.M.A. managed to win the elections) and the sad fact is sufficient to give some idea of the clout of jihadist outfits in Gujranwala that in the general elections even the Peoples Party and Muslim League, the political parties of national stature are obliged to ask them for help in order to get their candidates elected. Lashkar-e-Jhangvi is so strong there that Muhammad Ashraf Marth the former police chief of Gujranwala was assassinated at the main gate of his own house. At that time a very close relative of the said police officer was sitting Federal Interior Minister but nobody had the courage to start any operation in the centres of Lashkar-e-Jhangvi located in Gujranwala.[77]

It was in Gujranwala that a female provincial minister (Ms. Zile Huma Usman) was assassinated in broad daylight by a fanatic of a jihadist outfit and he had already been involved in the cold-blooded murder of many alleged sex workers and the terror of jihadist organisations prevented the local police to take any action against him. It is worth mentioning here that Harkat-ul-Mujahedeen was pioneer in Gujranwala to establish its office and tradition of "public donations" for the outfits engaged in jihad for Kashmir also started from the same city.[78]

District Gujrat of Gujranwala division is facing a similar situation that is generally considered a city of different castes engaged in perennial mutual feuds and murders of personal vendetta. According to a conservative estimate, almost four to five hundred people become cannon fodder during these feuds every year. Gujrat had the fame of these gory hostilities well before the advent of sectarian and jihadist culture in Pakistan due to protracted ancestral disputes. When the jihadist and sectarian culture became well established in Gujrat, innumerable criminals joined these organisations for their "better" protection.

The arrest from this city of Abu Khalfan, one of the most wanted operatives of Al-Qaeda could give an idea of the might and vast links of the sectarian and jihadist organisations here. Abu Khalfan was living in Gujrat for a considerable period of time and these outfits had taken upon themselves to protect him.

On 24th July 2004, the life was going at its normal pace in Mohalla Islam Nagar of Gujrat, the ancestral city of former caretaker Prime Minister Chaudhry Shujaat Hussain and the former chief minister Punjab Chaudhry Pervez Elahi. Some foreigners were living in a bungalow in this area but the majority of the people there were unaware of their presence as their movement had been quite limited. One evening, intelligence agents in plainclothes and the police with state-of-the-art arms, surrounded the bungalow.

Movement in the area was restricted, electric supply was cut off and the D.P.O. Gujrat Raja Munawar Hassan appeared with a megaphone to announce that all the routes to escape had been blocked and it is better for the residents of the bungalow to surrender to the police. This announcement made it clear to the inmates that they had been identified and already under siege and they are to either surrender or to fight till the end and this operation was launched in a jiffy.

After getting some cues from a terrorist of Al-Qaeda apprehended at Lahore Airport, some intelligence officials headed to Gujrat, took some senior police officers into confidence and identified the place. A task force was formed and the operation was executed. Even the intelligence officials were not fully aware of the significance of their intended target. However the level of resistance by the inmates of the bungalow was a clear proof of the high value of that target. As soon as the announcement was made on the megaphone, the inmates took their positions and started firing on the police. It was the biggest operation in the history of the Gujrat police and continued for more than 16 hours. It was after that that the police managed to apprehend the foreigners. Among the arrested terrorists, Abdullah, Saleem and Feroze hailed from Kenya, Sudan and South Africa whereas the women accompanying him were from Pakistan, Saudi Arabia and Uzbekistan. Later on it was known that among the arrested people included a "very high value target" and an important operative of Al-Qaeda known as Abu Khalfan who was a most wanted person to F.B.I. and there was reward money of five million dollars for his arrest.[79]

The world community was astonished to hear the news of his arrest. In the meantime a computer engineer Muhammad Saleem aka Noor Khan was also apprehended. With the arrest of both the militants of Al Qaeda, intelligence agencies managed to get hold of a highly valuable treasure of information and the attempts of some huge terrorist acts were foiled. However, how these operatives of Al-Qaeda remained active in Pakistan; what are their past and their status in Al-Qaeda; apart from their well-wishers in Pakistan were there any collaborators who played an important role in the operation and; what interesting developments took place after the arrests. Some mind-blowing and remarkable information was obtained while trying to look for answers to these questions.[80]

According to the documents available with the U.S. officials Ahmed Khalfan Gilani, Ahmed Khalfan Ahmed, Abu Bakar Ahmed, Ahmed Khalfan, Ahmed Khalfan Ali, Abu Bakar Khalfan Ahmed, Ahmed Gilani, Ahmed-al-Tanzani, Abu Janar, Abu Bakri Khalfan, Abdullah Husain, Sharif Omer Muhammad, Fopi, Fepi and Ahmed Tanzanian all were jihadist name of the same person. There is a marked difference in his date of birth in different documents. According to one, he was born on 14th March 1974 whereas in the others there are dates of 13th April 1974, 14th April 1974 and 1st August 1970. He was involved in the bombing on U.S. embassies in Tanzania and Nairobi where 224 people had died and around 5,000 injured. One of his accomplices Muhammad Sadiq Audhay was convicted in these bombing whereas Ahmed Khalfan remained an absconder. Sadiq Audhay told F.B.I. that Ahmed Khalfan headed for Pakistan through Kenya Airways just one day before the attacks and he was never seen afterwards.

Ahmed Khalfan was also convicted in absentia by an American court. He was alleged to have purchased the trucks used in the attacks on both the embassies. He also provided oxygen and other chemicals to raise the intensity of the blasts. He came to Pakistan after the attacks. American intelligence agencies were after him as he was a senior operative of Al-Qaeda having direct links with Khaled Sheikh Muhammad but he remained at large for a considerable period of time.

When the F.B.I. issued the list and posters of most wanted persons in May 2004, Ahmed Khalfan was sixth on the ranking with a reward of five million dollars on his arrest. According to some sources, after arresting a terrorist on Lahore Airport the intelligence agencies raided a hotel in Gujrat upon his cue. A cousin of a former member national assembly from Mandi Bahauddin was arrested from the hotel who had rented the bungalow to the foreigners for rupees 12,000 per month.[81]

At the start of operations, the foreigners were ordered to surrender but they put up stiff resistance. The police threatened to bomb the house if they did not surrender. The foreigners responded with a counter threat that all of them would come out with bombs attached to their bodies and would blow up everyone. However, they agreed to surrender after a long hold-up. At the time of surrender one woman was wearing a suicide jacket equipped with sophisticated ammunition.

All of them were brought to Lahore under strict security and transferred to a 'safe house' (private premises where high value terrorists are detained for investigations).

The other people arrested in the Gujrat operation included Habiba (Uzbek wife of Abu Khalfan) Saudi citizen Talha Zubair, Muhammad Kashif from Lahore, Mushtaq aka Abdullah, driver Asif Iqbal aka Faisal from Mandi Bahauddin, Aasia Bibi wife of Asif Iqbal, Fatima wife of Javed from Baluchistan and a ten-day old baby girl among other children. Some sources claim that Talha Zubair was trained for suicide attacks on General Pervez Musharraf. In the investigations the arrested persons disclosed that they had President General Pervez Musharraf, Chaudhry Shujaat Hussain, Faisal Saleh Hayat and Chaudhry Pervez Elahi on their hit list.

The material confiscated from Abu Khalafan and his companions included explosive matter, arms, hand grenades, mobile SIMS, world maps in Arabic, English and Urdu, Arabic literature, books, currency notes worth eight million Pakistani rupees, computer hard disks, laptop and scanner. Some highly sensitive information about Al-Qaeda and its future plans was obtained from the data on laptops and hard disks.[82]

The e-mails sent and received by Abu-Khalfan disclosed that he was planning attacks on important commercial centres of U.K. and U.S. There were photographs of important centres and buildings. Maps of Chaklala airbase and Karachi airbase (used by General Musharraf), Karachi International Airport and vital military installation in Karachi, Lahore and Islamabad were also retrieved.

According to an official statement Abu Khalfan was handed over to the U.S. in January 2005. However, some other sources insist that a plane took him to an unknown destination soon after his arrest. The U.S. intelligence called it an important achievement on the part of Pakistani Intelligence agencies but did not forget to assert that one Libyan and four Egyptian in the F.B.I. most wanted list of 22 persons were still at large anywhere in the Pakistan.[83]

Lashkar-e-Jhangvi and Sipah-e-Sahaba are still considered most powerful sectarian outfits in Gujrat with their most wanted terrorists busy not only in eliminating the people from opponent sects but also providing their 'services' to the groups engaged in local hostilities. The most powerful criminal gang of Gujrat that also has the backing of the ruling party of Punjab has taken refuge in Pabbi the deserted border area in Azad Kashmir. According to general perception, the group not only provides shelter to sectarian killers from all over the country but also provides support to Al-Qaeda and Taliban. Many members of this group were involved in a life attempt on Musharraf but later on they were released on the intervention by some powerful circles and an influential political family from Gujrat. A similar situation is found in district Mandi Bahauddin where jihadist organisation and sectarian elements enjoy the full support by local politicians, landlords and the trader class.

Sialkot, another important district of Gajranwala division is also ruled by sectarian and jihadist outfits. Lashkar-e-Jhangvi and Sipah-e-Sahaba can target the places of worship and the people from opposing sects whenever and wherever they like. Scores of people have been killed in suicide attacks on Imam Bargahs and mosques. The affluent industrialist and trading classes of Sialkot are very generous when it comes to financial aid to sectarian and jihadist outfits.

The story of a semi-backward village of district Sialkot vividly portrays the religious violence and sectarian tensions. Aadiwal was a semi-developed and traditionally secular village. The Line of Control is just 200 yards away from the village.

There were 109 families including 77 Muslim, 23 Hindu, eight Christian and one Ahmadiyya family living here till 1990. There were 60 Sunni (Ahle-sunnat Barelvi) and 17 Shiite kinfolks among the 77 Muslim families. Quiet and adhering to traditions, the village was a good example of religious harmony and tolerance. One of the Hindu families was land owners whereas the rest of 22 were landless peasants working for Muslim landowners. The women worked as housemaids and some of the youth were employed in the sports goods manufacturing factories and earning reasonable wages.

Nobody could claim that there had been any incident of religious or sectarian intolerance in the three hundred year history of the village. Even during the hard times of partition of the Indian sub-continent when both the Muslims and Hindus were suffering horrible attacks, the Muslim inhabitants of the village not only provided complete protection to the Hindu population but also provided them with shelter in their own houses in order to save them from attackers of other areas. That had been an important factor in motivating them to stay here and none of them migrated to India.

In 1992, these Hindu families were made to realise that Aadiwal, where they have been living for centuries with Muslims in an atmosphere of fraternity, was no longer a safe place for them. On 5th February 1992 on the occasion of "Kashmir Solidarity day" about 200 persons arrived on rented buses and vans from Sialkot city which is not very far from the village and attacked on the houses of Hindu families. Armed with batons and hockey sticks, they were headed by the leaders of Jamaat Islami Sialkot and were shouting that they should be sent to India as they are Hindus.

The villagers were not willing to cede their demand, so they decided to face the attackers and forced them to flee. The attackers were told that despite being Hindus they were natives of the village living here for centuries, and that they had no connections with India. They were brethren and they would never allow anyone to attack or harass them. There was only one mosque in the village where, apart from the Eid and Friday congregations, the average number of regular visitors never exceeded four to five persons and it is also worthy to mention that there were neither any place of worship for Hindu and Christian families nor did they ever wish to construct any. However, everyone in the village used to send them gifts on the festivals of Baisakhi, Diwali, Dussehra and Christmas either in cash or kind. On the occasion of marriages and other celebrations in Hindu and Christian families, Muslim households always contributed in them. The marriage of any Hindu or Christian girl was considered a collective responsibility of the whole village.

Till the end of 1992 the Hindus of the village were deeply shocked and harassed as two attempts had already been made to eliminate them; first on the 5th of February and then another in December after the gruesome incident of the demolition of the Babri mosque in India. Although the Muslim families tried their best to protect them. The Hindu young men going everyday from the villages to work in Sialkot city became so afraid that they started looking for odd jobs in the village. A Hindu villager Karam Das said that they had an acute sense of insecurity at the job and a constant fear that they might be murdered at any time.

Presently, there are only five Hindu families left in the village who do not have the means to migrate to India whereas 18 Hindu families have already drifted in the previous years but they are equally helpless there. In almost every letter to Muslim families in the village they call the migration to India the biggest mistake of their lives. Twelve persons of these migrated families have passed away in India as they could not bear the shock of leaving their ancestral abode.

The last was received in January 2008 written by Sant Ram most popular Hindu person of the village. He had written this letter from a hospital in Jalandhar and had expressed his earnest desire to breathe his last in his ancestral place. He said nobody knew them in India and they were financially unstable. All of them were desirous of coming back to the village and they do not mind even if any jihadist group assassinated them. They were willing to accept death provided it came in their ancestral land. This was his last letter for his village fellows and news about his death was given in March by his son Harish Chand.

These Hindu families would never have fled the village if it were only the external attackers but the real cause of their migration to India were the jihadist youth who after getting training in jihadist camps of Afghanistan and Kashmir had ordered the Hindu minorities of the villages Anola, saleem, Beeni Sulehrian, Jodhay wali, Karishna Wali, Mainderwal, Ramoo Chak, Akhnor, Bhalor, Chaubara, Ratowal and other villages of district Sialkot to either convert to Islam or to emigrate to India.

The jihadists had a special focus on this village and one night two young Hindu girls Kamlaishwanti and Lajwanti were abducted. At one hand the local police station refused to register the complaint by the Hindu families and on the other hand the kidnappers were communicated to take the abducted girls to any other town.

After three days, there was news that the girls have converted to Islam. Armed men of a jihadist outfit distributed sweets in the village and shot aerial gun fires as a gesture of delight. It was known after two weeks that Lajwanti had strangulated herself to death whereas Kamlaishwanti has shifted to Peshawar with her husband. The local people insist that both the girls had been murdered because they were not willing to change their religion and they should be allowed to go back. But this time the families of the girls did not lodge any complaint with the local police and started to sell their livestock and household goods.

One morning, the people of the village came to know that 18 Hindu families had left the village for good. After some days, they received letters informing that those families had reached Jalandhar in India. The houses left by them were occupied by the local influential people whereas the Rangers took the control of the five acres of land by the only Hindu landowner, Ummi Chand.[84]

The story of the only Ahmadiyya Family is a bit different. The head of the family was a retired school teacher and a respectable fellow of the village. When he passed away, some people contacted a jihadist organisation and got an edict that being a non-Muslim the deceased could not be buried in the village cemetery meant for Muslims. The same organisation arranged a rally in the evening and threatened to exhume and cremate the dead body if he were buried in the cemetery of Muslims. The next day this Ahmadiyya family went away from the village along with household goods and off course, the coffin of the deceased head of family. People came to know after a few days that they have shifted to Rabwa (the head-quarter of Ahmadiyya sect in Pakistan) and rented a house there.

Now it was the turn of the Christians. The poor fellows were terribly afraid after the blasphemous incidents in Gujranwala and Sumandrı and they were intress to the fate of the Hindus and Ahmadiyyas of the village. When a student organisation together with a jihadist outfit took out a rally on the name of honour of the Holy Prophet Muhammad at the highway near the village and demanded death penalty for the perpetrators of blasphemy, the Christian community decided to leave the village. Six out of eight families migrated immediately and the remaining two are too poor to move their residence elsewhere.

The 'elders' as well as some zealots of the village maintain that the Hindus migrated only because they were not able to find suitable matches for their adolescent girls and they had better prospects for them in India; by shifting to their sacred place the Ahmadiyya family fulfilled their religious obligation and for Christian families they claim that one of the Christian youths had kidnapped a young Muslim girl and that is why they were ordered to leave the village.

The village has three mosques and one Imam Bargah now. The minister of the grand mosque boasted that "by the grace of Allah" theirs is an ideal village now where almost everyone is a Muslim. The followers of other religion have already left or will leave soon. It is the story of just one village. The Hindu minorities living for centuries in around 64 villages of district Sialkot are faced with more or less the same situation and trying hard to migrate either to interior areas of Sindh or to India.

On 1st October 2004, a suicide bomber killed 35 people by blowing himself in a Shiite mosque, Jamia Zainabia in Sialkot city. Lashkar-e-Jhangvi claimed responsibility for the incident, however all the persons arrested for investigations were eventually released for want of sufficient evidence. Sialkot also has had a long record of sectraian killings and the cleric of the same Masjid-e-Zainabia was target killed by a militant of Sipah-e-Sahaba. Many Shiite and Deobandi were murdered in innumerable similar incidents.[85]

In September 2009, a Muslim mob set a church ablaze in village Jaithike in tehsil Sambarial of district Sialkot. Police sources claim that tensions were created as a Muslim girl was a victim of stalking by a Christian youth. One day while she was coming back from madrassa she was followed by the youngman, Fanish Massey and a part of Holy Koran carried by her was also desecrated in the process. Upon hearing this local religious extremists set the village church on fire.[86]

According to local media correspondents, the boy himself arrived at the police station to get his father freed. He was the only accused for charges of stalking and blasphemy and the police sent him to jail under judicial custody where he was kept in a separate security cell. The deputy superintendent of district jail Sialkot said that there were ten security cells in a separate block of the jail that were meant for people accused of crimes with a 'religious' colour, so that they could be saved from the wrath of other inmates. There were five prisoners at that day including two activists of Jamaat Ahmadiyya, two accused of desecration of Holy Koran and one for blasphemy.[87]

Jail authorities claim that one official went to call the cleaner and when he came back he found the dead body of Fanish Massey suspended by a noose. According to that official he used the cord belt of his shalwar (trousers) to strangulate himself. Deputy Superintendent Jails declared it to be a suicide. Local Special Magistrate Abu Bakar Siddiq and the District Police Officer inspected the venue. According to Emmanuelle Athar Julius, president of Pakistan Christian Alliance, Fanish Massey did not commit suicide and it was a case of 'religion-based murder'. He told BBC that he was murdered collusion of through the police and jail officials and that their organisation would pursue the case.[88]

MULTAN DIVISION

Whenever one tries to take a serious account of sectarian carnage, Multan is one of the most important and vulnerable divisions in Punjab. For many years Lashkar-e-Jhangvi, Sipah-e-Sahaba and Sipah-e-Muhammad have "ruled" different districts of Multan divisions. Hundreds of people have been killed in Multan, Muzzafar Garh and Khanewal on sectarian motives only. In Multan Lashkar-e-Jhanvi attacked on Iranian Culture Centre "Khana-e-Farhang" and turned it into shambles. Imam Bargahs, mosques and other places of religious significance, have been a special targets. The arrested militants of Lashkar-e-Jhangvi like Malik Muhammad Ishaq and Akram Lahori had confessed of having been involved in scores of attacks and killings in Multan, Muzaffar Garh, Khanewal and other areas of the division. In response the banned Shiite outfit Sipah-e-Muhammad never relented in this war either and kept on targeting the people from other sects to its full capacity. It would not be imprudent to say that the Multan division has been worst affected in the sectarian war in Punjab.

Maulana Masood Alvi of Multan is called the founder of jihad in Pakistan and he had the 'honour' of establishing the very first jihadist organisation of the country named Jamiat-ul-Mujahedeen at Madrassa Khair-ul Madaris, Multan. Maulana Masood Alvi was the son of the famous Deobandi cleric Maulana Muhammad Sharif Kashmiri who was Sheikh-ul-Hadith (Scholar and Head teacher in the discipline of Traditions (sayings) of Holy Prophet Muhammad) in Khair-ul-Madaris. Maulana Masood Alvi was a student in that madrassa and he managed to spare some time for physical exercise and to learn militant techniques in order to prepare himself for jihad. He often talked about jihad and kept himself busy in contemplating upon different war techniques. In March 1973, he founded the jihadist organisation Jamiat-ul-Mujahedeen in the grand mosque of Jamia Khair-ul-Madaris in the presence of some like-minded clerics. To prove the military might of Islam to the whole world was its main objective and to pull the Muslims out of the pit of humiliation and passivity was also mentioned in its manifesto.[89]

The Ahmdiyya Sect was the first target of this outfit. A training centre was established in the forests near Alipur Jatoi to impart militant training to the students of Khair-Ul-Madaris and other seminaries. When Khatam-e-Nabuwat movement (The finality of prophet-hood of Prophet Muhammad) culminated, the activists of Jamiat-ul-Mujahedeen also dispersed and organisation became almost inactive. Maulana Masood Alvi tried his luck in various seminaries but none of them allowed him to arrange for militant training due to pressure from the government. At last Khawaja Khan Muhammad of Kundian Sharif, permitted him to train the student in militant skill in his seminary, where Maulana Alvi started militant training of students apart from regular seminary education. Weapons were arranged and the practice of shooting became a regular component of everyday training. It did not take him very long to make a militant battalion ready in all aspects. When Maulana Mufti Mahmood was Chief Minister of N.W.F.P. (present Khyber-Pakhtunkhwa) he came to see Maulana Khawaja Muhammad Ahmed Khan, an important leader of Khatam-e-Nabuwat movement, at his seminary in Kundian Sharif. Masood Alvi presented him a guard of honour through the battalion of these newly trained mujahedeen. The guests were amazed at these skills of Maulana Alvi because during the era (well before the advent of Afghan Jihad) it was almost impossible to form a jihadist outfit in private sector and to get military training. At this, Pakistani intelligence agencies started his pursuit and eventually he left the seminary and went to the border areas of Kashmir. After crossing the Line of Control, Maulana Masood Alvi killed 12 Indian soldiers in an operation in Indian-held Kashmir. After leaving the seminary at Kundian he also established a madrassa in Chichawatni where militant training was an essential component of curriculum. It could be called the first jihadist madrassa of Pakistan. Maulana Irshad Ahmed was also one of his disciples who took the first ever private troops to Afghanistan in 1980. When Harkat-ul-Mujahedeen was formed in Afghanistan, he was appointed as central commander. In 1988 Maulana Masood Alvi was severely injured by a landmine in Paktia, Afghanistan and succumbed to injuries.[90]

Commander Nasarullah Mansoor Langrial is one of the most prominent commanders of Harkat-ul-Jihad-ul-Islami and languishing in Indian jails since 1992. He was the pioneer in demanding Jazia (The mandatory tax from non-Muslims in an Islamic state in exchange for full protection by the state) in Indian held Kashmir. He hails from District Chichawatni of Multan division. When he was studying in Khair-ul-Madaris it was a centre of jihadist activities. Many students had already proceeded for jihad in Afghanistan. Nasar ullah Mansoor Langrial also enrolled his name for militant training in 1982 and went to Afghanistan. He came back after one year and went again in the beginning of 1984 and dedicated his whole life for jihad. Many attempts were made for his release from Indian jail but none has proved fruitful.[91]

On 17th January 1997 the police raided the house of one Raj Massey in Village Shanti Nagar of district Khanewal in the charges of illegally selling alcohol. No liquor could be recovered but the Holy Bible was desecrated during the raid. The Christian community took out a protest rally and the local administration suspended some police officials after the incident. The police officials threatened them of dire consequence if the Christian community did not withdraw its charges. After three weeks there was an announcement from the local mosque of Shanti Nagar that some Christians had set a copy of the Holy Koran on fire and had thrown the burnt pages in front of the mosque. Upon hearing the announcement, a rally of about 20 thousand people from

14 surrounding villages started marching towards Shanti Nagar and Toba and set on fire about 1500 houses, 12 churches, one hostel and a dispensary of the village. According to a news report, the police first demanded that the Christian community leave the village and shift to a safer place and then gave a free hand to the angry mob. That was perhaps the worst incident of sectarian frenzy after the partition of the Indian sub-continent. It was later learnt that the militants of Lashkar-e-Tayyba and Jaish-e-Muhammad played a prominent role in the incident and houses of poor victims were burnt through a highly inflammable chemical. It was a well-planned attack and a large number of people were prepared for arson and pillage. There were inflammatory announcements from the mosques and the helpless minority community was under attack in no time.[92]

The seminary of Dar-ul-Aloom Eidgah Khanewal and its graduates have a special distinction in promoting sectarian tensions in Pakistan. When in the 1990s the government started a pursuit of terrorists in Punjab, the name of Kabirwala was repeatedly mentioned in the media. This town, about 15 km north-west of Khanewal, also has the shameful distinction of providing shelter to most wanted terrorists. In the sectarian context, Maulana Haq Nawaz Jhangvi is the greatest identity of this town who founded Anjuman Sipah-e-Sahaba in the 1980s. Before establishing that organisation Haq Nawaz Jhangvi had been a student of seminary of Kabirwala for seven years. This madrassa was founded by Maulana Abdul Khaliq in 1953 who was a graduate of Dar-ul-Aloom Deoband. There are 1,500 students in this four-storyed seminary whereas the number of its teachers exceeds 80. Working without any financial assistance by the government, this seminary has an annual budget of approximately 15 million rupees. In 2009, a businessman of Karachi gave a donation of 10 million rupees on the condition of anonymity. This seminary is considered to be a centre of anti-Shiite activities in Punjab.[93]

On 30th July 2009, about 200 shopkeepers and 35 educational institutions received letters in district Muzaffar Garh of Multan division that demanded them to adapt themselves into an atmosphere of 'Sharia' as soon as possible and quit all the anti-Sharia and evil ways. Initially, these letters were considered to be written by the local sectarian elements, in habit of writing this type of warning letters to Shiite Muslims of Muzaffar Garh from time to time. But later on it was discovered that these letters were sent by the militants who had come back to their home town after "jihad" in Swat and tribal areas. The letters sent by 'Tahreek-e-Taliban Punjab warned cable channels operators and owners of internet cafes to shut down their "filthy businesses" within 24 hours or face dire consequences. Educational institutions for girls as well as working ladies and ordinary housewives, were also warned in tehsil Kot Addu of district Muzaffar Garh that if they ever came out of their houses without wearing a hijab, acid would be thrown on their faces. Tahreek-e-Taliban had issued an ultimatum of five days to observe the restrictions of hijab whereas the shopkeepers were given only 24 hours to 'mend' their ways. The local police declared these letters "vague and anonymous" and not worth taking cognizance of.[94]

After one week the Tehreek-e-Taliban Punjab sent letters to the houses of Shiite Muslims in the town of Daira Din Panah, Sanawan and Mahmood Kot declaring the Shiite non-Muslims and their beliefs as apostasy to Islam, with severe warnings that they would be exterminated if they did not quit their 'false' beliefs and ritual. However, no deadline was mentioned for them and after a severe criticism of their beliefs, they were ordered to revert towards 'real and true' Islam, failing which they would get eternal punishment in the life after. They would also have to face serious consequences in this world as well. The punishment suggested in these letters for the Shiite Muslims include killing their males and incinerating their dead bodies, turning their women and children into slaves and dividing their properties and other valuable among the mujahedeen of Islam as bounty. It is worth mentioning here that the text of these letters was similar to that issued by the spokesperson of Tehreek-e-Taliban Pakistan Muslim Khan and that was published by all major newspapers of Pakistan.[95]

On the morning of 13th July 2009, in the village Chak No. 129/15L, tehsil Mian Chanon, district Kahnaewal of Southern Punjab, 17 people were killed and 150 injured due to a heavy blast in the house as well as the compound of the madrassa run by Riaz Ali an activist of banned extremist outfit Sipah-e-Sahaba. The blast was so severe that around one hundred houses of the surrounding area were demolished. This sad incident is a solid evidence of the strong network of extremist organisations in Southern Punjab. Earlier on 11th July, one terrorist was killed in an encounter between police and the terrorists hiding in a seminary at Shadan Lund in district Dera Ghazi Khan, whereas two of his companions were arrested and a huge quantity of weapons was also recovered from the madrassa.[96]

It is reported about Raiz Ali the activist of banned Sipah-e-Sahaba that he had been a companion of Taliban in Afghanistan during the 1990s and managed to get a job of a primary teacher after coming back from Afghanistan. He was working in the primary school of Chak no. 15/B and was a president of the primary school teachers' association as well. According to Abid Ali Sandhu, the union council nazim of Chak no. 129, Riaz Ali, was running a madrassa as well, where his sister Fatima was teaching around 150 students. On the day of that sad incident children were going back to their houses when that big blast occurred. A majority of the killed people were the children of that madrassa. The Nazim of union council said that a big quantity of mobile phone SIM cards, rocket launchers, suicide jackets, CDs, magazines of jihadist outfits and pamphlets were also recovered from the spot. Fatima, the sister of master Riaz was also killed in the blast, while master Riaz, along with two of his brothers Yousuf and Imtiaz, was arrested and three of them were severely injured.[97]

About one year ago, eight family members of one Saif Ullah Khan Niazi were killed in broad daylight in the village Kaccha Khoo of district Khanewal. In April 2010 some activists of a banned outfit arrested from Dera Ghazi Khan confessed during investigations that they were involved in that incident of firing at Kaccha Khoo. There was evidence of the involvement of master Riaz as well and District Police Officer Khanewal had instructed Mian Channon police to have a strict monitoring of master Riaz but the local police proved negligent as usual and master Riaz remained engaged in his nefarious activities.[98]

This area of Southern Punjab, for more than two decades, has been a stronghold of extremist outfits like Sipah-e-Sahaba, Lashkar-e-Jhangvi, Jaish-e-Muhammad, Harkat-ul-Jihad-ul-Islami and Lashkar-e-Tayyba etc. It is sufficient to judge the clout of these extremist organisations in Southern Punjab by the fact that scores of such terrorists hail from South Punjab that have been the main characters in almost every serious incident of terrorism and most wanted criminals with huge amounts announced as their head money. Shakeel, Gohar Iqbal and Maulvi Jallel Ahmed from Bahawalnagar, Qari Akram aka Ikram, Shahab Uddin and Abdul Wahid of Multan, Shahnawaz of Muzaffar Garh, Ahson Shah from Rahim Yar Khan, Nasar Ullah aka Fazal-ur-Rahman of Fort Abbas, Haji Abdul Mannan, Abdul Majid and Hafeez ur-Rahman of Layyah, Hafeez Ullah aka Israr of Kot Sultan, Layyah, Qari Ramzan Qaisarani of Dera Ghazi Khan, Zakria and Aslam from Khairpur Tamaywali, Anees-ur-Rahman and Akram Habib from Vehari, Maulana Abdullah Jan of Ahmedpur East, Qari Abdullah from Sarai Sadhoo district Khanewal, Mahmood Ahmed aka Sohail from Bahawalpur, Zafar Iqbal aka Bala and Abu Bakar from Jhang and Qari Hayat from Khanewal are but a few examples.[99]

Jaish-e-Muhammad and Lashkar-e-Tayyba have thousands of jihadists and trained militants in Multan who are always waiting but a call from their organisation. According to some reliable sources Jaish-e-Muhammad has at least twenty seminaries in Multan where not only jihadists are recruited but they are also used for "help" to their ally Lashkar-e-Jhangvi. Militants of Jaish-e-Muhammad have been active in many incidents of sectarian killings in Multan and still there are scores of its extremist activists behind the bars under the charges of murder and other serious crimes in Multan Jail. Lashkar-e-Tayyba has similar position in Multan that is considered a strong jihadist outfit here and many of its martyrs also hailed from different towns and cities of Multan Division. After Faisalabad, Lashkar-e-Tayyba gets biggest donations from the Multan division and hundreds of jihadists from this division are still under training in Muridke and Chehla Bandi Azad Kashmir training centres run by Lashkar-e-Tayyba.

Sipah-e-Sahaba and Lashkar-e-Jhangvi killed an important government officer from the rival sect, posted in Khanewal just because he had a hostile attitude towards sectarian killers of Sipah-e-Sahaba who were under arrest. It could be safely claimed that the general identity of Multan division is that of a sectarian and jihadist region. There are grand centres of jihadist outfits like Lashkar-e-Tayyaba and Jaish-e-

Muhammad that impart a proper training of terrorist activities. Innumerable madrassas are promoting sectarian hatred and religious intolerance. A comparatively new Sunni Barelvi organisation is rapidly gaining popularity and boasts of hundreds of thousands of affiliates. It gathers as many people in "Madina-tul-Aulia" and constructing a vast new headquarters in the suburbs of the city with a cost of hundreds of millions of rupees. Some observers guess Multan in the near future would no longer be divided on Shiite-Deobandi grounds only but Barelvis-Wahhabis, Barelvi-Deobandi, and Wahhabi-Deobandi conflicts would also intensify. So its primary identity of a city of Shiite-Sunni or Shiite-Deobandi conflicts would give way to ever increasing force of other sects. Local political elite that include different dynasties of caretakers of shrines, feudal lords and businessmen, rely upon their religious and sectarian identities in order to succeed in elections.[100]

DERA GHAZI KHAN DIVISION

The Dera Ghazi Khan division is located at the crossroads to four provinces of Pakistan with Khyber-Pakhtunkhwa in the north, Sindh in the south, Baluchistan in the east and some parts of Sindh in the west along the river Indus as well although major portion of its western borders comprise the mountain ranges of Koh-e-Suleiman. Over the years, Dera Ghazi Khan has also turned into a region sans peace, crippled with terrorist activities and bomb blasts. Although security arrangements here are said to be comparatively better due to the presence of the Uranium Processing Plant, Airport and a huge industrial area but still ever increasing bomb blasts, sectarian killings and incidents of detonating railway tracks are going beyond the control local administration and the police. Terrorists have repeatedly targeted oil supply lines, commercial and trade centres, installations of national significance and thickly populated residential areas. Despite registering cases in such incidents, not a single accused has ever been arrested.

District Dera Ghazi Khan has its boundaries with Khyber-Pakhtunkhwa on one side and Baluchistan on the other and terrorists just disappear into the Tribal Areas. In a 'bicycle bomb' blast on 23rd September 2006 at Bakra Mandi two persons had died. Police also issued the sketch of the possible accused but no clues were found afterwards. The blasts on 24ᵗʰ July 2006 at a snacks shop, 23ʳᵈ September 2006 in Bakra Mandi, 26ᵗʰ December 2006 at minibus stand in Taunsa Sharif and 4ᵗʰ January 2007 in a motorcycle rickshaw strengthened that sad reality that terrorists are now targeting populated areas with the only aim to reinforce a sense of insecurity among ordinary citizens.[101]

The intensity in sectarian violence and terrorist activities by the Taliban could be judged by the fact that the two accused arrested in the charge of a suicide attack on a Moharram procession on 5ᵗʰ February 2009, were activists of Tehreek-e-Taliban Pakistan (T.T.P.). Police chief Dera Ghazi Khan Mubarak Ali Athar told the media that a suicide attack was made on a chehlam procession at Imam Bargah Johar Wadani on 5ᵗʰ February 2009 that killed 27 people and injured more than 50 (later on the number of deceased persons reached 35) and Commander of Tehreek-e-Taliban Pakistan Bait Ullah Mehsood claimed responsibility for the attack.[102]

During the police investigations, close links of a local seminary with Taliban were unearthed when phone calls of some management personnel of madrassa were traced. Some important leaders of T.T.P. have been visiting Dera Ghazi Khan from times to time and there are recruiting centres for T.T.P. in five most prominent seminaries of the city, whereas about 2000 jihadists from Dera Ghazi Khan have already joined Taliban.

During the investigations on the suicide attack of 5ᵗʰ February, some maps and video clips were also recovered from a local Taliban Qari Muhammad Ismail resident of tehsil Taunsa Sharif that include addresses of some sensitive state installations as well as important personalities of the Shiite sect whereas security targets and local people were highlighted with special signs. Qari Ismail confessed that he had been a disciple of Maulan Azam Tariq. He was looking for 'opportune moments' for revenge as Shiite people had rejoiced of the murder of Maulana Azam Tariq. He had his training from different jihadist camps and told the police that during 2008 he stayed at jihadist camp in South Wazirsitan where he managed to get contact with Bait Ullah Mehsood and also established relations with Qari Imran aka Hakeem Nasir an important commander of Bait Ullah Mehsood Group.[103]

The plan to attack the chehlam procession was prepared in the same training center of Bait Ullah Mehsood. Qari Ismail also disclosed that Ghulam Mustafa Qaisrani and Qari Imran were also accompanying him in the camp and facilitated in the planning. The suicide attacker along with his suicide jacket and other explosive material was accommodated for some days at the house of Ghulam Mustafa Qaisrani. The name of the suicide bomber was Abdullah aka Arshad Pathan, who was a resident of South Waziristan, and specially trained by Qari Hussein the first deputy of Bait Ullah Mehsood. The go-ahead for that attack was also given by Bait Ullah Mehsood.[104]

During the process of investigations, the accused apart from the said suicide attacker, also confessed to having murdered five people from Shiite sect on 3rd August 2006 at Kachha Khoo, district Khanewal. They had also done a recce of Dhodak Oil field and planned to capture the field to get the demands by Bait Ullah Mehsood fulfilled was ready that included to blow up the oil plant and to kidnap Chinese engineers working there in case their demands were not met.

Due to a scarcity of their own resources, hundreds of seminaries present in South Punjab could prove a recruiting ground for the extremists. There are thousands of students in these hundreds of seminaries in southern Punjab and most of them are faced with shortage of sources. The number of registered seminaries in only one district of Dera Ghazi Khan in Southern Punjab is 185; while 90 of them belong to the Deobandi sect, 84 to Barelvi, six to Wahhabi whereas only five are run by Fiqah-e-Jafarria (the Shiite sect). Thousands of students are boarding there whereas hundreds are day scholars. The age of students varies from five to 25. Some seminaries, apart from religious education, have also made arrangements for regular education from primary to high schools. Although these seminaries get donations from gulf countries, local religious charities and from philanthropists, a majority of them face a shortage of finances, teachers and other resources and a few of them manage to get sufficient funding and a reasonable number of teachers. The same situation prevails in the seminaries of Rajanpur, Rahim Yar Khan and other districts of South Punjab. There is an urgent need to make these madrassas a part of mainstream education and to create better prospects for their students, otherwise there is a sure danger of these seminaries falling into the hands of extremist elements.

Famous defense analyst Dr. Shireen Mazari maintains that military operation alone cannot solve the serious issue of extremism and the real solution lies in provision of justice, restore dignity of deprived classes and to give them hope for a better future. The position of Dr. Mazari is similar to that of "flexible" right wing intellectuals, who under a specific bent of mind and despite knowing so many facts keep themselves busy in providing various apologies and justifications to the extremism that springs from these seminaries. The reality is that the situation in South Punjab had gone out of control a long ago; where the mighty institutions of the state are completely responsible for this situation, the extremist and jihadists of Pakistan are also well aware of the processes that promoted and nurtured the Talibanisation of this region.[105]

The Deobandi seminaries of Dera Ghazi Khan have their direct links with T.T.P. and they also keep themselves busy in sectarian killings in other parts of the country. Tehsil Taunsa Sharif of Dera Ghazi Khan has turned into a stronghold of Taliban and sectarian mercenaries as according to some safer estimate thousands of students (Punjabi Taliban) from about a dozen Deobandi madrassas of Taunsa are not only heading towards training centres in South Waziristan and Afghanistan but there are also continuous drives to recruit students from the local madrassa and to send them to Waziristan and Swat. The majority of seminaries in Rajanpur and other districts of Dera Ghazi Khan Division also belong to Deobandi Sect where the campaign to recruit Punjabi Taliban is in full swing. Like Bahawal pur Dera Ghazi Khan Division is also being considered as a land of jihadists and staunch supporters of groups like Taliban, Jaish-e-Muhammad, Sipah-e-Sahaba and Lashkar-e-Jhangvi etc.

The areas of Kacha (the belt that continues along the riverbed of Indus) in district Rajanpur is called a haven for sectarian elements and jihadists. The "Ghazi Borthers" of Rojhan, Abdul Aziz the ex-imam of Lal masjid (red mosque) and younger brother Abdul Rasheed Ghazi, who was killed in Lal Masjid operation, also hail from the same area. Presently hundreds of their supporters are active in the area of Rojhan and a majority of them are affiliated to Lashkar-e-Jhangvi and Jaish-e-Muhammad and they also have close ties with the Taliban present in

Tribal Areas of Waziristan and Pak-Afghan border. Some of them are also fighting in Afghanistan alongside Taliban.

SARGODHA DIVISION

The Sargodha division also has its own significance regarding sectarian massacre and jihadist culture. Jihadist outfits like Jaish-e-Muhammad and Lashkar-e-Tayyba have a dominant position here, with thousands of youth affiliated with these outfits. Many of them lost their lives during jihad in Indian-held Kashmir. A considerable number of these youth are also engaged in fighting in Afghanistan alongwith Taliban against troops of Western countries. In district Bhakkar of Sargodha division many recruiting centres are active in providing cannon fodder for sectarian killings as well as for Taliban fighting in Waziristan. The security installations of Pak army face the greatest danger by the hands of Jaish-e-Muhammad and Lashkar-e-Tayyba, which could give some idea of the clout of these jihadist outfits. It was also in Sargodha that a bus of Pakistan Air Force was hit in a suicide attack.

An Anti-Terror Court passed a sentence of a record 870 years of imprisonment to Umar Farooq a student of Jamia Miftah-ul-Aloom even the charge of a suicide attack on Air Force bus on 1st October 2007. The seminary of Miftah-ul-Aloom is located in Satellite Town, Sargodha where the total number of students is one thousand one hundred whereas the number of Pashtun students from age 10 to 25 is around four hundred. The administrator of the seminary claims to have expelled a number of students who were found involved in sectarian, terrorist or political activities. This Seminary was founded by Mufti Abdul Latif in 1950 and prominent role of this seminary in the promotion of extremism and sectarian violence could not be ignored.[106]

On 1st November 2007, a suicide bomber hit his motorbike to a bus of Pakistan Air Force at Faisalabad Road, Sargodha that killed seven air force officers and three ordinary citizens. The number of severely injured was 28. The bus was carrying the air force staff from Mus'haf Air Base to ammunition depot when a suicide attacker targeted it at about 6:45 a.m. Later investigation by the police revealed that the suicide attacker was provided with full details of the movements of air force buses by local jihadist organisations and he had also stayed at a seminary affiliated with Jaish-e-Muhammad in order to have a complete recce of this movement.[107]

Riaz Basra, the most important character of sectarian killings in Pakistan also hailed from Sargodha. The terror of Riaz Basra could be assessed by the fact that he was wanted in the murder of 300 people of the Shiite sect. The government of Punjab had announced a 'head money' of five million rupees for him whereas the amount announced by government of Sindh to apprehend him dead or alive was three million rupees. Once in 1998 he went into an 'open court' by then prime minister Mian Muhammad Nawaz Sharif in a changed get-up and got his snapshots taken while accepting donation from the prime minister. The same evening the Prime Minister's Secretariat received a parcel containing that photograph along with a stern warning that if the government of Mian Nawaz Sharif did not stop the killing of Lashkar-e-Jhangvi activists in fake police encounters, the Prime Minister himself could be killed in a suicide attack.[108]

After that warning Mian Nawaz Sharif stopped this routine of 'open courts' at his residence in Model Town, Lahore. In the meantime, Lashkar-e-Jhangvi also issued a press release to the newspaper announcing that Riaz Basra the chief of Lashkar-e-Jhangvi will give cash reward of 14 million rupees if somebody succeeded in killing Mian Nawaz Sharif and Mian Shahbaz Sharif. During that period 36 most wanted terrorists of Lashkar-e-Jhangvi and Sipah-e-Sahaba were eliminated in police encounters. Lashkar-e-Jhangvi held the view that the federal government of Mian Nawaz Sharif and Punjab government of Mian Shahbaz Sharif are involved in the killing of activists of Sipah-e-Sahaba and Lashkar-e-Jhangvi.[109]

Riaz Basra was secretary information for Sipah-e-Sahaba and a staunch disciple of Haq Nawaz Jhangvi, who was murdered by a Shiite youth in 1990. He along with a few others, tried to establish a new group that is not directly under the control of Sipah-e-Sahaba and that has its own 'arrangements' of eliminating the Shiite of Pakistan and sustaining heavy losses to Iranian interest that is also supporting Shiites of Pakistan. Riaz Basra eventually succeeded in this aim and managed to form a proper group comprising only 'professional mercenaries' and it was named "Lashkar-e-Jhangvi" after Haq Nawaz Jhangvi, the assassinated founder of Sipah-e-Sahaba. In the meantime, the break away factions of Sipah-e-Sahaba had in fact formed six new groups namely Lashkar-e-Jhangvi, Al-Haq Tigers, Tanzeem Al-Haq, Al-Farooq, Al-Badar Foundation and Allah-o-Akbar group. Al-Badar Foundation was formed in Karachi whereas the five were established in different cities of Punjab like Jhang, Faisalabad, Sargodha, Samnadri and Chiniot.[110]

Later on all these groups merged into Lashkar-e-Jhangvi headed by Riaz Basra, who firmly believed in the philosophy of sheer power and its timely utilisation. Intelligence agencies of the country insist that the formation of Lashkar-e-Jhangvi had the full consent of Sipah-e-Sahaba so that it could have an independent platform for its militant activities. Initially, Riaz Basra was provided with a troop of twelve persons, who were considered the most cold-blooded mercenaries in the inner circles of Sipah-e-Sahaba and even the organisation had to face some serious problems because of their reckless activities. The strength of Lashkar-e-Jhangvi never exceeded eight hundred members but it always managed to retain the "title" of the most dangerous group of Pakistan. Riaz Basra had parted ways with Sipah-e-Sahaba as according to his opinion it had deviated off the mission of Haq Nawaz Jhangvi.

In January 1997 an important leader of Sipah-e-Sahaba, Zia-Ur-Rahman Farooqi was murdered in a bomb blast in the Session Court of Lahore where he had come in the hearing of a case against him. That was the point where Lashkar-e-Jhangvi properly started to target Shiites. The revenge of Farooqi's murder came in the shape of a fierce attack on Iranian Cultural Centre (Khana Farhang-e-Iran) and killing all the seven persons present in it. Soon after it the building of Khana Farhang-e-Iran in Lahore was also torched and a spate of target killings of Shiite was unleashed. On 3rd January 1999, the chief of Lashkar-e-Jhangvi planted a bomb under a bridge at Raiwind road Lahore where Prime Minister Mian Muhammad Nawaz Sharif was due to pass in a few minutes. It was a matter of sheer luck that a police officer parked his vehicle near the bridge and happened to see that the planted bomb. A police official also lost his life while trying to de-activate the bomb.[111]

Riaz Basra also murdered the brother of Lieutenant General (R) Moeen-Ud-Din Haider the former Federal minister for Interior Affairs. Earlier he had killed four U.S. citizens in Karachi. He had also worked as in-charge Khalid Bin Waleed Camp Sarobi (Kabul) where he developed close links with the Taliban. Whenever he came back to Pakistan from Afghanistan a new killing spree of Shiite started. In Momenpura Lahore Riaz Basra and his cohort Akram Lahori opened an indiscriminate fire on a Shiite congregation and killed more than 30 persons. In May 2002 Lashkar-e-Jhangvi killed 11 French citizens in a bomb blast mistaking them as Americans.[112]

On 14th June 2002, Lashkar-e-Jhangvi murdered 12 people in an attack on Karachi seaport. Earlier in March it has killed five Christians including one U.S. citizen in an attack on a church in Islamabad. In July 2002 Shaukat Raza Mirza (A Shiite) Managing Director of Pakistan State Oil was assassinated in Karachi. Lashkar-e-Jhangvi was involved in all these incidents.[113]

Riaz Basra became a symbol of terror in Pakistan and from 1996 till his killing on 14th May 2002, a total of 300 cases were registered against him in which Shiite were murdered, bomb blasts happened, Shiites were kidnapped or personnel of law enforcement agencies were killed. Riaz Basra had the fame of developing very close relations with some politicians, army generals and high-ranking bureaucrats of Pakistan who were always willing for his "timely" help whereas many business tycoon of country generously provided him with finances. Although his death closed the chapter of a highly dangerous terrorist, still he left behind many of such followers who are engaged in the promotion of his 'mission'. Some of them have been eliminated in police encounters whereas others are still running Lashkar-e-Jhangvi as an underground organisation and with the collaboration of Taliban are engaged in suicide attacks in Pakistan, especially in Punjab.

Bhakkar, another district of the Sargodha division is not less significant when it comes to sectarian violence. It has also been a target of many suicide attacks. In a suicide attack on the house of "Nawanis", a famous political family of the city, many innocent lives were lost. As Nawanis belong to Shiite sect, they are facing the perpetual danger of being attacked by Lashkar-e-Jhanvi and Sipah-e-Sahaba. Moreover

Bhakkar is also an important centre jihadist outfits and Lashkar-e-Tayyba and Jaish-e-Muhammad have their strongholds there that are known for "exchange" of jihadists from nearby district of Dera Ismail Khan. In other words it provides an easy access to jihadists to and fro Tribal Areas. According to reliable sources the manpower being provided from Punjab to Taliban and Al-Qaeda engaged in fighting in Waziristan use the route of Bhakkar. Syed Tajummal Abbas Shah, Commissioner Sargodha division who belonged to Shiite sect also was murdered by Sipah-e-Sahaba. So Sargodha division has its own significance in sectarian tensions in Punjab and many of the terrorists involved in sectarian killings and other activities of sabotage hailed from the Sargodha division.[114]

RAWALPINDI DIVISION

The Rawalpindi division is also considered a division that is hostage to Lashkar-e-Jhangvi and Sipah-e-Sahaba; the outfits that have been persistantly involved in sectarian massacres. Moreover jihadist organisations like Lashkar-e-Tayyba, Jaish-e-Muhammad, Harkat-ul-Ansar and Harkat-ul-Mujahedeen are also deeply rooted in this division. The Chakwal and Jhelum districts of the Rawalpindi division have been a target of hundreds of incidents of sectarian violence where not a single place of even the smallest of religious significance, from Imam Bargah to mosques and cemeteries, was spared of suicide attacks or bomb blasts. The number of seminaries run by Lashkar-e-Tayyba and Jaish-e-Muhammad in Rawalpindi division is more than hundred with the recruitment for jihad in Kashmir and Afghanistan as their main activity. Madrassa Hauzia Ilmia an important seminary of the Shiite sect is also located in the city of Rawalpindi, the headquarters of the division, moreover a renowned Shiite cleric Allama Hamid Ali Musvi also ran a seminary in the centre of the city. He is the head of his own faction of Tehreek-e-Nafaz-e-Fiqah-e-Jafria and allegedly he is being supported by the powerful secret agencies of Pakistan. Both the factions of Tehreek-e-Nafaz-e-Fiqah-e-Jafria desire implementation of Shiite shariah in the country but still harshly criticise beliefs of each-other and each of them claim to be true Shiite Muslims.

Always divided on sectarian grounds, the district of Chakwal has played a prominent role in the sectarian politics of the country. The Shiite Zakirs and religious scholars as well as the preachers and clerics from Deobandi and Wahhabi sects have all contributed to the intensification of sectarian war. Apart from Takfeer (declaring non-Muslim) of other sects, youth in large numbers were also recruited for sectarian killings. Maulana Akram Awan, an important character in the promotion of jihadist culture in Pakistan also lives in the same district. He has a long history of establishing linkages between the Pakistan Army and jihadists. He has also established a militia of his own that has to go through strict training in order to be ready at any time, in case there was a "bloody revolution" in Pakistan.[115]

Maulana Akram Awan is Ameer (Chief) of Tanzeem Al-Akhwan (The brotherhood organisation) and aims to launch a jihad for a change in the system, apart from working for the promotion of militant jihad in the country. He hails from district Chakwal that serves as a nursery for recruitment to the Pak Army. He is related with Silsala-e-Awaisia (an important sect in Sufi traditions) and there are a great number of followers of Silsala-e-Awaisia in Pak Army. Maulana Akram Awan became a disciple of Maulan Allah Yar in 1964 and he was appointed as a Khalifa-e-Majaz (A deputy that after his Sheikh's death is entitled to step into his shoes) there was a propaganda against him that he had links with Mohammad Khan the all-time notorious bandit of the area, but his organisation Tanzeem Al-Akhwan always denies such charges.[116]

He established Tanzeem Al-Akhwan in 1986 which was declared a non-political entity at the outset. A link in the chain of Sufi traditions that encouraged a reasonable number of memberships from the circles of retired as well as serving army and civil officers. In 1995, during Benazir Bhutto's premiership, Brigadier Mustansar Billah and Major General Zaheer-ul-Islam Abbasi attempted a coup d'état to establish in Islamic system of state. The name was Maulana Akram Awan which was also mentioned in this failed conspiracy however he was not indicted with sedition charges due to his links with the high-ups in the army. In 1998 he started re-organizing his group on political lines in order to pay attention towards public mobilisation for an 'Islamic Revolution'. In the same year in a grand rally in Lahore he took an 'oath to die' from his followers for the struggle to implement Islamic Sharia in Pakistan. He also focused on armed jihad and played a prominent role in promotion of this aspect of Islam. A large number of youth from Tanzeem-al-Akhwan were sent to Afghan jihad and to support Taliban about whom he said in an interview: "All who have gone have gone for good. May Allah accept their sacrifices; nobody of them has come back yet. The other day a General was asking me whether some of your boys are (fighting) there? When I responded in the affirmative, he inquired about their fate. I said they have gone after bidding adieu. They will stay there till their last breath. If they turn martyrs, Allah will accept them. They had sought a final permission from us to become martyrs, so we have never inquired about them."[117]

In December 1999, Maulana Akram Awan announced the formation of "Al-Akhwan Jihad Force" to participate in jihad in Indian-held Kashmir and this outfit was collaborating with Lashkar-e-Tayyba regarding financial resources and manpower. The Vice-Chairperson of Tanzeem Al-Akhwan Major (r) Maqbool Ahmed Shah also affirmed that our organisation was in close co-ordination with Lashkar-e-Tayyba and we are contributing financially to the Jihad of Kashmir and in manpower resources, according to our full capacity.[118]

Maulana Akram Awan has his prime focus on jihad in Pakistan so that Islamic sharia could be implemented here at the earliest possible. In this context, he has his reservations about the jihad in Kashmir as well. In an interview to an international journal "News Pakistan" New York in August 2000 he said: "No jihadist outfit has the capacity to snatch Kashmir from India. Operations by these outfits like killing four, eight or ten Indian soldiers from time to time only have the repercussions of further atrocities on the people of Kashmir by Indian forces. Their houses are looted and their women are raped. Who is responsible for this situation? And there is another aspect of the problem; what we are going to do with Kashmir if we manage to free it from India? Any of these jihadist outfits might establish a separate state of Kashmir. Moreover where there is (social) justice in Pakistan so that Kashmiris would like to have an accession with us?"[119]

As Maulana Akram Awan is primarily focused at the internal system of Pakistan and he had made quite an aggressive attempt in December

2000 for the change in system. In December 2000 he called his followers to assemble at his Headquarters at Manara, Chakwal so that they could march towards Islamabad and would carry on their sit-in and siege of the federal capital till implementation of sharia laws. About six thousand of his disciples gathered at Manara and Maulana Akram Awan issued an ultimatum to the government of General Pervez Musharraf "If you do not announce the implementation of sharia laws, I will start towards Islamabad along with 30 thousand of my followers; we would come unarmed with copies of the Holy Koran and rosaries in our hands, and we would come reciting Kalima but if anybody tries to point guns towards us, we would snatch them and enter into the city"[120]

Maulana Akram Awan first issued the deadline of 24th December 2000 for the enactment of sharia that was extended till 7th March 2001 on the special request of Corps Commander Rawalpindi and a negotiation team headed by Federal Minister for Religious Affairs Dr. Mahmood Ahmed Ghazi reached Manara. The team held talks with Maulana and reached an agreement with the approval of General Pervez Musharraf and a committee was formed in order to finalise the basic points for enactment of sharia laws. So the programme for the long march and the siege of Islamabad was postponed for the time being. Maulana was quite firm in his determination and the axis and focal point of all his speeches and sermons remains jihad within the country for which he can give a call of direct action at any time.[121]

Rawalpindi also has the unique 'honour' that Khaled Sheikh Muhammad, the third most important person of Al-Qaeda after Osama Bin Laden and Ayman Al-Zawahiri was also apprehended here from the house of a prominent leader of the Women's Wing of Jamaat-e-Islami Pakistan. House number J-18, located at Nisar Road, Rawalpindi belonged to a Nazima (lady president of a town or city) of Jamaat-e-Islami. Her husband was a famous physician and one of her sons was a high-ranking army officer posted at Kahuta at that time. When the prominent leader of Al-Qaeda and the planner of 9/11 attacks Khaled Sheikh Muhammad was captured in a raid on this house he was fast asleep. All the arrested people were immediately shifted to a 'safe house'. The American participating in the operation informed the C.I.A. chief

George Tenet of this important development as soon as the name of the arrested person was confirmed. At the time the U.S. president George W. Bush was at Camp David, the official place for vacation. George Tenet informed Condoleeza Rice, the national security advisor to the President, about this important breakthrough. It was 7:00 a.m. U.S. time and Dr. Rice rushed towards the room of George Bush and woke him up to inform him about that remarkable acheivement.[122]

Khaled Sheikh Muhammad being one of the most important leaders of Al-Qaeda and the mastermind of the 9/11 attack, his arrest was an important achievement on the part of intelligence agencies. The fact that he was arrested from the residence of a women leader of Jamaat-e-Islami was also significant for U.S. officials. The hide-and-seek between U.S. intelligence agencies and Khaled Sheikh Muhammad was on much before the incidents of 9/11. The foiled conspiracy of 1995 to wreak havoc on U.S. ships in the Pacific Ocean, special attentions of F.B.I. and C.I.A. were focused on him. According to the officials he exerted his best possible skills to materialise his terrorist plans and he had tried every technique from traditional car bomb blasts to political assassination, bombing from planes, hijacking, poisoning reservoirs and hitting aero-planes through guided missiles. It is not hard to assess how significant his arrest from Rawalpindi was. Although the Nazima of Jamaat-e-Islami who provided a hiding place to Khaled Skehikh Muhammad still claims "He was not apprehended from her house and that it is not possible to provide refuge to any stranger in her small household that steadfastly observes the restriction of hijab. It is a cantonment area comprising offices and residences of army officers only with a very strict security check for strangers. It is not possible that the most wanted terrorist of the world would have been living very comfortably in a military area". However this arrest was a joint success of the U.S. as well as Pakistani intelligence agencies as he was the person that could provide some clues of the shelter and the plans of Osama Bin Laden and Ayman Al-Zawahiri.[123]

A political leader of national stature, Sheikh Rashid Ahmed, who hails from Rawalpindi and has many times served as federal minister, has the fame of patronising a jihadist training camp for Kashmir in the suburbs of Rawalpindi. It is pertinent to mention here that Sheikh

Rashid never denied the fact categorically. Once while serving as a federal minister, he was refused visa permission by Indian authorities due to his alleged links with a seminary-cum-training camp. Rawalpindi is also considered a "Hub" for Jihad in Kashmir and the Jihadist caravans enter into Kashmir from here after a complete "gear up".

There are various "operational" offices of jihadist outfits in Rawalpindi and according to sources, the activities at these offices are in full swing. Lashkar-e-Tayyba and Jaish-e-Muhammad get a substantial portion of financial aid from this city whereas the centres and offices of both the outfits are fully operational in different towns and cities under different names.

4

A Paradise for Jihadists and Sectarian Hatemongers

It is often commented about Punjab that it is a province of the ruling elite of the country, army generals, national players and athletes, artists, politicians and clerics or to put it plainly, a province of people with tendencies of leadership and upward mobility in almost every sphere of life. Smaller provinces have this constant complaint that Punjab due to its antogance and bullying, controls all resources of the state. While, the nationalists desirous of creating a separate province in South Punjab claim that it is the provincial capital of Lahore that eats up all the resources and development allocations meant for remote and underdeveloped areas of the province. A majority of the powerful politicians and army generals from Punjab keep themselves busy in Islamabad in the tussle for authority and share in central government. In the milieu of all the apprehensions and objections by other regions and provinces, Punjab has very silently promoted a new but distinct "identity" in the past three decades or so and all aspect of individual and collective life, political, socio-cultural or others have been cast in this new mould. This new identity of Punjab is all about the rise of bigot religious parties, extremist militant outfits and sectarian groups as well as a rapid crumbling of the writ of the state in the face of these groups and the situation is fast turning into a deep crisis. Presently Punjab is hostage to various bigot groups that are much more powerful and lethal than the sans-control tribal people and the terrorists of troubled areas of Khyber-Pakhtunkhwa and FATA, the killer and extortionist gangs of Karachi and the rebellious tribal lords of Baluchistan. These zealots are not only bent upon destroying the venation of social fabric but their target seems to be something much more than the mere control of Islamabad. Still they enjoy a tacit support by the powers to be and according to more recent experiences also from the public circles to greater extent. From media to powerful institutions of state, their supporters and apologists are present everywhere that not only keep them busy in churning out a variety of arguments in their favour but also in expanding the circle of their implicit support.

Presently every city and town of Punjab is trembling with suicide attacks while the groups and organisations involved in terrorist activities from India to Afghanistan are more powerful and influential than most of the law enforcement institutions of the state. From Mumbai attacks to any future possible act of terrorism in London one would ultimately find their links and the supply line of manpower from Punjab. If the operational chief of Al-Qaeda gets arrested from a city in Punjab then Aimal Kansi, the person involved in the assassination of C.I.A agents in Virginia also gets apprehended from the Southern Punjab city of Dera Ghazi Khan. The secret agencies support their claims with facts and figures that there are more than one hundred and fifty thousand militants of various jihadist and sectarian outfits roaming around without any fear of reprisal; If on the one hand, a group of them is found involved in fatal Mumbai attacks, thousands of them are fighting against the Pakistan army in Swat and South Waziristan at the other.[124]

The strangest aspect of this phenomenon is that the elements, who are presently a hard target of the operations by the state machinery were its "strategic asset" not a long time ago and the state institutions have not only been in providing them with an adequate training of guerilla warfare but also given them safe sanctuaries in Punjab in the shape of mosques, seminaries, centres and a variety of other shelters. Even at present, it is as simple as ever for them to simply rise from any of these safe havens and to launch an easy attack on the nerve centre of the defence mechanism of the state (GHQ), kill many high-ranking army officers and take hostage scores of them. While in such a situation of panic, the secret agencies are forced to contact the chiefs of any banned sectarian and jihadist outfits that are still fully functional in Punjab, in their underground sanctuaries and most of them are still waiting for the call that they were used to get from the establishment every now and then.

What made Punjab face such circumstance and what are the real motives behind it? The back drop of this long and tragic tale is also a reflection of the gradual deterioration of state institution as well as an eventual failure of the state of Pakistan. How the extremist and the fanatic sectarian elements were fully supported and materially aided in different parts of Punjab by the omnipresent institutions of the state, who have not only succeeded in establishing strong links with Al-Qaeda but also inscribed a big question mark on the sovereignty of the Pakistani state and they also have played an important role in presenting Pakistan as a pariah state in the eyes of international community. The details of this long history are quite mind-boggling; that how these elements who are also responsible for worst kind of religious violence in Punjab, managed to fortify them, the same elements are also desirous of controlling the whole world by dint of their nuisance value based on sheer violence.

When during the 1990s the construction of a grand centre under the title of Markaz-e-Dawat wal Arshad for the promotion of jihad in Kashmir and Bosnia was started on a vast tract of agricultural land in Muridke near Lahore, a majority of the people had no idea of the organisation or its financial sponsors. Initially, the local people and media was kept in the dark about the organisation and its leadership. Any case, the media was not even keen to get information about that centre. So it is safer to observe that nobody in the administration of the provincial capital of Lahore just 30 km away, was well-informed about this development either. The people from Ahle Hadith sect (Wahhabis) in Punjab generally conducted their congregations and rallies in the cities like Sialkot, Gujranwala and Faisalabad and apart from their central rallies in the area of Mochi Gate, Lahore we did not have much information about their religious activities.[125]

On the other hand, the activities of religious parties from Deobandi sect and the extremist outfits like Sipah-e-Sahaba actively working for the promotion of sectarianism were easily noticeable in different cities and towns of Punjab. The activities of sectarian killings were like a routine matter in Punjab and the armed extremist groups from Sipah-e-Sahaba were specifically targeting the Shiite religious leaders and zakirs, bureaucrats and well-educated and professional people from other walks of life. On the opposite, front armed activists of the Imamia Students Organisation (I.S.O.) and Sipah-e-Muhammad (both Shiite outfits) were taking their revenge on people of the Deobandi sect. Sipah-e-Sahaba was getting a considerable number of mercenaries from troubled cities and town like Jhang, Kabirwala, Sargodha, Faisalabad, Multan, Khanewal and Bahawalpur while Sipah-e-Muhammad was getting its quota of recruits from Jhang, Multan, Rawalpindi and Lahore especially from the suburban areas of Thokar Niaz Beg. In the comparison of manpower and other material resources, the killer outfits of the Deobandi sect undoubtedly, had an upper hand over their opponents and both their number and capacity to strike were on the rise with every coming day.

It is interesting to note that the majority of the mercenaries from both the sides comprised of hardened criminal elements and according to the record of law enforcement agencies, most of them were wanted in theft, robbery, murder and other serious crimes. During a press conference in Rawalpindi, a vigilant officer of Punjab Police, Dr. Shoaib Suddle disclosed that sectarian killers from both Sipah-e-Sahaba and Sipah-e-Muhammad are wanted in the crimes of bank holdups and robbery. If on the one hand, the close aides to Azam Tariq and Zia-ur-Rahman Farooqi were involved in bank muggings, the associates of Ghulam Raza Naqvi, Dr. Muhammad Ali and Munawwar Alvi of Sipah-e-Muhammad were trying to even their scores of amassing wealth through other criminal activities. Although Dr. Shoaib Suddle provided media representatives with detailed statistics of nefarious acts committed by these criminal elements, next day the entire information was "killed" in almost every newspaper. Later, it was known that a 'high up' from the I.S.I. had instructed the newspapers not to publish the details of the high-handedness of these sectarian gangs.[126]

In the initial period of this sectarian frenzy, there is evidence that the sectarian killers from the Deobandi sect had the support of the passionate youth from Ahle Hadith and in certain cases from Barelvi sects as well. This could be attributed to a clear difference in religious perspectives of Shiite and Sunnis sects (Deobandi, Barelvi and Ahle Hadith, etc.). Although the historical differences about the sacred personalities of Islam were the underlying initial motives for this sectarian massacre but Sunnis and the Shiite could also be loosely divided into two main classes. Almost all the sub-sects of Sunnis have equal reverence for the Sahabas (the companions of Holy Prophet Muhammad) as well as His wives while the Shiites hold quite a different point of view that has its roots in the clamoured history of Islam. Their views about the first three Caliphs of Islam, the wives of Prophet as well as some of His companions have been always quite painful for the Sunnis. While praising the Ahle-Bait (direct descendants of Prophet Muhammad) as well as discussing the hardships faced by the progenies of the Prophet during the era of Umayyad's and Abbasids, a criticism of the personalities revered by Sunnis has also been a prominent part in the strong tradition of Shiite Majalis in the Indian sub-continent. The collective opposition to the Shiite point of view had persuaded most of the Sunnis to support Sipah-e-Sahaba in the initial incidents of sectarian violence in Punjab and in the sectarian pillage from 1980 to 1990. The agitated elements from Ahle-Hadith and Hanfi Barelvi have been extending a regular support to extremist sectarian elements from Deobandi sect rather have been helping them in the incidents of killing of Shiite and damaging or looting of their properties.[127]

In reaction, the Shiite extremists and sectarian elements have been responding in the shape of scattered groups that helped this vicious circle of sectarian hatred to gain momentum. The Shiite were getting a clear material and moral support from Iran and other Shiites of the Gulf region and the 'Pardaran-e-Inqilab' (Revolutionary Guards) of Iran established formal militant training centres for Pakistani Shiite youth. Saudi Arabia and other middle-eastern countries including Libya and Iraq were engaged in financial support of anti-Shiite sectarian elements. In the same period, an Ahle-Hadith mullah from Lahore obtained visas for Libya and Iraq through recommendation from the I.S.I. and met the officials of these countries to get direct financial support from them. Later, this religious leader working as an operative for I.S.I., joined Benazir Bhutto and other opposition leaders in their agitation. However, his real identity remained that of a provider of financial resources to militants of Sipah-e-Sahaba and Lashkar-e-Jhangvi for the killing of Shiites.

On one hand, Punjab was engaged in sectarian war and on the other Ahle-Hadith of the province who liked them to be identified with a rather hardliner and distinct title of 'Salafi'; started to organise and arm themselves with financial support from rich Arab sheikhs, apart from the support from the secret agencies of the country and the "remnants" of Afghan Jihad. Towards the end of the 1980s Hafiz Muhammad Saeed and Zafar Iqbal, two professors from the "Dawat wal Irshad" organisation formed a jihadist outfit under the title of "Lashkar-e-Tayyba" in the K████ vince of Afghanistan. Two housing projects of 'Mecca' and 'Me████ lonies for the staff of the centre in Muridke were completed ████ some modern bungalows were also constructed, adjacent to th████entre. These bungalows were to accommodate the rich Arabs who were providing financial aid and training to the "Seventh Brigade" in Bosnia. It is interesting to note that while the newspapers coming to 'Mecca' and 'Medina' colonies were thoroughly censored and even matchbox, cigarettes and photographs were confiscated from the visitors, special arrangements of swimming pools were made in the residence of Arab sheikhs. As a horse is symbolic to jihad, a horse farm with latest facilities was also constructed in the centre and horse riding was made compulsory for all under training mujahedeen.[128]

In the beginning of 1991, the I.S.I. engaged three Deobandi outfits in jihad of Kashmir. Youth were recruited for Harkat-ul-Mujahedeen, Harkat-ul-Jihad-ul-Islami and Jamiat-ul-Mujahedeen-ul-Almi that were entered into Indian-held Kashmir after different phases of training in Kunar, Jalalabad, Khost and Kandhar apart from the training camp in Mansehra. It is significant that three of these organisations earlier had vast experience of jihad in Afghanistan under guidance from the I.S.I. and that agency was mainly responsible for providing them with all material resources. Three of them also had the credit of bringing Pakistani and Afghan mujahedeen in Kashmir. They were granted authority to recruit fresh mujahedeen from Pakistan and a considerable number of people from different religious parties of the country joined their ranks within no time. Through the efforts by the I.S.I., all three outfits were joined together on a common platform in 1993 under the title of Harkat-ul-Ansar and seminaries of N.W.F.P. were given a special task of providing jihadist manpower for this new alliance. Initially the influence of Maulana Sami-ul-Haq and Maulana Fazal-ur-Rahman was also exploited and thousands of youth from seminaries were provided militant training. It is worthy to note that it was Maulana Mufti Mahmood, the father of Maulana Fazal-ur-Rahman, who in 1979, issued the fatwa (edict) in favour of Jihad in Afghanistan and demanded that all the Muslims of Pakistan participate in this jihad in person as well as through their financial resources.[129]

After a year's "hard work", Lashker-e-Tayyba was also ready to enter its mujahedeen in Kashmir and launch successful operations. In 1991, it sent its first ever jihadist troops to Kashmir and most of these mujahedeen belonged to different areas of Punjab. As prospective recruits Lashker-e-Tayyba targeted unemployed and nominally literate youths instead of students from schools and colleges. After the basic training at Muaskar-e-Tayyba (militant training centre) at Kunar they were sent to Murdke where they were introduced to the blessings of jihad and the great bounties in paradise in the life after death including more than 70 exceptionally beautiful virgins. They were told that not only would they but their parents and other family members as well, would be granted with divine bounties in the heavens while on the day of judgment they would be lodged in the camps for highly-favoured people if they succeed to become a martyr in "Ghazvi-e-hind" (a hadith from the Prophet Muhammad that predicted the eventual victory of mujahedeen in a future battle in India). They will be granted with 72 vigins headed by a queen virgin and honoured with a crown decorated with precious diamonds and rubies while seventy family members of a martyr could enter in the heavens upon his personal recommenda-tion.[130]

Till the formal beginning of sectarian war in Punjab Shiite youth were also ready to enter into "battle field" as they also had established some strong "militant ties" with "Pasdaran-e-Inqilab (the revolutionary guards) after the successful revolution in Iran. On the other hand, a fiery Shiite cleric from Parachinar Allama Arif-ul-Husseini had been appointed the chief of Tahreek Nifaz-e-Fiaqah-e-Jafferia on the recommendation of Ayatollah Khomeini. Allama Arif-ul-Husseini, who enjoyed the full support from Shiite Toori tribes of Parachinar, had experienced the worst kind of sectarian partiality on the part of Pakistani establishment during Zia-ul-Haq era and he wanted to organise Shiite youth of the country in the face of ever-growing force of Deobandi jihadist outfits. If Doebandi and Ahle-e-Hadith youths of Pakistan were flocking for jihad in Afghanistan, Arif-ul-Husseini also dispatched youth of Imamia Students Organisation for the support of Hazara tribes of Afghanistan while Shiite youth were also sent to Kashmir for the support of Shiite militant outfits. From 1989 to 1992, there were about one dozen jihadist groups from the Shiite sect with their base camps in Baltistan and Skardu apart from Muzaffarabad where they had several sources for arms and manpower.[131]

In the light of available fact and statistics it would not be wrong to say that it was Punjab that turned into a crossroads for extremists, terrorists and adventurists of every genre. First a favourable atmosphere was created for jihad in Afghanistan and Kashmir and then extremist groups and organisations established camps in different cities and towns of Punjab and recruited un-employed young men and youth from poverty-ridden families. Some jihadist outfits were being paid per person for the recruitment of jihadist organisations like Jamaat-e-Islami and Al Dawat-wal-Irshad recruited thousands of young men for training of jihad. First of all a training camp with the support of the I.S.I. was established in Mansehra, then for militant training of prospective mujahedeen by Lashkar-e-Tayyba a vast tract of land was acquired in Chehla Bandi near Muzaffarabad. This area of Chehla Bandi was selected so that the new recruit mujahedeen from the plains of Punjab could fare better in real 'jihad' after completion of training here. The chief of Dawat-wal-Irshad Hafiz Muhammad Saeed and his associated Professor Zafar Iqbal started conducting lectures for local traders and rich classes on the blessings of jihad at places selected by the I.S.I. and appealed to them for financial support. Some of them were directly instructed by the I.S.I. and other secret agencies to extend financial support to mujahedeen of Lashkar-e-Tayyba and pretty soon it turned into the biggest organisation engaged in militant activities in Indian-occupied Kashmir.[132]

Harkat-ul-Ansar, Hizbul Mujahedeen and other outfits were also engaged in their militant operations with support from "Rawalpindi", apart from Lashkar-e-Tayyba. Lashkar-e-Tayyba used to conduct its annual jihadist conference that was attended by every sympathizer of jihadist ideology from former Director General I.S.I. Lieutenant General (r) Hamid Gul to Chief of Jamaat-e-Islami Qazi Hussein Ahmed, editors and owners of right-wing newspapers and magazines, rich political elite of Punjab, ex-army officers and businessmen. Harkat-ul-Ansar and other Kashmiri jihadist organisations also continued to collect funds. In the meantime, Urdu newspapers from Lahore used to publish special editions to highlight the blessings of jihad and blew out of proportion, the exploits of mujahedeen in Kashmir and the loss incurred by the Indian Army in the Valley of Jammu and Kashmir. Lashkar-e-Tayyba established its media cell at Lahore. It used to issue exaggerated stories and un-realistic statistics on a daily basis. If the figures issued by the said media cell are tabulated, one gets the impression that a few scores of mujahedeen murdered thousands of Indian troops in the span of just three years while only a handful of mujahedeen were martyred in the process.

The sectarian organisations on the other hand, were engaged in the worst killing in Punjab, not sparing anyone from the opposite groups. The mosques, imam bargahs even cemeteries of every sect were under attack in district headquarters and towns of Jhang, Shorkot, Chiniot, Faisalabad, Sargodha, Multan, Mianwali, Rawalpindi, Gujrat, Gujranwala, Sialkot, Narowal, Lahore, Khanewal, Vehari, Bahawalnagar, Bahawalpur, Rahim Yar Khan, Layyah and Muzaffargarh. The militants from Sipah-e-Sihaba and Sipah-e-Muhammad never missed any occasion to kill the members of opposite sects. Successive governments in Punjab, intelligence agencies and law-enforcement institutions, all seemed helpless in this killing spree. In Lahore, Sipah-e-Shaba murdered Sadiq Ganji, a very popular Iranian diplomat in broad daylight. The assailant took flight on a motorbike. After a chase by the police the two were arrested and one of them turned out to be a low-ranking official of the I.S.I., especially dispatched for this mission by his superiors.[133]

Shiite politicians and feudallords were constantly under attack in different cities of Punjab and Sipah-e-Muhammad was launching retaliatory attacks on Sipah-e-Sahaba. In the meantime, Riaz Basra an important leader of Sipah-e-Sahaba, was arrested in the murder charge of the Iranian diplomat. At that tune, Mian Manzoor Wattoo was the chief minister of Punjab and many leaders of Sipah-e-Sahaba were present in his cabinet of ministers. Riaz Basra had no difficulty in escaping from the court and later it came to light that the official facilitating his escape was acting upon 'special' instructions from one of the most important high-ups in the Punjab government. Although the government functionaries categorically denied the allegation, the accomplices in this escape were never taken to task either. The same Riaz Basra later on committed the murder of so many important personalities including Commissioner Tajummul Abbas, Deputy Commissioner Syed Ali Raza and Senior Superintendent Police Muhammad Ashraf Marth. The former officers belonged to the Shiite sect whereas the latter had some very important information about the terrorists of Sipah-e-Muhammad and he had arrested many of them after getting intelligence about their biggest network.[134]

At the time when Punjab was a victim of the worst kind of sectarian extermination and was at its lowest ebb in the law and order situation, the fund-raising for jihad in Kashmir was at its peak. The style of advertising campaign by Lashkar-e-Tayyba and Jamaat-ud-Dawa, as well as the rapid expansion in its network of schools, madrassas, centres and offices often gives rise to suspicions and objections about the sources of funding; whether these funds were generated from abroad and what was so special about these resources that the organisation succeeded in expanding such an established network. The monthly expenses for the militant training camp of Lashkar-e-Tayyba itself, are said to be around 350 million rupees. The cost of land of the centre at Chauburji was estimated to be 75 million and construction charges were 20 million rupees, in interior Sindh the Aqsa muaskar (militants training centre) at Hyderabad was constructed with a cost of 50 million rupees whereas capital investment on the centre at Muridke is worth much more.

It is noteworthy that before a ban on fund-raising and collection of donations for jihadist outfits was imposed, Lashkar-e-Tayyba had deposited about six hundred thousand collection boxes at various points all over country whereas one thousand persons were deputed with the responsibility to empty the boxes and take the collections to the secretariat. They were paid monthly remunerations apart from a motorcycle from the organisation. In January 2002, a prominent member of L-e-T lamented in Muzaffarabad that previously the daily collection in small bazaars was from 15 to 50 rupees per box whereas in big markets it was from 200 to 500 rupees per box. There was an overall average of rupees 200 with a total collection of 120 million rupees per day. After the ban L-e-T is deprived of such a huge source of daily income. Professor Hafiz Muhammad Saeed also claims "from its creation to every day's operations, no foreign country had any role to play in this organisation. We have never sought financial help from any country nor any other kind of support. Much is said about the aid of Saudi Arabia to L-e-T but I must clarify that Saudi Arabia had never sponsored us, rather I have my complaints with all the Muslim countries and especially Saudi Arabia that they are lagging far behind in terms of their support for jihad. We get all our support from the citizens of Pakistan. Those who are offering the sacrifice of their lives are also willing to offer their financial support. Our organisation does not comprise people with any sources of income or those who neither have anything to eat nor of the people about whom it is also alleged that they go to Kashmir instead of committing suicide; who are also called Fedayeen. This sort of propaganda comes from the West. Our organisation is made up of every segment of society including doctors, engineers, PhDs and young men from affluent families. There are names of Masters of Arts, M.B.B.S. and Engineers in the list of martyrs in jihad. The youths with PhD from abroad have also sacrificed their lives. At present, young men of some prominent and affluent families from Punjab and Sindh have been also participating in jihad."[135]

There is another allegation against Lashkar-e-Tayyba that instead of focusing on the jihad in Kashmir it pays more attention to "correction" of the beliefs of the local population (the majority of Kashmiri Muslims is Sunni) and preach their Wahhabi version of Islam after getting hold of their mosques. The refugees in the camps at Pakistani-controlled Kashmir, generally complain about such kind of behaviour but L-e-T holds that the belief of people cannot be changed by force but if somebody is convinced of the 'truth' than others should not have any objection to our preaching it. Abu Osama, a mujahidin from Shahdadkot confided that Ameer Sahib (Hafiz Muhammad Saeed) has clearly forbidden them to interfere in such issues but if someone becomes a part of our organisation, "correction" of his/her beliefs gets prime importance for us as it is essential for their future life and for participation in jihad. Lashkar-e-Tayyba already known for its fatal guerilla operations in Indian-held Kashmir and the infamous suicide attacks on Red Fort Delhi, once again became the focus of global attention when its Fedayeen launched a carnage on innocent people in Mumbai on 26th November 2008.

Zaigham Khan in his research titled "Religious militancy and sectarian violence in Pakistan", in the monthly "The Herald", Karachi of January 1998, has written about 'Askari (militant) Wing' of Al-Dawa Markaz, Muridke that more than one hundred thousand people participated in the convention of Al-Dawa in 1997 held at Muridke (about 30 km north of Lahore on the Grand Trunk Road). The area of this centre is more than 190 acres, where a grand mosque, a big pool, a university campus and a big stable are constructed, apart from many garment, steel and woodwork factories in the surroundings. Residential colonies are also developed there. The foundation of this centre was laid by three university teachers in 1987. Both Hafiz Muhammad Saeed and Professor Zafar Iqbal taught at the University of Engineering and Technology, Lahore, whereas Professor Doctor Abdullah Azzaam (of Palestinian origin) was a teacher at International Islamic University, Islamabad. Abdullah Azzaam was killed in a bomb attack near Peshawar in 1989 and Hafiz Saeed and Prof. Zafar Iqbal are leading this organisation. According to Hafiz Saeed "the centre is serving two main objectives; preaching of Islam and promotion of jihad. There are various Muslim organisations working for preaching of Islam in and outside Pakistan but their organisation has also disseminated an awareness of jihad among the people apart from that object of evangelisation. Although the significance of jihad is everlasting, at present its need is much more heightened". Adding to this Prof. Zafar Iqbal said that "jihad is a way of life that opens doors of success for whosoever that follows its path. As you can observe the presence of thousands of people in this convention is a clear evidence of the success of the jihadist way of life."[136]

It is claimed that Jamaat-ud-Daw is engaged in various fields of education and social uplift. The extraordinary work by its jihadist wing gives the organisation an international 'recognition'. Lashkar-e-Tayyba sends its activists for jihad after a reasonable training. Although it participated in Afghan jihad earlier but, now the focal point of its activities is Indian-held Kashmir and presently it is the largest jihadist organisation of Pakistan. So many other local groups are also engaged in jihad in Kashmir but all these local groups have support by foreign militants who had got their training in Pakistan and Afghanistan.

According to the sources of Lashkar-e-Tayyba, 80 percent militants from these groups come from different countries but L-e-T has 80 percent of its militants from Pakistan. The organisation never likes to show off its numerical strength. The number of mujahedeen to be sent in Kashmir is the discretion of Ameer (chief) and only the relevant office can tell their exact number. Although people are recruited keeping in mind the casualties during jihad or it is subject to change according to circumstances or any possible variation, the capacity of the organisation however, the number of recruits and trainees always exceeds that of actual requirements. In Kashmir the 'success rate' for Lashkar-e-Tayyba has remained much higher than other jihadist outfits.

In order to get widespread support through its schools, groups of social uplift organisations and religious literature, the L-e-T always exaggerates the atrocities against Kashmiri Muslims to a mythical proportion, so that a high spirit of jihad could be infused in people. The youth aspiring to join the jihad have to go through two phases of exclusive training. This first phase finishes in three weeks whereas the second one comprises a demanding and harsh training of three months that is also called 'daura khasa' (special phase). Guerilla warfare, use of small conventional arms, ambush of the enemy and the techniques to expose oneself to minimum of afflictions are some salient components of this training. The militants training by the other jihadist outfits is comparatively different and harder than that of L-e-T. According to sources of Jamiat-ul-Mujahedeen (it is worth mentioning that Jamiat is still engaged in jihad of Kashmir), the first phase of training takes around forty days. Second and third phases are of four and six months respectively. The first phase gets the trainees seasoned for harsh conditions through a rigorous physical exercise and they also take training of 0.32 pistol, 303 rifles and Kalashnikovs. In the second phase the militants get the training of anti-aircraft guns as well as dissembling and re-assembling of available weapons. The also learn how to make a grenade and bombs comprising a mixture of calcium carbonate and petrol. In the third and the last phase which is generally called 'commando training', militants get used to living without food for longer spells, bearing harsh weather conditions, walk on a rope, fire at the enemy while then legs are fastened with a cord or with only one hand and of course crawling is an essential part throughout this phase.[137]

The names of new entrants in L-e-T are immediately replaced with that of companions of Prophet Muhammad or other legends of Islamic history. They are called by new names in the organisation and even the martyrs in Kashmir are remembered by the same jihadist names. The appearance of militants under training is also altered and they start sporting a long beard and long hair. Before the jihad in Afghanistan and Kashmir and the arrival of Arab mujahedeen, religious elements in Pakistan never had this type of identity of long hair and beard. The trainees of L-e-T also wear their trousers ankles high as it is an essential part of their creed and longer trousers are considered anti-Islamic and they become much particular about it at the time of prayers. Not everyone is dispatched to Kashmir soon after the completion of training and some of them are engaged in other organisational activities like the collection of funds, to look after the offices and to introduce the new entrants to the organisational structure and culture.

A majority of the newcomers in L-e-T are graduates from government schools or colleges and students from seminaries are very few. For example Azhar Sawar, a militant in the Lashkar, had graduated from a college and he was in search of a job when he became a member of L-e-T and his name was changed to Abuzar Basri. He got his militant training and went to Kashmir where he lost his life. Similarly Abu Shaheed aged 12, from Vehari became a member of Lashkar after listening to a fiery speech from Major Mast Gul the commander of the militant outfit Hizb-ul-Mujahedeen. The charismatic personality of Major Mast Gul instilled a spirit of jihad in Abu Shaheed and he got military training after joining the L-e-T. Before that he was running a music centre but later he burnt all the CDs in his shop. Manzoor Ahmed 34, of Hafizabad had a similar story. He was a mechanical engineer but participated in jihad with the title of Abu Hamza after winding up his business. He got his training in 1996 and had fought in Kashmir for one year. Ten of his companion became martyrs but he remained safe. He claimed that he would go to Kashmir again and will keep fighting until his martyrdom.[138]

However, people outcast by society such as drug-addicts, criminals and people engaged in anti-social activities, also joined and were welcomed in L-e-T. Young man Abdullah is a good example of it who was in jail in a murder charge where his thinking underwent a drastic transformation as the result of interaction with members of L-e-T. Abdullah was assigned the responsibilities of care for persons injured during jihad. Likely Tariq from Shadbagh Lahore was addicted to heroin before joining L-e-T and he lost his life in 1997 in the jihad of Kashmir. L-e-T has a clear policy of sending to jihad only those who have permission from their parents. That is why there is no mourning or crying whenever anyone of them is martyred. As a norm, a delegate from L-e-T goes to the family of the martyr and felicitates them for that honour on the part of their son or brother. On such occasions, expressions of kudus replace the crying or lamenting and guests coming for this purpose are served with good food.[139]

At the loss of his son, Muhammad Sarwar, an ex-bank officer, said "In a society where people lose their lives in so called 'honour killing' or in incidents of terrorism or roadside accidents, I'm glad that the sacrifice of my son did not go in vain. Hafiz Abdul Ghafoor, an old man from Lahore, after losing two of his sons in Kashmir, expressed his feelings in these words "I have a great desire to turn young again so that I can fight for L-e-T alongside my sons". Hundreds of such examples were abundantly quoted in the monthly organ "Mujalah Al-Dawa," published by Jamaat-ud-Dawa (the magazine has since been banned).[140]

The militants killed during the fight against Indian forces in

Kashmir are buried by the local people with honour and respect. When any militant of L-e-T gets martyred, troops of the Indian Army or Border Security Force hand over the dead body to the local police station. The local people receive the body and after performing all the funeral rites, bury it in the cemetery specially meant for martyrs. Such cemeteries are found in almost every village of Indian-controlled Kashmir. In the meantime in Pakistan funeral prayers for the martyrs are also observed. Blessings of dying a martyr's death are discussed. Generally Lashkar manages to find many new recruits on the occasion of such funeral prayers. According to the policy the militants of Lashkar prefer death instead of being caught alive.

Till the end of the 1990s, the number of militants of L-e-T in Indian jails was around 20 and it is impossible to bring them back through any negotiation so they would be executed there. In turn when militants capture any of the members of the Indian troops they kill them by slitting their throats. However highly brutal psychological tactics like beheading the captured soldiers or cutting the organs of teen body are also used in order to pressurise Indian forces. Once a militant called Abu Haibat brought the head of an Indian soldier to Pakistan. The Ameer (chief) of Lashkar in Indian Controlled Kashmir Abdul Rahman Aldakhil claims "Koran orders us to hit each and every knuckle of them and instructs us to treat them in the same manner as they treat us"[141]

Till the end of 2001, about 1,100 militants of L-e-T were martyred while the number of killed Indian troops exceeded 15 thousand. Some sources claim that this militant outfit of Wahhabi creed got financial aid from many Arab States including Saudi Arabia. Prince Abdul Aziz, a prince of the Saudi royal family, had spent huge amounts for promotion of Wahhabi-ism all over the world. The business people of Wahhabi sect in Pakistan donated generously to this organisation. Moreover billions of rupees were also generated as funds for jihad in Kashmir. A report was published in the Pakistani media in the beginning of 2004, with a host of disclosures about the assets of Jamaat-ud-Dawa-wal-Irshad and Lashkar-e-Tayyba. The list of assets held by these organisations was as following.[142]

Annually 30 million rupees are spent on the training camps of Lashkar-e-Tayyba.

The value of its property in Chowk Chauburji exceeds 35 million rupees.

Aqsa Training Camp at Hyderabad was completed with a cost of rupees 50 million whereas rupees 180 million have already been spent on Markaz Dawa-wal-Irshad at Muridke. Before the ban, rupees 120 million were collected on a daily basis as Jihad-e-Kashmir fund. In the heydays of jihad in Kashmir, in the 1990s, when slogans were chanted in every town and village of Pakistan in favour of jihad, the leading personalities of these outfits were moving around in luxurious SUVs and were enjoying every imaginable comfort of life. It took these mujahedeen just a couple of years to graduate luxury vehicles from their old bicycles.

In 1997, Lashkar-e-Tayyba shifted its headquarters from Kashmir to Jammu and there was a sharp increase in the activities of militants especially in the border districts of Doda and Poonch. Although Jammu and Kashmir is the focus of L-e-T activities it has already targeted many other states and cities of India including New Delhi, Mumbai, Bangalore, Hyderabad, Varanasi, Kolkata and Gujarat. The network of Lashkar-e-Tayyba is not limited to Jammu and Kashmir and it expands to Andhra Pradesh, Tamil Nadu, Maharashtra, Karnataka and Gujarat. India. The allegations have been repeated time and again that Lashkar-e-Tayyba, on the behest of Pakistani intelligence, is involved in terrorist activities in Maharashtra, West Bengal, Bihar, Hyderabad, New Delhi, Haryana and Uttar Pradesh.[143]

Suicide attacks are forbidden in the strategy of Lashkar-e-Tayyba. In the Wahhabi jurisprudence these attackers are called Fedayeen as the attackers are not always martyred and could come back alive sometimes, whereas at present in Pakistan, Afghanistan and Iraq the suicide attackers target their enemy with explosive material attached to their bodies so their own death is certain. But when in 1999, Pakistani troops and militants were forced to retreat from Kargil. Fedayeen of L-e-T launched suicide attacks on Indian posts. So the first Fedayeen attack by L-e-T was made in district Bandi Pura in mid-1999 after the retreat from Kargil. From 1999 to 2002, a total of 161

Indian troops and ordinary citizens as well as 90 Fedayeen lost their lives. Pakistan and India were at the brink of a deadly war due to such activities by the L-e-T.[144]

First, when after an attack on Indian Parliament on 13th December 2001, General Pervez Musharraf was forced to impose a ban on all jihadi outfits, L-e-T was also affected by that ban. After this Lashkar-e-Tayyba changed its name to Jamaat-ud-Dawa and Hafiz Muhammad Saeed in a press conference at Lahore distanced himself from the Lashkar by appointing Abdul Waheed Kashmiri, a rather unknown militant as the next Chief of L-e-T. The central executive council of Lashkar appointed Maulana Zaki-ur-Rahman Lakhvi as the new Operational Supreme Commander in place of Abdul Waheed. After a few days Hafiz Muhammad Saeed was put under house arrest. Earlier he had announced the formation of a new outfit named Jamaat-ud-Dawa and he was sure of his ultimate arrest due to his fiery speeches and inciting people to defy the state laws.[145]

When the statements about the relations between Osama Bin Laden and Hafiz Saeed were constantly being published in the U.S. media, the security of Hafiz Saeed was further tightened. However, the Lahore High Court quashed his house arrest after one year. After his release, he started gathering youth from all over the country through his student organisation "Talba Jamaat-ud-Dawa". So both the outfits dodged the ban imposed in 2002. Jamaat-ud-Dawa being a new set-up formed after the ban while Lashkar-e-Tayyba by going underground.

Hafiz Saeed has always been a favourite of the Pakistani establishment and while declaring him "more amiable and supportive" than the chiefs of other jihadist outfits, intelligence circles are confident that they could launch a 'controlled jihad' in Kashmir through Hafiz Saeed wherever, whenever and whatever level they like. It is also often said about him that he is much more determined and enthusiastic to get Kashmir freed as compared to other jihadist outfits and he has a greater number of Punjabis among his mujahedeen who get mixed up with the local population of Jammu and Kashmir. Their language and dress code is more or less similar with that people of Jammu and Kashmir. Most interesting fact is that Jamaat-ud-Dawa continued collecting its funds and recruiting new blood notwithstanding all the bans and restrictions by the U.S. administration and the Pakistani government. Despite all these sanctions banners and other publicity material from Jamaat-ud-Dawa and Lashkar-e-Tayyba was quite visible in rural as well as urban Punjab with a clear provocation for jihad against infidels. The names of local group leaders and their contact numbers were also published in these advertisements.

The leadership of Jamaat-ud-Dawa is fully aware of the abject poverty in remote rural areas of Pakistan that is why these advertisements tempt prospective recruits with free boarding lodging and transport. Unemployed and semi-literate youth, in the hope of getting free military training and these facilities, become their easy target. The young volunteers of Jamaat-ud-Dawa and Lashkar-e-Tayyba could be seen distributing pamphlets and booklets in front of mosques in towns and villages, glorifying the blessings of jihad in Kashmir, Palestine and Chechnya. The literature gives an impression that pretty soon they would to hoist flags of Islam in New Delhi, Tel Aviv and Washington. The leadership of L-e-T is quite emphatic about the point that Hindus and Jews are the worst enemies of Islam. The annual report of the U.S. state department for 2008 has noted that despite all restrictions Jamaat-ud-Dawa and Hafiz Saeed are free to collect funds as well as to incite Pakistani population against the U.S., Israel and India.[146]

The report also states that Jamaat-ud-Dawa and Lashkar-e-Tayyba are providing logistic support to Al-Qaeda; the arrest of Abu-Zubaida, an important member of Al-Qaeda from the house of a worker of Lashkar-e-Tayyba in Faisalabad is a clear evidence of the fact. On 11th July 2006, more than 200 people were killed in seven bomb attacks on Mumbai suburban railways. According to Abu Anas, the arrested bodyguard of Zaki-ur-Rahman, the mastermind behind these attacks, regular monthly meetings take place between the leadership of Lashkar-e-Tayyba and officials of I.S.I. in Muzaffarabad. Abu Anas told A.N. Roy, the Police Commissioner of Mumbai that there had been regular monthly meetings between Zaki-ur-Rahman Lakhvi, other higher leaders of Lashkar-e-Tayyba and Brigadier Riaz, brigadier Haji and Major Wajahat of I.S.I. An interim ban was imposed on Jamaat-ud-Dawa after one month of this incident at Mumbai and Hafiz Saeed was put under house arrest for one month.[147]

It is true that Jamaat-ud-Dawa had raised an amount of 10 million pounds from ex-patriot Pakistani after the devastating earthquake of October 2005 for the aid and rehabilitation of affected families but only half of that amount was spent for aid. On the other hand, secret agencies of the U.S. and the U.K. claim that there was a real threat of an incident bigger in scale than that of 09/11/01 and 07/07/05 bombings, if the plot to destroy a plane of Atlantic Airlines was not foiled. It is worth mentioning that here the air tickets and other expenses of the operatives of this plot were paid by Jamaat-ud-Dawa. The U.S. state department, in its report, has disclosed about "Idara Khidmat-e-Khalq" a welfare wing of Jamaat-ud-Dawa that it is in fact a part of Lashkar-e-Tayyba formed to continue its operations under disguise.[148]

After sometime during the address on 5th February 2007 (Kashmir Day) at Qadsia Mosques, Hafiz Muhammad Saeed said "Jihad in Kashmir will reach its logical end when all the Hindus in India are terminated. Jihad is a diktat by Allah, not an order by any army general that could be started one day and halted the next day upon his orders". Addressing a Kashmir solidarity conference in Lahore exactly on the same day next year Hafiz Saeed declared "While India, the U.S. and the U.K. are together engaged in a proxy war against Pakistan, it is high time to get Jammu and Kashmir liberated by waging a jihad against India. The Government of Pakistan should declare an all-out jihad in order to ensure integrity and unity of the country. After five months of this speech, India accused the I.S.I. and Lashkar-e-Tayyba for a suicide attack on the Indian embassy at Kabul (Forty people were killed in this attack including an Indian Brigadier). It is claimed in the investigative report that the 22-year old suicide attacker, who was driving a car, Hamza Shakoor was a Punjabi jihadist trained by Gujranwala wing of Lashkar-e-Tayyba.[149]

Lashkar-e-Tayyba resurfaced again after some months and launched a deadly attack on very busy business districts of Mumbai on 26th November 2008, killing 175 persons. On 10th December 2008, the U.N., upon a plea by India, banned Jamaat-ud-Dawa declaring it a terrorist organisation and a front runner of Lashkar-e-Tayyba. The U.N. Security Council included the names of Zaki-ur-Rahman Lakhvi and

Haji Muhammad Ashraf (the in-charge of financial affairs of Jamaat-ud-Dawa) in the list of terrorists. Muhammad Ahmed Bahaziq, the chief of Lashkar-e-Tayyba in Saudi Arabia and the main fund-raiser was also declared a terrorist. In spite of all these sanctions by the U.N., the educational institutions and medical centres run by Al-Dawa, continued working without any restriction. However, the government of Pakistan, in the second week of December 2008, appointed its own administrators on the headquarters at Muridke and many leaders and activists including Hafiz Saeed and Zaki-ur-Rahman Lakhvi were arrested. In reaction to that the spokesperson for Jamaat-ud-Dawa, Abdullah Muntazar threatened the government with dire consequences for damaging the infrastructure of Jamaat. However, the F.B.I. had by that time identified him as Abdullah Ghaznavi who had served as the spokesperson of the Lashkar-e-Tayyba in Sri Nagar. It is pertinent to note that he had been persistently calling in newspapers' offices from some unidentifiable numbers.[150]

Earlier, Pakistani intelligence officials shared with the F.B.I that Mantazar had shifted to Sri Nagar. Blocking the English and Urdu websites of Jamaat-ud-Dawa was the only concrete step against it by the government of Pakistan. However, "Ghazva" the weekly organ of Jamaat-ud-Dawa, continued publishing its hate-mongering features and articles. In the first week of December, "Ghazva" published a cover story on the Mumbai attacks declaring them not only a 'historic victory' for Muslim militants but also a befitting revenge for the atrocities perpetrated against Muslims in India and Kashmir. It was also claimed in the same issue that during 2008, four thousand five hundred mothers in Pakistan dedicated one of their sons each to Jamaat-ud-Dawa whereas 83 of them devoted two sons each; all of them have an aim of waging an armed jihad against Indian Armed Forces apart from promotion of Islamic values, defence and preaching their religion.[151]

At present, all the experts on global terrorism agree that Jamaat-ud-Dawa (read Lashkar-e-Tayyba), greatly inspired by Al-Qaeda aspires to expand its operations much beyond India as it perceives itself to be the guardian of Islam. They maintain that lashkar-e-Tayyba that started its operations with some low-intensity skirmishes in Kashmir, presently has acquired the capacity to launch terrorist attacks on a global scale. Its leadership operates camps for the training of foreign nationals.

Experts hold that there is a possibility of Afghanistan inspiring Western Muslims towards jihad for a limited period of time but the training camps in Pakistan and the jihadists 'graduating' there could pose long-term threats for Western world.

On 3rd February 2009, the director of C.I.A., Michael Hayden included Lashkar-e-Tayyba among the outfits that potentially pose serious security challenges at global level. In an interview with Fox News he said "The world community still has the greatest threats from Al-Qaeda that has spread a network of terrorism all over the world through its affiliated organisations. The situation is quite painful. Its subsidiaries include Lashkar-e-Tayyba that was involved in terror attacks in Mumbai. First it declared India as enemy number one, now it plans to target Israel and the U.S. In order to achieve that goal, some members of the Lashkar-e-Tayyba have merged themselves into Al-Qaeda"[152]

Zaki-ur-Rahman Lakhvi, the chief planner of the Mumbai attacks, was born at Chak (village) No. 18 L, Renala Khurd; district Okara on 30 December 1960. His father's name is Hafiz Aziz-ur-Rahman, who has the fame of a hardliner Wahhabi among the people of the area. Ajmal Kasav the lone survivor among the Mumbai attackers captured alive, also hails from this district. Lakhvi got affiliated with jihad after his sister got married to a rich Saudi citizen, Abu Abdul Rahman, a long-trusted associate of Osama Bin Laden. It is said about Abu Abdul Rahman that he donated 10 million rupees in 1988 for the construction of Markaz-ud-Dawa near Muridke. He also founded an organisation at Kunar Afghanistan that had an arrangement for militant training of Pakistani and Afghani youths at Bajaur. Here a large number of the youth from Wahhabi sect were imparted militant training. Lakhvi worked as an instructor in this camp and in 1991 he was made a 'Commander-in-Chief' by the Pakistani establishment for operations of Lashkar-e-Tayyba in Indian-controlled Kashmir.[153]

After assuming the role of a supreme commander for militant operations in Jammu and Kashmir, Lakhvi had additional responsibilities of searching for new young men, to train them and to make requisite preparations for 'missions' in Kashmir. On 12th April 1999, about four weeks before the Kargil operation, Lakhvi said in an interview with the daily 'The Nation' that they had already made all the arrangements for a full-scale Pak-India war and were preparing to send mujahedeen to Himachal Pradesh in order to attack important Indian installations. They had the target of preparing the maximum number of mujahedeen within India. He said "We are getting the Muslims of India ready, when they would be fully prepared it would prove be the dooms day for India"[154]

While addressing a rally at Muridke he declared that after the retreat of Pakistan from Kabul and the statements by Bill Clinton and Nawaz Sharif, it is essential that the morale of the Kashmiri brethren as well as the mujahedeen for Kashmir be boosted. We have already dispatched Fedayeen to teach a lesson to India and New Delhi would be our next target. It is significant that he turned this threat into a reality by attacking the Indian Parliament on 13th December 2001. Within ten days, General Pervez Musharraf enforced a ban on Lashkar-e-Tayyba on 24th December 2001. Although Hafiz Saeed resigned as chief of Lashkar-e-Tayyba the same day and formed a new religious welfare organisation titled Jamaat-ud-Dawa, Lakhvi was still retained as the operational chief of Lashkar-e-Tayyba. Lakhvi had apprehensions that Hafiz Saeed wants to embezzle funds of jihad in Kashmir. He also claimed that as Jamaat-ud-Dawa was a religious and welfare organisation, it had no right on the funds. Lakhvi also established a separate organisation named "Khair-ul-Nas" (welfare for people) and shifted to Muzaffarabad. Some close aides to Lakhvi swore upon eliminating Hafiz Saeed but some officers of the army and intelligence agencies experienced patch-up between the two.[155]

Lakhvi kept himself busy in the training of militants and sending them to India-controlled Kashmir. In July 2006, India assented that the wing leader of Lashkar-e-Tayyba, Azam Cheema was responsible for the death of 209 people in bomb attacks at the Mumbai Railway Station. The Police Commissioner of Mumbai claimed in a press conference that the attacker was trained and prepared in a house near Bahawalpur. He further stated that the arrested person claimed to be a bodyguard of Zaki-ur-Rahman Lakhvi. On 28th May 2008, the four persons banned by the U.S. department included the name of Lakhvi as well, who had close ties with Al-Qaeda and Osama Bin Laden. The other three were Hafiz Muhammad Saeed, Haji Muhammad Ashraf and chief financer of Lashkar-e-Tayyba Haji Muhammad Mahmood Ahmed Bahaziq. The two sons of Lakhvi, Abu Qatal and Abu Qasim had been killed in Kashmir by Indian security forces in 2003 and 2005 respectively. His wife performs the responsibilities of carry for the mothers and the widows of militants fighting by Lashkar's side and killed.[156]

While swapping restrictions on these four persons, the U.S. department of finance also made it clear that the group had close ties with Al-Qaeda and that it was involved in the killing of innocent people. India repeated its allegations after 26/11 that Zaki-ur-Rahman Lakhvi who is residing at Muzaffarabad, went to Karachi in August 2008 where he dispatched mujahedeen of LeT for Mumbai and carried on issuing instructions through telephone to the terrorists about this operation. Some close circles also confide that Lakhvi was quite annoyed at the statement made by Hafiz Saeed that Hafiz Zaki-ur-Rahman Lakhvi and Zafar Shah do not have any more relations with Jamaat-ud-Dawa and Hafiz Saeed.[157]

The Mumbai attacks launched by Lashkar-e-Tayyba have not only thrown Pak-India relations into an abyss but all the progress so far made on the issue of Kashmir has also been dumped into a cold storage. When India accused Pakistan for these attacks it was categorically denied in the beginning but the confession made by Ajmal Kasav turned the tables. Pakistan, on an official level not only recognised Kasav as a Pakistani citizen but many among the leadership of Lashker-e-Tayyba were also arrested under the charge of Mumbai attacks. At present the case of Mumbai attacks tops the list of bilateral issues between India and Pakistan and it is being seen by the international community in various aspects but mainly in the perspective of widespread extremism in Pakistan.

Similarly fingers are also pointed on the militants of Lashkar-e-Tayyba regarding attacks on the Sri Lankan cricket team. Some sources of police and secret agencies draw attention towards the fact that the presence of an ample stock of edibles with the attackers of Sri Lankan cricket team proves that the assailant wanted to hijack the bus of Sri Lankan players so that release of Zaki-ur-Rahman Lakhvi could be bargained who was due to appear in Anti-Terrorist Court no. 2 of

Rawalpindi the same day while four of his accomplices were locked up in the Special Investigations Cell. It is interesting to note that Hafiz Muhammad Saeed was leading prayers of Eid for eight years in the same ground of Qaddafi stadium where the Sri Lankan team was playing. It is also worth mentioning that here hearing against the accused of Mumbai attacks was in progress inside Adiala jail Rawalpindi, when attackers were engaged in their assault on the Sri Lankan team. Government had decided so for security reasons.[158]

On 12th June 2009, the Lahore Police, while showing the footage of attackers killing the traffic warden at Liberty Roundabout, claimed that it had unearthed a network of Punjabi Taliban. The chief of Lahore Police Pervez Rathore told the press that the police had arrested Muhammad Zubair, Ilyas and Nek Muhammad, who came from Dera Ghazi Khan to reside in Medina Colony, Lahore (near the place of attack) and were a part of the team of seven attackers. The assailants had a plan to abduct the Sri Lankan cricket team. Pervez Rathore also disclosed that Aqeel Ilyas aka Dr. Usman resident of Kahuta is mastermind of this attack. Terrorists who planned the attack at Toheed Hostel, Wahdat Road had rented a house in Medina Colony Gulberg Lahore. Zubair told the police that he worked as a waiter at a restaurant in Rawalpindi whereas Saifullah, who was a regular customer there, persuaded him to participate in jihad. According to police sources, the rest of the attackers had escaped to Waziristan. On 25th July 2009 the Ministry of Interior sent a report to National Assembly's Standing Committee on Sports and Culture stating that assailants of the Sri Lankan cricket team were activists of Lashkar-e-Jhangvi who wanted to hijack the bus in order to pressurise the government for the release of their leaders Malik Ishaq and Akram Lahori.[159]

'Jaish-e-Muhammad' is also one of the most dangerous militant outfits of Pakistan that has continued a low intensity war (or jihad) in Jammu and Kashmir. It was created by Maulana Masood Azhar on the behest of the I.S.I. in February 2000, when he came back to Pakistan after getting released from an Indian jail as a bargain in the hijack of an Indian Airliner. Some Kashmiri militants brought that plane from Kathmandu, Nepal to Kandahar, Afghanistan in the last days of 1999. Soon after his release, Maulana Masood Azhar established Jaish-e-

Muhammad that had 'fighting against Indian security forces in Jammu and Kashmir' aspect of their higher goals. Earlier he had been performing the responsibilities of 'ideological guidance' to another jihadi organisation 'Harkat-ul-Ansar' that was banned by the U.S. State Department in 1997 due to its alleged links with Osama Bin Laden.[160]

Jaish-e-Muhammad is undoubtedly an ideological extension of Harkat-ul-Ansar that had changed its name to Harkat-ul-Mujahedeen after one year of its ban. Jaish-e-Muhammad, in comparison to Harkat-ul-Mujahedeen, went through a phase of rapid expansion due to its links with two Sunni Deobandi outfits, Sipah-e-Sahaba and Lashkar-e-Jhangvi. Similarly, two Deobandi clerics played a vital role in the formation of Jaish-e-Muhammad. One of them was Mufti Nizamuddin Shamzai who had his inclinations towards Taliban and the other was Maulana Yousaf Ludhianavi who was heading Sipah-e-Sahaba at that time. The newly-formed organisation also enjoyed the support of other prominent clerics like Maulana Mufti Rasheed Ahmed and Maulana Sher Ali Khan, Sheikh-ul-Hadith of Darul Aloom Haqqania, Akora Khattak.

Maulana Masood Azhar was the general secretary of Harkat ul Mujahedeen before his arrest in Sri Nagar. After the creation of Jaish-e-Muhammad, 90 percent of Harkat-ul-Mujahedeen militants joined the new organisation and 'captured' more than one dozen offices of Harkat-ul-Mujahedeen in Punjab. Such a remarkable number of offices by any of the jihadist outfits in Punjab point towards the fact that jihadist culture had already penetrated in Punjab in the decade of the 1990s. The leadership of Harkat-ul-Mujahedeen branded Maulana Masood Azhar an Indian agent when he formed Jaish-e-Muhammad. They claimed that this action had greatly undermined the jihad in Kashmir. When Masood Azhar made a visit to Lahore among hundreds of his Kalashnikov carrying bodyguards, thousands of young militants welcomed him and took an oath of loyalty to him. That marked a record expansion in the manpower of Jaish-e-Muhammad.[161]

All the movements by Maulana Masood Azhar were banned at the time when his statements against Pervez Musharraf became increasingly aggressive and provocative and were given a prominent coverage in Pakistani media. Hardliner Deobandi youth served as a nursery for

Jaish-e-Muhammad, those were affiliated with Sipah-e-Sahaba, Lashkar-e-Jhangvi and Deobandi seminaries, in the same manner the nine thousand students from the seminaries of Jamiat-ul-Ulmae Islam (the mentor of Jaish-e-Muhammad as well) played a critical role in Taliban Movement. When Masood Azhar went to Kandahar to thank Taliban for their streauous efforts for his release from the Indian jail, he took an oath of loyalty towards all who graduated from Pakistani seminaries and who had been fighting alongside Taliban against Ahmed Shah Masood.[162]

On the formation of Jaish-e-Muhammad a leader of Harkat-ul-Mujahedeen declared "Maulana Masood Azhar had a great desire to become an undisputed leader of all Deobandi militants fighting in Jammu and Kashmir". Masood Azhar, after the establishment of Jaish-e-Muhammad, repeatedly declared during his visits to different cities and towns of Pakistan that his organisation would assassinate the Indian Prime Minister Atal Bihari Vajpayee sooner rather than later. In his speeches he also emphasised that his organisation would not only free Kashmir but also get the control of the historic Babri mosque situated in the Indian city of Ayudhia.

Jaish-e-Muhammad launched its first operation in Jammu and Kashmir on 19th April 2000 just two months after its inception. One of his activists hit an explosive laden car at the main gate of Badami Bagh Cantonment. It was the first suicide attack in 13 years of the armed insurgency in Kashmir. Since then J-e-M is engaged in jihad against Indian forces. After 9/11 the name of J-e-M was changed to Tahreek-al-Farqa. When the U.S. declared Tahreek-al-Farqa, a terrorist outfit as well, the new name was Khudam-e-Islam but still the organisation is commonly known as Jaish-e-Muhammad.[163]

The government of Pakistan arrested Masood Azhar under pressure from India and some other countries and his outfit was also banned by Pervez Musharraf in January 2002. However he was released on 14th December on orders by the Lahore High Court. The former Director General I.S.I. and a close aide to Pervez Musharraf Lieutenant General (r) Javed Ashraf Qazi said (*Daily Times*, 7th March 2004) "We must not hesitate to accept the reality that JeM has been involved in murder of hundreds of innocent Kashmiri Muslims, attack on Indian

Parliament, murder of Daniel Pearl as well as life attempts on Pervez Musharraf." He further said that Jaish-e-Muhammad and Lashkar-e-Tayyba had incurred greatest losses to the Kashmir cause.[164]

After about three months of the two successive life attempts on General Pervez Musharraf in Rawalpindi, it was also stated that one Muhammad Jamil was among the assailants and he was an activist of J-e-M. After that some officers of intelligence agencies started taking him as an Indian agent who was giving a bad name to Kashmiri freedom movement on a directive by India. After 9/11 and life attempts on Pervez Musharraf, Masood Azhar had to go underground on counsel from the I.S.I. but by that time the U.S. officials were sure that he was providing Al-Qaeda and Taliban with support and facilities of movement within Pakistan. Before that he had been a highly-trusted jihadist for the establishment and it is also important to remember that the government of Pakistan had rejected a plea by Interpol for the arrest of Masood Azhar.[165]

Interpol had made the request for custody of Masood Azhar and Ahmed Umar Saeed on demand by the U.S. Department of Justice as both were charged with the murder of two U.S. citizens. One of them was Daniel Pearl, who was serving as South Asian Bureau Chief for Wall Street Journal and other was Jeanne Moore who was stabbed by the hijackers after the commandeering of Indian Airliner (IC-814) towards Kandahar in December 1999. The U.S. assented to Pakistan that according to the U.S. laws it had the authority to have an inquest about the crimes perpetrated against its citizens anywhere in the world. However, the government of Pakistan rejected both the pleas of investigation as well as of custody. The government of General Pervez Musharraf, while defending Masood Azhar, argued to the U.S. officials that he was not involved in the murder of Daniel Pearl and Sheikh Ahmed Omer Saeed and three other accomplices were facing sentence of life imprisonment decreed by Pakistani court.[166]

The government of Pakistan rejected the plea by Interpol by declaring that Masood Azhar was not involved in the hijacking rather the Indian government had illegally put him in jail. When the plane was hijacked he was already in jail so how he could have committed any crime. The government of the time extended full support to Jaish-e-Muhmmad and Maulana Masood Azhar but the ban again by Musharraf government in 2003 caused considerable loss to J-e-M. After a few days, the government also enacted a ban on Jamiat-ul-Ansar, Khuddam-e-Islam, Jamiat-ul-Farqa, Lashkar-e-Tayyba and Hizb-ul-Tahrir as well. That new ban on jihadist outfits was imposed after one day of a visit by a U.S. diplomat in Karachi. He maintained that jihadist outfits in Pakistan are creating a lot of trouble for the U.S. by changing their names every other day. He specially urged on Pakistan to curtail the activities of J-e-M and L-e-T. The intelligence agencies of Pakistan sealed the offices of Jaish-e-Muhammad all over the country, arrested hundreds of its workers and banned the organisation. This was not a result of yielding to American pressure but simply a curt reaction to suicide attacks on General Musharraf.[167]

Many activists of J-e-M had been already arrested for launching various attacks in Murree, Islamabad and Taxila. A majority of them had continued their activities under the patronage by Maulana Abdul Jabbar, who had been already expelled for not following the discipline of organisation. When Maulana Abdul Jabbar and 12 other commanders were expelled from J-e-M they formed a new organisation named Jamaat-ul-Furqan and entered into direct rivalry with J-e-M. Maulana Abdul Jabbar was the chief of the new outfit and Abdullah Shah Mazhar was appointed Nazim-e-Aala (chief administrator). The activists of the new outfit were ready to launch suicide attacks against U.S. interests as a revenge for termination of the Taliban government in Afghanistan, and Maulana Masood Azhar briefed his mentors in I.S.I. that they are merely sectarian elements and J-e-M would not be responsible for their actions; rather arresting them would be a better option. However, some militants maintained that Abdullah Shah Mazhar was the first person to leave Masood Azhar for Maulana Abdul Jabbar. On the other hand Abdullah Shah Mazhar held the view that Masood Azhar had lost his credibility in J-e-M and all the leading Deobandi 'elders' including Mufti Shamzai, Maulana Shabbir Ali Shah and Maulana Wali Ullah had lost confidence in him although all of them were at the forefront in the creation of J-e-M. Abdullah Shah Mazhar also said that Maulana Masood Azhar had refused to continue with jihad in Kashmir but we cannot quit just because of funds. Seven out of ten members of supreme council have already parted ways; I being one of them.[168]

When Maulana Abdul Rauf, the younger brother of Masood Azhar, was interrogated in connection with suicide attacks on Pervez Musharraf in 2003, he alleged about Maulana Abdul Jabbar and his companions "They only want to grab the assets, whereas Jaish-e-Muhammad is a torch-bearer of jihad on a global scale". When Jaish-e-Muhammad was formed, Al-Rashid Trust donated 20 million for its initial operating expenses. However Al-Rashid Trust was blacklisted because of this donation to J-e-M. Afterwards it was estimated that when the number of its affiliates started to increase, its fund-raising reached to rupees 10 million per day. These donations were used for establishing training camps and for regular aid of heirs of militants lost their lives in Jammu and Kashmir. But at the same time the lifestyle of many leaders of Jaish-e-Muhammad also underwent remarkable changes. For example, Masood Azhar who belonged to the lower middle class and used to live in the shanty town of Bahawalpur, shifted to Model Town, a posh area of the city and started riding on Land Cruisers and Range Rovers with a motorcade of armed bodyguards. His brothers and close associates also adopted a lavish lifestyle. People who had spent very hard times with him in Afghanistan and Kashmir were astonished at this transformation in Masood Azhar's lifestyle.[169]

The slow pace and fruitless exercise of Pakistan-India peace dialogue in New Delhi persuaded the government of General Musharraf to force Jaish-e-Muhamamd to rejuvenate. The aim was to restart militants' activities in Jammu and Kashmir. According to intelligence circles of Pakistan Jaish-e-Muhammad was reorganised under the supervision of Mufti Abdul Rauf, younger brother of Masood Azhar who got acclaim through his successful operations in Kashmir. Mufti Abdul Rauf was also allowed to establish his camps in Rawalpindi for transit stay of militants coming from South Punjab. These jihadists were to be taken to Kohat for training. It was also decided that Mufti Abdul Rauf would oversee the training camps as caretaker Ameer (chief) of J-e-M, whereas Masood Azhar would look after the organisational affairs of J-e-M while remaining underground so that he would remain in touch with his organisation somehow or other.

The British investigation officer for the 07/07/2005 bombing of London shared with his Pakistani counterparts that two culprits named Shehazad Tanveer and Sadiq Khan of the four accused of 07/07 London Bombings, had a meeting with Osama Nazir of Jaish-e-Muhammad at Faisalabad two months before these attacks. Osama Nazir has the destinction of training the suicide attackers of Jaish-e-Muhammad. Osama Nazir disclosed after his arrest that during his visit Shehzad Tanveer had stayed at another extremist seminary Jamia Manzoor-al-Islamia located at Lahore Cantonment. The administrator of this seminary is Pir Saif Ullah Khalid who is considered a close aide of Masood Azhar.[170]

Once again Jaish-e-Muhammad became a focus of global attention when it was disclosed in August 2006 that Rashid Rauf, who was one of the younger brothers of Masood Azhar's brother-in-law and an alleged operative of Al-Qaeda, was among the planners of a plot to detonate a U.S. bound flight of British Airways. He was also accused of training terrorists for preparation of liquid explosives. Rashid Rauf was apprehended from a seminary 'Medina-tul-Aloom in Model Town Bahawalpur on 9th August 2002. This arrest was made just a few days before a massive crackdown against terrorists by the British police in London and the capture of their mastermind. On 17th August 2007 a Pakistani intelligence officer found out that approval for the plot to wreak havoc on the British airport was given by the vice-chief of Al-Qaeda Ayman-al-Zawahiri while the planning was made by Rashid Rauf.[171]

Rashid Rauf was born in Mirpur (Pakistan) and went to the U.K. in 1981 when he was only a year old. In 2002, he had to come to Pakistan to evade an inquest about the murder of his uncle. He was constantly in touch with the U.K. through his mobile phone that helped his capture. On 12th August, British officials made it clear to Pakistan that Rashid had a key role in these attacks and he should be handed over to the U.K. After his arrest, Allah Bakhsh Sabir, father of Masood Azhar told media in Bahawalpur that Rashid Rauf had been a member of Jaish-e-Muhammad but later he had joined Jamaat-al-Furqan. Hafiz Allah Bakhsh shared with daily Dawn "Al-Furqan was active in Afghanistan whereas J-e-M operates for the freedom of Indian-occupied Kashmir. They are against the U.S., we are not". However Rashid Rauf was acquitted by the British anti-terrorism court on 13th December 2006, for lack of sufficient evidence."[172]

Rashid Rauf was arrested when he came to Pakistan. When British officials mounted pressure for his repatriation to the U.K. he was made to flee from police custody in Rawalpindi in quite a mysterious way. However in a rather disputed inquiry report by the Islamabad Police it was said that the story of his escape was totally fake while he was still under custody in Adiala Jail. Later media reports pointed towards the fact that the story of the escape by Rashid Rauf pointed towards a secret "deal" between Jaish-e-Muhammad and officials in Islamabad. According to a general perception, Mufti Abdul Rauf was among the people who helped Rashid Rauf to run away from police custody. There was also news of his death in North Waziristan on 22nd November 2008 in a predator attack by the U.S. forces.[173]

After four months in April 2009 British officials once again requested Pakistani agencies for help in arresting Rashid Rauf and handing him over to the U.K. It was also pointed out in this request that earlier reports (or guesses) about his death would have to been seen in the perspective of the credible intelligence information made available recently. According to British officials an activist of Al-Qaeda arrested in Belgium has confessed that Rashid Rauf, after giving him training, had sent him for suicide attacks in the summit of European heads of governments and states at Brussels, apart from assignments of terrorist attacks in Belgium, France, England and Holland.[174]

Jaish-e-Muhammad also had close ties with Lal Masjid of Islamabad. J-e-M had been a staunch supporter of Ghazi brothers in their attempts for implementation of sharia in the country, as long as Musharraf had not ordered to deal with the issue with an 'Iron hand'. Maulana Abdul Rauf denied any link with the activists of J-e-M hiding in Lal Masjid and declared them to be truants of the organisation. On the second day of operation he again branded Ghazi brothers as favourites of the establishment and said they had succeeded in bringing a huge quantity of arms in the premises of Lal Masjid with the tacit approval of the government. A few days before the Lal Masjid operation Maulana Masood Azhar wrote in 'Al-Qalam' the organ of J-e-M that

"At present hundreds of jihadist outfit have mushroomed and such computer operators have assumed the role of chiefs of these outfit who have turned to jihad by just watching CDs of jihad. They got their jihadist training through websites. They perceive that they could become rich through the internet. Some jihadists are involved in drug trade, kidnapping for ransom and human trafficking. Jihad has been turned into a lucrative business and it is becoming increasingly difficult to control such groups". At the time of 26/11 Mumbai attacks Maulana Abdul Rauf was in the twin cities of Rawalpindi and Islamabad and was engaged in supervision of jihadist training camps whereas Maulana Masood Azhar was looking after the affairs of organisation while staying at Bahawalpur.[175]

On 23rd June 2008, an article was published in 'The News' with a caption of 'Another Lal Masjid'. The writer of this article had been living abroad for several years and he tried to limelight the activities of Masood Azhar and Jaish-e-Muhammad through a visit to Bahawalpur. He wrote thus "Bahawalpur is a town where almost everyone knows each other. Maulana Masood Azhar lives in the neighborhood of one of my cousins and lives in a house that is not so visible from the main road. I remember when he came home after his release. The crew of B.B.C. wanted to have his video coverage from the verandah of my cousins' house but was not allowed to do so because of the restrictions of hijab. He was not mentioned much in the media as such and people never gave him much importance either. At that time there was a lot of graffiti against the U.S. whereas slogans of 'Al-jihad wal Qital' were also inscribed on the walls of the central mosque of city.[176]

It was not the same Bahawalpur I had known for ages. When we went near the mosque we saw its adjacent ground was full of bearded people and a majority of them had arrived there after a long journey by buses. The whole city was full of graffiti. Some uniformed officials had closed one way of the road to facilitate the arrival of participants at the convention. This rally-cum-conference was in fact the launching ceremony of a book on jihad by Masood Azhar. There was an air of tremendous excitement among the participants; they seemed as if they just had just been granted permission for the jihad mentioned in the Holy Koran. We reached our friends' house with mixed feelings. I asked my friend and cousin what was happening around the city. They told me it had been going on for quite a long time then. It is a matter of so many years now that the small house of Masood Azhar has been converted into a multi-storeyed building and there are around seven hundred gunmen in its compound and a majority of them spend the day moving around the area. All this is happening in the heart of the city that is called Model Town. The police have never dared to question them. Local politicians hire the services of these gunmen during election campaigns. When we arrived at the cousin's house from our friend's, we noticed a big white flag on top of another building that was visible from a long distance. It was Masood Azhar's compound where we noticed a group of bearded young men performing the duties of security guards. They cast a sceptical glance at us as we went past them. We feel like strangers in our own town. One of our companions took it as a normal situation and in his view there was nothing to be tense about. While talking to people about the situation, I had a chance to get some interesting information as well; they included politicians of local as well as of national stature. They thought Masood Azhar was simply a cleric similar to Ghazi Abdul Rashid of Lal Masjid"[177]

After the 26/11 attacks, Masood Azhar was confined to the boundaries of his house at Bahawalpur and all the activities of J-e-M were remarkably curtailed. It was done because the government of India had demanded the custody of three persons including Masood Azhar, besides Dawood Ibrahim and Tiger Memon. It was decided, in an agreement between Director Generals of Indian Central Bureau of Investigation (C.B.I.) and Pakistani Federal Investigation Authority (F.I.A.) in 1989 that the agencies of both the countries would not only assist each other to search for terrorists and criminals but also hand over the wanted personnel to each others country. The list of wanted persons by India also included the name of Maulana Masood Azhar who was accused of December 2001 attacks on Indian Parliament.[178]

According to a news report of 18th January 2009, Maulana Masood Azhar had vacated the headquarters of J-e-M in Bahawalpur and shifted to Waziristan. However on 13th April 2009 the government of Pakistan officially announced that Masood Azhar was not in Pakistan. Earlier Interior Minister Rahman Malik declared on 13th January 2009, that neither Masood Azhar nor Dawood Ibrahim were in Pakistan nor our country had provided shelter to any wanted criminal but Indian Interior Minister Pranab Mukherjee pointed towards the fact that evidence about the presence of these people in Pakistan had been repeatedly provided and expressed surprise about Pakistani denial.[179]

There are reports about militants of J-e-M fighting against the Pak army in Swat. When on 7th May 2009, Prime Minister Yousaf Raza Gilani directed the army to launch an operation against terrorists, Major General Athar Abbas of Inter Services Public Relations said in an interview with "Daily Dawn" that there are also five thousand militants of J-e-M fighting alongside Taliban. So far J-e-M has not denied the allegations about the involvement of its jihadists engaged in fighting against the Pak Army in Swat, Waziristan and other tribal areas side by side with Al-Qaeda and Taliban. At present J-e-M is considered the biggest supporter jihadist outfit of Al-Qaeda and Taliban in South Punjab that is not only providing them safe havens in Punjab but also extending support for terrorist activities in Islamabad and Punjab.[180]

On 17th June 2009, five members of J-e-M were arrested from Sialkot and it was reported in the newspapers that Masood Azhar was one of them but the Government of Pakistan immediately denied the reports and said particulars of those arrested were not yet ascertained. Pakistani establishment never repudiated that the Chief of J-e-M was still living in a safe refuge provided by I.S.I. in Rawalpindi. Sources claim that there is a general consensus among intelligence circles that the Chief of J-e-M would never be handed over to India at any cost.[181]

Sipah-e-Sahaba, an extremist and sectarian outfit, was formed in the district Jhang at central Punjab in mid-1980s. This Sunni organisation was established in reaction to Iranian Revolution by the intelligence machinery of Pakistan. Sipah-e-Sahaba killed many people from Shiite minority and constantly raised the demand to declare them non-Muslim in Pakistan due to their beliefs. This organisation desirous of turning Pakistan into a Sunni state and establishing Caliphate in Pakistan, had its ideological affiliation with Tehreek-e-Taliban Pakistan while targeting Shiite citizens and Iranian interests in the country is its main objective. Sipah-e-Sahaba is like a sub section of Jamiat Ulemae Islam (a Sunni Deobandi religious political party). It is worth noting that Sipah-e-Sahaba has always influenced electoral politics in Pakistan since its inception and many of its important leaders not only got elected in national and provincial assemblies but also have had representation in provincial cabinet.[182]

Aipah-e-Sahaba was formed by Maulana Haq Nawaz Jhangvi, Maulan Zia-ur-Rahman Farooqi, Maulan Israr-ul-Haq Qasmi and Maulana Azam Tariq in September 1985. In the beginning it was named Anjuman Sipah-e-Sahaba and at that time sectarian hatred was increasingly on the rise in Punjab. Its main founder was a graduate of a seminary of Darul Aloom Eidgah, Kabirwala and was famous for his fiery anti-Shiite speeches. Haq Nawaz had been a vice-chairman of Jamiat Ulemae Islam as well and played a prominent role as an active member in anti-Ahmadiyya movement. He remained affiliated with Jamiat Ulemae Islam till 1989 and parted ways when he announced a violent struggle.[183]

In district Jhang a majority of Sunni peasants working for big Shiite landlords, joined this organisation thinking that they were heading towards the goal of turning Pakistan into a Sunni state. At that time anti-Shiite sentiments intensified to such an extent that Sipah-e-Sahaba openly started to declare Shiites as non-Muslims.

Fatal Sunni-Shiite clashes also started from this city and tension over the dispute to change the name of ancient Khewa gate turned into a full-scale Sunni Shiite riot. Curfew was imposed in Jhang but sectarian violence also spread to other cities of Punjab. Sipah-e-Shaba apart from Jhang started to organize itself in other cities and towns of Punjab as well and Shiite Zakirs and clerics became the main target. Leadership of Sipah-e-Sahaba alleged that the Iranian government is engaged in the promotion of Shiite religion in Pakistan and supporting Tehreek-e-Nafaz-e-Fiqah-e-Jaria in every possible way.

Sectarian riots became more intense and Haq Nawaz Jhangvi was murdered in Jhang on 23rd February 1990. Zia-ur-Rehman Farooqi, a cleric from tehsil Samandri, district Faisalabad took the control of Sipah-e-Sahaba but later he was killed a bomb attack in Lahore on 19th January 1997 when he was brought to the sessions court for a hearing. Afterwards, Maulana Azam Tariq was also murdered in Islamabad in October 2003 by his Shiite opponents. Sipah-e-Shaba was among five outfits that were banned by General Pervez Musharraf on 12th January 2002.[184]

Maulana Azam Tariq had changed the name of his organisation from Sipah-e-Sahaba to Millat-e-Islamia Pakistan a few days before he got killed and also announced that his organisation would launch a political struggle through parliament to change Pakistan into a Sunni state. Azam Tariq, who had earlier survived two assassination attempts, was considered a staunch supporter of Taliban in Pakistan. He won the 2002 elections of the National Assembly from Jhang as an independent candidate. He frequently visited Afghanistan without any restriction. According to intelligence agencies of Pakistan, Sipah-e-Sahaba had five hundred thousand militants in December 1999 that were trained for terrorist activities in Jammu and Kashmir.[185]

Maulana Azam Tariq was at the forefront in the protest along with Afghan Jihad Council against the U.S. occupation of Afghanistan after 9/11. Sipah-e-Sahaba together with Jamaat-e-Islami, Jamiat Ulemae Islam (Fazal-ur-Rahman group) and Jamiat Ahle Hadith had declared American invasion as anti-Islamic. Sipah-e-Sahaba under the leadership of Maulana Azam Tariq, developed close relations with Harkat-ul-Mujahedeen (Fazal-ur-Rahman Khalil group) and Jaish-e-Muhammad, two of the biggest jihadist outfits of the country as many activists of both the organisation have also been extending 'help' to Sipah-e-Sahaba in the ongoing sectarian frenzy in Pakistan. Sipah-e-Sahaba had established its strongholds at Jia Musa (Shahdara Lahore) apart from Bahawalnagar (Faqir Wali) and Jhang that are still operative at present. Till 2002 it had established 300 units all over the country. Azam Tariq was arrested in 2001 and he contested the elections of 2002 from jail and won. He was assassinated in 2003 near Islamabad and Allama Sajid Naqvi, leader of a Shiite party was accused of this murder.[186]

Sipah-e-Sahaba demanded the implementation of Sharia in country through a grand rally in Islamabad on 7th April 2007. It is imported to that videos of U.S. troops being beheaded in Iraq and Afghanistan were also shown. About that rally, political analysts opined that the Musharraf government had probably decided to give political space to Sipah-e-Sahaba and allow it to contest the next general elections. According to media reports it was decided between the Ministry of

Interior Affairs and the leadership of Sipah-e-Sahaba that they would go underground after the rally and would not fan sectarian hatred anymore. The decision was greatly opposed by Shiite leadership and dubbed a 'license to kill' the Shiite community.[187]

However, it is a fact that Sipah-e-Sahaba had never stopped its activities even for a single day despite the ban on 12th January 2002. Neither its network of terrorism was broken nor its offices were sealed and it continued providing manpower to hardliner anti-Shiite outfit Lashkar-e-Jhangvi, that had already established direct links with Al-Qaeda. All these activities have sustained a dent to sympathies with Sipah-e-Sahaba at least at the Jhang level. That is why the present chief of Sipah-e-Sahaba Muhammad Ahmed Ludhianavi lost the election of 2008 with a margin of five thousand votes.[188]

The alleged links of sectarian outfit Sipah-e-Sahaba and Ramzi Yousaf, the person involved in 1993 bombing of World Trade Center was captured in 1995 from a hotel in Islamabad and subjugated to a long and very hard investigation by the U.S. officials. It was said in a report by "The News" on 27th March 1995, that Pakistani agencies are increasingly led to believe that a majority of the trainees in the military camps in Afghanistan hail from Pakistan. Pakistani agencies were able to trace Abdul Shakoor, a young man of 24, from Liyari area of Karachi who had close relations with Ramzi Yousaf. Abdul Shakoor was also involved in the 20th June 1994 bombing at shrine of Imam Ali Raza in Mashhad Iran. Some analysts suggest that Ramzi Yousaf, due to his Iraqi background, had close ties with the Irani insurgent group Mujahedeen-e-Khalq. Iran first accused said organisation for bombing at the shrine. Ramzi Yousaf had fled to Iran in 1995 via Turbat. Abdul Muqeem another terrorist from Karachi, who had been identified as the brother of Ramzi Yousaf, had affirmed the involvement of Ramzi Yousaf in these attacks. In 1994 Ramzi Yousaf was also assigned the task to eliminate Saleem Qadri, a prominent leader of the Barelvi sect. Officials deputed on investigation, said that Abdul Wahab owner of Chand Bakery in Liyari, was also an aide of Ramzi Yousaf, who was a unit in-charge for Sipah-e-Sahaba as well. It was also disclosed in the report that Ramzi was also engaged in a Saudi network working to weaken the royal family of Saudi Arabia.[189]

According to the July 2002 issue of "South Asian Analytical Report" on terrorism, thousands of activists from Sipah-e-Sahaba and Lashkar-e-Jhangvi had been sent to Afghanistan through facilitation by the I.S.I. in order to make attacks by Taliban on Kabul and Jalalabad a success. After the capture of Kabul by Taliban in September 1996, these activists stayed on in Afghanistan and started supporting Taliban against the Northern Alliance. These were the elements that also killed a large number of Shiites in the Hazara belt of Afghanistan and assassinated Iranian diplomats in Mazar Sharif. When Osama Bin Laden came back to Afghanistan in 1996 he started leading an already established network comprising Pakistani and Arab militants. He established the International Islamic Front in 1998 to launch a jihad against the U.S. and Israel which also consisted of a great number of jihadists from Sipah-e-Sahaba and Lashkar-e-Jhangvi.[190]

When the U.S. launched an attack against the Al-Qaeda and Taliban in Afghanistan, all the parties of International Islamic Front including Harkat-ul-Mujahedeen, Lashkar-e-Tayyba, Jaish-e-Muhammad, Sipah-e-Sahaba and Lashkar-e-Jhangvi fled towards the tribal areas of Pakistan along with all their jihadists. Secret agencies estimated the members of Lashkar-e-Jhangvi to be around one thousand and that of Sipah-e-Sahaba approximately one hundred thousand with its attackers between two to three thousand. Although both groups came into being in a sheer hatred against Shiite, their members have also been active in jihad in Kashmir and Afghanistan. For example, an ex-activist of Sipah-e-Sahaba that has been identified as Commander Tariq is an in-charge of Dara Adam Khel wing of Taliban in Orakzai agency near Kohat in Khyber Pakhtunkhwa. He was a most wanted person by law enforcement agencies in connection with various attacks on people from the Shiite sect. He had also been involved in cases of abduction of foreign nationals for ransom moreover he was allegedly indicted in the murder of a Pole engineer who was working at an oil field.[191]

A large number of seminaries and mosques had been turned into such strongholds of Sipah-e-Sahaba and Lashkar-e-Jhangvi that served as centres for "Punjabi Taliban". Recently the police chief of Karachi had disclosed after an investigation with some office bearers of Lashkar-e-Jhangvi that they had confessed to have attacked many security personnel, army troops and NATO forces. For this purpose they selected youth from Karachi and trained them in Mansehra and Waziristan to prepare them for attacks against the Pak army. Both Lashkar-e-Jhangvi and Sipah-e-Sahaba had been active all over the country defying all the bans on a national and international scale. It is true that Lashkar-e-Jhangvi has been a target of civil and military agencies of the country but Sipah-e-Sahaba has proved wiser as it managed to save itself from official crack down through a better and comprehensive strategy. Their repeated entry in national and provincial assemblies by winning general elections is a clear proof of that policy.

5

Extremist Elements of Punjab and their Political Linkages

A fter all the barbaric acts and ferocious behaviour of extremists was exposed, questions were raised as to where this increasing supremacy of bigot elements was going to end. Various incidents of violence in different cities of Punjab have a common factor among that all the local extremist elements have "acted" under a proper planning and disseminated their message of religious and social cleansing while on the political, front their prominent identity is still that of a marked affiliation with local religious-political parties. People from different walks of life have tried to bring forward various interpretations for these incidents in order to vent out sentiments of frustration and concern dominant among the masses, while the media outlets that enjoy maximum control over the population, never tried to go beyond sensational reporting of the incidents. Electronic media working in an atmosphere of tough business competition also did nothing more than bringing forth incidental details. This situation could be attributed to the fact that the nexus of religious-political parties has become a symbol of power in Punjab and it also provides backing to violent and sectarian elements, who in return ask for complete protection from the authorities while their show of militant power is considered an essential part of the drama of dominance staged by political actors.

Neither any serious dialogue nor a research-based report has ever been presented by the media reporting these incidents. All that the audience gets in the name of analysis is nothing more than some statements of condemnation by Human Rights organisations or some expressions of concern by the intellectuals who are totally ineffective religiously and politically. Or there are comments by some unknown people who are otherwise almost irrelevant in society. While the presence and influence of people with extremist religious views and sectarian tendencies in every sector of life is considered the main reason for it, the concerns by media houses about their security is an equally important inhibitor. Extremist religious outfits have not only fortified themselves in Punjab at a fast pace, but they have also sent stern messages to the provincial administration, so that the situation compels the concerned quarters to be highly prudent. There are a number of precedents where the present government of Punjab and high-ranking officials of the central government were "warned" after many heinous acts of terrorism and, advised to avoid showing any "investigative impartiality". The administration of affected districts were also given various verbal orders from Chief Minister's House that were aimed at saving his party members from any sort of harmful criticism for their connection with the extremists and also requesting the media for not being so harsh on party workers.

If we remove the tradition of informed and research-based points of view from all the conspiracy theories presented in the name of analysis, the facts that are available on the situation in Punjab all point towards the grim reality that it seems quite justified to call it the most dangerous region in South Asia. Every aspect of the rapidly changing scenario of Punjab is easily discernable with the help of statistics and analytical reports by different department non-governmental organisations as well as some research-based books published during the last decade. At present, nobody can deny the "effectiveness" of the strategy of extremist and sectarian outfits, having incredible power and an overwhelming presence in almost every part of Punjab. And the responsibility for all the serious incidents that cannot evade media coverage can inevitably be fixed on these extremist organisations that are working for very 'high' aims. These outfits are equipped with a greater strength of manpower than ever before and local communities seem to have decided to adopt a submissive attitude towards them as various political and social factors are involved in this policy.

Because of the peculiar political atmosphere of Punjab, some religious outfits of certain sects managed to establish strong ties with the Muslim League (Nawaz) during the Musharraf regime. The complicity of the local leadership of the Muslim League (N) in the gruesome incidents of Gojra, Sialkot and Phool Nagar points towards the same sad reality. If the "services" rendered by these people, who apparently are considered activists of the Muslim League (N), are taken into account, it is not difficult to trace their extremist and sectarian linkages. These elements are following a policy of not openly accepting their sectarian inclinations as the imperatives of present circumstances force them to do so although they have linked their identity with Muslim League (Nawaz). While they had a host of complaints against the leadership and governments of the Muslim League (N) in the heydays of sectarian feuds, they never hesitated to express these grievances openly.[192]

Another vital question is that what is so special and "accommodative" in the composition of the Muslim League (N) that most of the extremist groups and sectarian outfits are automatically attracted towards it. There is plenty of evidence that some prominent personalities, who otherwise belong to minority and discriminated-against communities, are also affiliated with this party and they had served on higher public offices during different stints of government by the Muslim League (Nawaz). Certain research-based reports and other documents also give the idea that financial needs of a number of religious extremist and sectarian organisations of Punjab have obliged them to develop their relations with the Muslim League (Nawaz). The countrywide network of businessmen, especially the traders, having a long history of giving generous donations to local religious parties and sectarian outfits could also be the main reason for it. According to a general estimate about fifty percent of the newly-constructed mosques and seminaries in cities and towns of Punjab during the last fifteen years were financed by local traders who have affiliations with the Muslim League (Nawaz) marked as their specific identity while a few of them are members of the Muslim League (Quaid).

What great lessons the leadership of the Muslim League (Nawaz) had learnt by the example of the "support" lent during the agitation movement of Pakistan National Alliance (P.N.A.) in 1977 by the right wing traders' community, could be assessed by the fact that the party had always tried to give every possible importance to traders among its local cadres and it has made the best use of their power to further its role of opposition in national politics. The tradition of getting members of the trader class elected in national assemblies was also started by the Muslim League (Nawaz) and donations of these traders were utilised for buying political loyalties during the power play and numbers game in national and provincial assemblies.

For the Muslim League, that has a long tradition of multiplying and regenerating like a star fish, those "political traders" play a key role in its strong grip in Punjab who always managed to get a best possible price for their political proclivities and a majority of them are inclined towards a (apparently) puritan religiosity; may be it is an effort to purge them of their past. It does not require going much further in the past to know that the local jihadist organisations and militant groups were given generous donations by these politically motivated traders in jihad of Kashmir. In this regard certain evidence is available as to how interlinks of these jihadist outfits and "political" traders were created through support by the Muslim League, the powers to be in Islamabad and some strong characters in the establishment. So within no time, there were donation boxes for jihad in Kashmir in every business centre of Pakistan and tens of millions of rupees were collected every day for training and support of militants. However it could not be assured what portion of these donations was actually spent on jihad in Kashmir and what was apportioned for local sectarian element in order that they could organise themselves in Punjab.

Moreover, a considerable number of these traders got attracted towards "Tableeghi Jamaat" and they used to make long evangelisation visits to far-flung areas on their own expense and managed to develop strong links with people having similar political and religious perceptions. The annual conference of "Tableeghi Jamaat", essentially a congregation of Deobandi sect, also played a vital role in an effective interaction among sectarian elements. The leadership of the Muslim League carried forward the tradition of special interest in the patronage of Tableeghi Jamaat that was set by General Zia-ul-Haq; so it did not take long that all the 'like-minded' people from tribal areas to Afghanistan managed to fortify themselves with the support from central government and establishment and a specific world view got promoted within Pakistan. There is hard to find anything similar to the precedent of extending 'support' to Raiwind congregation from the national exchequer, set by Mian Nawaz Sharif and Mian Shahbaz Sharif. In return the Sharif brothers also benefitted from all axis of power in the establishment.

Similarly, the Sharif brothers were also engaged in the 'service' of every promising cleric and scholar and were busy accommodating their like-minded religious leaders in the power politics at the central government level apart from the Punjab level. Every religious leader from Professor Sajid Mir to Dr. Israr Ahmed was provided with opportunities of growth according to their own whims. It is hard to ignore the attachments with Tableeghi Jamaat and the love for Sharif family by Rafiq Tarar (former President of Pakistan) that eventually bore fruit and he (Rafiq Tarar) became president of Pakistan on recommendation by Abbaji (father) of Nawaz Sharif. Similarly Lieutenant General (r) Javed Nasir ex Director General of I.S.I., an important office bearer of Tableeghi Jamaat as well, was promoted to this post by the special affections of the Sharif family. Some were made members of the Senate, while others were made ready to extend their support in that 'vague sharia based legislation' that was used in a bid to gain total and long-term control of state institutions. Meanwhile, the leadership of the Muslim League started following a policy of a "free hand" to a certain extremist outfit as it required support from that outfit against Pakistan People's Party on the floor of the National assembly. Because of these tendencies on the part of the Muslim League, such discussions in National Assembly and Senate were very common. That which sect could be declared non-Muslim and a religious party came with a bill in the parliament that was aimed at declaring the opponents sect to be committing apostasy. The opposing sects, in response, also came up with similar drafts of legislation and after 1974 there was a strong feeling that the ruling party, for its short-lived political expediencies, is bent upon declaring a certain sect as non-Muslim.

All the prominent actors of sectarian warfare in Punjab got every kind of support during the tenures of the Muslim league in the Punjab government so much so that the Assembly Members from Faisalabad, Multan, Gujranwala and Sheikhupura have been providing shelter to innumerable 'most wanted' sectarian killers. In the meantime, some activists of an extremist outfit were captured in a raid at Faisalabad but the government of Punjab was forced to free them after some real time life threats to important leaders of the Muslim League while Prime Minister Nawaz Sharif was also obliged to give up his famous routine of 'open courts' at Model Town Lahore due to serious security concerns. However, the links in parliament of the Muslim League with the leadership of these outfits could not be cut off due to "political imperative" of maintaining numeric superiority against the Peoples Party.[193]

The Muslim League (Nawaz) has been playing a vital role in special relations between the leadership of banned outfits from Lashkar-e-Tayyba to Sipah-e-Sahaba etc. and Sharif brothers and also in establishing "working relationships" of army officials with those responsible for jihadist activities. At present, these old-time relations and the material interests attached thereof are the main reason for the popularity and widespread acceptance of the Muslim League (Nawaz) in Punjab. If some important personalities among its central leadership are evaluated in the light of their past attachments, comprehension of Muslim League's point of view becomes easier. This is the reason that the collective stand point of the Muslim League (Nawaz) on important national affairs and political issues resemble that of a hardliner religious party instead of a political party of national stature. At present, it is principally the dominant standpoint of the Punjab and it is also playing an important role in promoting extremist tendencies in different cities and towns of the province.

Today the hardliner religious parties have clear inclination towards the Muslim League (Nawaz) and the presence of former members of religious parties among its higher ranks is the main reason for it who consider the ruling party in the federal government neither true Muslim nor patriotic. They think that the Peoples Party and its allies are engaged in activities that are against our "Islamic identity and national integrity".

A certain section of the media is extending full "support" to them and the incumbent government is facing allegations of committing acts that are against "national honour". For example, it is quite surprising to note that the vague terminology of "national honour" is only being used in Punjab and none of the chief ministers from other provinces had attempted to link "Kerry Lugar bill" with it, while the leadership of the Muslim League in Punjab is trying to mobilise religious parties and extremist organisations for a movement against the federal government.

The Chief Minister of Punjab declared this disputed bill of U.S. aid, a trade-off between national integrity and short-term material ends. Jamaat-e-Islami had same point of view and a similar hue and cry was made by other religious outfits that otherwise had a long experience of turning financial support by the U.S. into their "personal aid". How weird it is that breach of any agreement and telling a lie were never considered against honour and national integrity and if the resources obtained in aid from any quarter were diverted to any other head in a clear contravention of agreement provisions, it is not against their integrity either. For example, does not it look strange that the Asian Development Bank provides heavy amounts every year for development projects in Punjab and a major portion of its allocations for 2009 were diverted from development projects to "Sasti Roti Project" (cheap bread project) on special instruction by the Chief Minister of Punjab? Now the officials of ADB have warned the government of Punjab that its aid would immediately be stopped if during the audit, it was revealed that ADB funds were utilised other than on development expenditure of the backward areas of Punjab.[194]

The present administrative dispensation of Punjab is reflective of its political tendencies and religious trends as the province is not only preparing itself for a sectarian warfare but there is also a huge gathering underway by Taliban and their sympathisers in Southern Punjab but provincial government keeps its eyes closed on such movements as these are possibly the best tactics to even the scores with the federal government. The remnants of jihad in Kashmir are fortifying themselves in Southern Punjab and there is a general perception that powerful circles in the establishment are still lending them full support. The decisive forces are divided in visibly distinct factions and the perceptions about the government of the People's Party are promoted that it has a 'lenient attitude' towards India and its policies towards the West are also 'quite sympathetic'.

People in Punjab have the common perception that the Muslim League (Nawaz) in comparison to the People's Party, is more patriotic and pro-Islam while the People's Party not only expects favours from 'national enemies' but it also has an attitude of amity with anti-Islam forces. That is why serious apprehensions about some proposed 'un-Islamic' changes in blasphemy and hadood laws were expressed and the People's Party is alleged to have committed an act of apostasy. Such accusations originate from right-winged pro-Muslim League quarters to help it gain political mileage and to intensify anti-Peoples Party sentiments in the general public. There is news of providing vast tracts of land to two extremist organisations in the outskirts of Lahore, Bahawalpur as well as in Cholistan and the clear objective of this move is to get support from retrogressive quarters of the country so that the 'forces' of these outfits could be utilised at the hour of need. The central leadership of the Muslim League (Nawaz) has, without doubt, been following a policy of appeasement of extremist circles so that there would be no trouble when their "support" in centre or Punjab is required. The listing of people and groups patronised by the Muslim League (Nawaz) is not a difficult task rather the long list of such persons could be made into a voluminous report.

The present national scenario also points to the fact that in the coming days Punjab will engage the central government on multiple fronts that are prepared with the help of right-winged elements as well as certain religious forces. Even the Muslim League (Quaid) with a considerable circle of district nazims, is associating itself with the political strategy of the Muslim League (Nawaz) and there are reports that Syed Mushahid Hussein General Secretary Pakistan Muslim League (Quaid) is trying to minimise differences with the Muslim League (Nawaz) in order to streamline the situation for possible 'common opportunities' in future. On the other hand the 'religious spokespersons' of the Muslim League (Nawaz), in the mosques all over Punjab, are blaming the central government for compromising on national interests and allowing 'enemies of Islam' to interfere in Pakistan. Although the federal government is trying to get support from "alternative" religious circles and the Federal Minister for Interior affairs, Rahman Malik by visiting Jamia Al-Muntazir requested clerics and other influential people for support but it was not only a gaffe in principle but also a stern message for other religious and sectarian organisations. But such efforts could give a new direction to sectarian warfare in Punjab and it could turn out to have very fatal consequences.

According to the Punjab Law Minister, Rana Sanaullah, there is no existence of Taliban in Southern Punjab and it was merely propaganda from the West that a great number of Taliban is migrating towards South Punjab from Swat and tribal areas. Two groups of terrorists had launched a simultaneous attack on the office of the Federal Investigation Authority (F.I.A.) and Badian Police Training Centre near Manawan and had taken several police officials as hostage at the same time when the honourable Law Minister was issuing that statement. In a way he rejected the reservations by his own government expressed through various reports sent to the federal government and sensitive agencies of state. As the provincial Law Minister has a hostile attitude towards the federal government, he took the allegations about the presence of terrorists in Punjab especially the Southern region, as an insult to the Government of Punjab and thought it proper to properly refute them.[195]

Setting aside the hate or opposition for the federal government, if the dangerous situation underlying such an attitude is not controlled, it could drastically damage the interests of province and affect the security of the people of Punjab. To ignore the presence of extremist elements in South Punjab, their ever increasing number and fatal acts of terrorism committed by them is next to impossible as various bits of evidence reinforce the fact that extremist and sectarian elements not only strengthened their network but also succeeded in committing serious acts of terrorism by utilising this network.

Although the nursery of extremist and sectarian elements in the south of Punjab was cultivated during Zia-ul-Haq era and some mighty institutions of the state were directly engaged in their proper nurturing and grooming, later on some influential political parties also exploited the nuisance value of extremist and sectarian elements to get their support on the floor of Parliament as well as to suppress political opponents in certain districts of Punjab. Ample funds were provided to them and they were given a free hand to crush their adversaries at the local level. For example, in Jhang and adjacent districts such leaders of a banned sectarian outfits were extended complete support that were not only capable to win elections and get into assemblies but also in supporting the election campaigns or launching effective movements against any 'undesirable' (read Peoples Party's) government in Islamabad. Certain activists of this organisation were provided immunity against court cases that were involved in the assassination of high-ranking officials in Punjab and very strong eyewitnesses against them were also available. But these witnesses were barred from testifying in courts of law. "Support" was also provided in the escape of many dangerous sectarian killers from police custody.

The circle emphasising the geographical differences of Punjab with that of Khyber Pakhtoonkhwa, especially its tribal belt, held the view that terrorists could not reorganise themselves in the plains of Punjab like they did in difficult and rugged terrain of north moreover it would be difficult to hide oneself in Punjab after committing any act of terrorism. It was rather easier for security agencies to launch an operation in Punjab, so that terrorists from Tribal areas would abstain from any serious act of terrorism in Punjab. There was also a general (mis)perception that unlike Tribal Areas, the tradition of providing shelter to criminals and wanted people is not so strong, so it would be easier to control the terrorists in Punjab and launch a crackdown against them. Present government in Punjab persistently claimed that there is neither any support for terrorists in their province nor they could find any refuge in seminaries of Punjab but the terrorists and their groups arc fully active in Punjab without any fear of reprisal, despite all these claims.

All the guesses and estimates in this context have proved wrong and terrorists have focused all their attention towards Punjab. Neither have they been stopped from their terrorist activities nor have their sanctuaries been eradicated in Punjab. Recently, a few incidents have revealed that terrorists were not only hiring residential buildings nearby their intended targets but they also used to keep that target under watch for many days so that the operation could be executed at the right moment. Al-Qaeda and Taliban have proved fully efficacious in turning Punjab into a war field and local terrorists are specifically targeting security agencies in different cities of Punjab.

There are reports about a seminary in Dera Ghazi Khan that is affiliated with an extremist organisation, that there is a full-scale recruitment drive for Swat and Waziristan and when functionaries of the local government tried to contact the administration of that seminary, the district officer was directed to 'mind his own business' and if any attempt was made to either conduct a raid on a seminary or to arrest the students, it would lead to dire consequences. When pressure on the seminary was mounted, an important leader of the Muslim League from Dera Ghazi Khan hushed up the provincial government in Lahore by claiming that if any bid to displease the clerics and seminaries was made, the Muslim League would suffer a lot. Presently the number of 'veterans' who have returned after 'serving' in Afghanistan and Tribal Areas is on the rise in seminaries of South Punjab. As soon as Hakimullah Mehsood took control of Tehreek-e-Taliban Pakistan after Baitullah Mehsood was eliminated in a drone attack, he increased the pace and intensity of suicide bombing and hostage attacks in different areas of Pakistan. Command of the squads that have trained for these attacks in Islamabad and Punjab has been vested to 'Punjabi Taliban' of South Punjab that not only make decision about important targets but gather initial information which is also their personal responsibility.

Present-day Taliban, who with the patronage from powerful military agencies were earlier engaged in sectarian war in the country and simultaneously were participating in jihad in Indian controlled Kashmir, have found a new sector to divert their energies and in the meantime they are well aware of the fact that they are dealing with a majority that for the time being does not have any ability to retaliate. No doubt the hardliner Taliban firmly believe that in Pakistan and specially in Punjab religious institutions and organisation from Barelvi sect are not following 'true Islam' and commit divergences that result in estrangement of ordinary people from the teachings of real Islam. Although traditionally in Punjab the real debate of such dogmatic arguments was between Ahle-Hadith and Barelvi sects, after extremist organisations like Sipah-e-Sahaba and Lashkar-e-Jhangvi gained strength and Jaish-e-Muhammad was formed, hardliners from the Deobandi sect also thought it imperative to prove their existence thus they soon entered into a direct confrontation path with Barelvi outfits in Punjab especially different caretaker dynasties of shrines and other sanctuaries. At present, clerics from both Deobandi and Barelvi sects are engaged in fierce theological and dogmatic battles among themselves and every day epic tales about the 'humiliating defeat' of the opponent sect are narrated in every mosque and seminary to inspire the adherents of their respective sects.[196]

Since under pressure from different international circles the fervour of Islamabad of patronising the Ahle-Hadith and Deobandi outfits that have been engaged in jihad of Kashmir has diminished remarkably, these outfits have started developing strong linkage among people of their own sect and there was not only an elaborate planning for the purpose but they were also provided adequate support from the adherents of their respective sects who are present in very strong institutions of the state as well as in different political parties. For example, when Lashkar-e-Tayyba and Jamaat-ud-Dawa were deprived of the patronage by the establishment after Mumbai attacks they were left with the only option of establishing contacts with their local cohorts and sympathisers. The chief of the organisation, Hafiz Muhammad Saeed, who has the fame of his hardliner stances against India and other non-Muslim world, in this situation decided to engage his organisation in issues of local significance. He activated 'Kissan (peasants) Wing' of his organisation that had a vigorous entry in the media by linking the shortage of surface water in Pakistan with "water terrorism" from India. Hafiz Saeed who earlier has been quite successful in generating fund by highlighting the plight of Kashmiri people, their massacre and gross human rights violation by Indian forces, now presented the issue of water between India and Pakistan as the most serious crisis of the day, although water treaties between both the countries totally refute the claims by Hafiz Saeed and the government of Pakistan as well as the Water Commission formed under monitoring by the U.N.O. and headed by Jamaat Ali Shah (a Pakistani) both reject any possibility of "water terrorism" by India and absolve it from such actions. As a result,

Jamaat Ali Shah is being harshly criticised by the powerful agencies of the state and the 'hawks' in the establishment and even he has been declared an 'Indian agent'. By activating his organisation on the issue of water, Hafiz Saeed to a great extent has managed to ward off the pressure his organisation was facing after the Mumbai attacks and has succeeded in transforming the stance by Lashkar-e-Tayyba into a collective stance of people as well as mighty institutions of Pakistan. As Pervez Musharraf, the number one enemy and hot target of Lashakr-e-Tayyba and other militant outfits of same genre, had lost his popularity and relevance, the other political adversaries of Pervez Musharraf also started supporting Lashkar-e-Tayyba and other militant outfits and the extremist religious and sectarian organisations once again had a chance to further their respective agenda.

On the other hand, Pakistani media, especially hardliner, right-wing TV anchors, in that atmosphere of competition with fundamentalist and anti-Pakistan Indian TV analysts, also played an equally important role in creating these new trends based on imprudence and bigotry. A remarkable example of it was seen just after the Mumbai attacks when Indian authorities alleged that Ajmal Kasav, the only surviving attackers who was captured alive, is a member of Lashkar-e-Tayyba, Pakistani official and its media immediately rejected the claim and categorically denied that there was neither a town named Farid Kot in Pakistan nor was Ajmal Kasav is a Pakistani citizen. The Indian media came up with further details about Kasav along with his confessional statement. The civil government of Pakistan was planning to enact further restrictions on Lashkar-e-Tayyba in the light of that statement, but it had to face enormous pressure and a harsh attitude from powerful establishment as well as the sympathisers of L-e-T thus the weak civilian government was forced to back out.[197]

Similarly, the outfits like Jaish-e-Muhammad, Sipah-e-Sahaba and Lashkar-e-Jhangvi that have strong connections with Taliban in Afghanistan and Tribal Areas also engaged themselves in invigorating their centres in various cities and towns of Punjab and wherever they to felt that a strong support from politicians, traders and local influential people was required they got it at any cost and in return never hesitated to provide "armed support" to these circles. These connections had already got matured in the course of the last general elections during

Musharraf era (February 2008) and according to the statistics presented on TV by Maulana Ludhianvi, chief of banned Sipah-e-Sahaba, more than forty candidates for the provincial assembly got support from banned jihadist outfits during the elections of 2008 only in Punjab and succeeded in becoming members of parliament. However, in the ensuring bye-elections, the ruling Muslim League (Nawaz) in Punjab openly got support from sectarian and jihadist outfits and provincial Law Minister Rana Sanaullah assumed the responsibilities of monitoring such constituencies where electoral success sans armed support by Sipah-e-Sahaba and Lashkar-e-Jhangvi was impossible. There were a number of such precedents that came to light during bye-elections in Faisalabad and Jhang and one fine morning Rana Sanaullah also succeeded in enrolling Maulana Ludhianvi and scores of his armed followers in the ranks of Muslim Laeague (Nawaz). When Rana Sanaullah was questioned by media representatives about this "electoral alliance", he claimed that Sipah-e-Sahaba is a 'democratic organisation' and there is nothing wrong with getting support from it. It is worth mentioning here that the government that Rana Sanaullah represents as a Law Minister had already banned Sipah-e-Sahaba after declaring it a terrorist outfit. A few days later there were reports about the Governor of Punjab, Salman Taseer (representing People's Party) and that he called on leaders of Sipah-e-Sahaba in connection with getting their support in bye-elections and took them on board his official helicopter that included some 'most wanted' personnel as well. There is no doubt that the Muslim League (Nawaz) and the People's Party, who are otherwise at odds with each other in Punjab, are constantly in touch with these extremist and jihadist outfits and do not find anything wrong in getting their support from time to time. To keep the secrecy of these links is no longer possible as the media takes no time to bring them to the limelight.[198]

The People's Party is also more inclined towards extremist Deobandi outfits because a powerful lobby in Islamabad is spreading the word through the media that President Asif Ali Zardari belongs to Shiite sect and there are proper arrangements of 'Majalis' in his ancestoral home whereas he is also a follower of Bawa Sada Hussein from a Shiite center at Bagum Kot Shahdara Lahore. Sipah-e-Sahaba has already revealed a lot about the beliefs of Bawa Sada Hussein. Moreover, the Peoples Party is well aware that Sipah-e-Sahaba and Lashkar-e-Jhangvi are most strong sectarian outfits and ignoring them could not do any help in realising the dream of political dominancy in the province. It is also not ignorant of the fact that Sipah-e-Sahaba and Lashkar-e-Jhangvi have much closer ties with Muslim League (Nawaz) and some of former leaders of these outfits are currently office bearers of the Muslim League (Nawaz) in many districts of Punjab. Rana Sanaullah declares them 'democratic people' while slain Governor of Punjab Salman Taseer used to call them 'terrorists' infiltrated in the ranks of Muslim League (Nawaz)'.

The heirs to Tehreek-e-Taliban in Punjab, who have already succeeded in almost eliminating disorganised and scattered Shiite outfits, see groups and organisations of the Barelvi sect as their next target, while rifts among Deobandi sub-sects in Punjab are also quite apparent, who are busy distinguishing their identities of 'Hiyati' and 'Mamati'. Dogmatic arguments, as well as tensions among them, are intensifying in different districts of Punjab. As most of the writers, intellectuals and analysts are least interested in the internal conflicts of various Muslim sects and a majority of ordinary people are not aware of the complicated nitty-gritty of these differences, there is very little information about these sectarian tussles and dogmatic rifts in the Pakistani media. For example, any analysis in the national Urdu or English press has never been published about the organisation boasting about conducting the second biggest congregation of Muslim after the Hajj (i.e. Tableeghi Jamaat) that it is apparently a Deobandi organisation but its relations with other Deobandi groups and organisations are never discussed. Although it is essentially an organisation of the Deobandi Hanafi sect, what are it basic differences with other Deobandi groups like Sipah-e-Sahaba and Jaish-e-Muhammad. In dogmatic terminology it falls in the category of 'Mamati' Deobandis whereas both the latter outfits are considered 'hayati' deobandis. Although both are followers of the Hanafi school of Islamic jurisprudence, 'hayatis' believe that after his death the Holy Prophet Muhammad is still alive in his mausoleum and hear all our implorations pleadings while 'mamatis' believe otherwise.

The ever-increasing number and influence of rigid religious parties, jihadists and sectarian fundamentalists could be judged by the fact that at present the provincial administration and law enforcement agencies, before taking any major or minor decision about them, are bound to apprise the Chief Minister of Punjab that activists of such organisation in such a district have political connections with which member of parliament or political dynasty. They would also discuss repercussions any impending action against them could have. According to information so far available, 163 members of the Punjab Assembly are directly involved in material support and aid of extremist religious organisations, jihadist outfits and sectarian groups because they also had sought the support from these powerful and well-armed outfits during their election campaign of 2008 on the promise of return the favour if got elected to the assemblies. A majority of these assembly members belongs to Muslim League (Nawaz) although there are a considerable number of parliament members from the Peoples Party and Muslim League (Quaid) who had also made such promises and accepted conditions by militants to get elected to assemblies.

This nexus between political leadership and extremist organisations was first disclosed by Sheikh Waqas Akraam, a member of the National Assembly from district Jhang belonging to Muslim League (Quaid). While giving a statement on the floor of the National Assembly he stated that in his constituency, Rana Sanaullah in collaboration with Maulana Ludhianvi, chief of the banned Sipah-e-Sahaba, is engaged in getting support for a candidate of his party. It is worth mentioning here that Sheikh Waqas Akraam had defeated Maulana Ludhianvi in election of 2008. His family is one of the famous families of Punjab, engaged in the business of transport, has been a staunch supporter of Sipah-e-Sahaba in the 1980s. However it did not take long for this amity to turn into enmity, which continues till today. A leader of the Muslim League (Quaid) Sheikh Waqas Akraam travels in the company of dozens of gunmen and central leadership of Sipah-e-Sahaba wants to eliminate Sheikh Waqas so that it could regain their constituency in Jhang that was lost with the murder of Maulana Azam Tariq. The present chief of Sipah-e-Sahaba Muhammad Ahmed Ludhianvi is on record on a TV channel for stating that during general elections of February 2008, his party had provided support to dozens of candidates from the People's Party and Muslim League (Nawaz) and most of them get elected to assemblies by dint of their 'armed support'.[199]

Maulana Ludhianvi also quoted a video tape where the Governor of Punjab Salman Taseer is shown travelling with armed persons of Sipah-e-Sahaba while some of these armed personnel had also travelled on the Governor of Punjab's special plane and provided support to the candidates from the People's Party in the bye-elections of Faisalabad as well as Sargodha. Rana Sanuallah, who hails from Faisalabad, had admitted to having relations with people from Sipah-e-Sahaba 'who are democratic' and fully support his party. As Sheikh Waqas Akraam pointed out, when some of the most wanted criminal would be travelling along with the Law Minister of the province, nobody among the law enforcement agencies would dare arrest any of them.[200]

There is nothing new in the nexus of politicians with sectarian terrorists nor do political leaders ever try to hide these ties. The most strange point is that many of the politicians and members of parliament from the Shiite sect have developed strong ties with extremist Deobandi outfits; Riaz Pirzada a member of the national assembly of the Muslim League (Quaid) from Bahawalnagar is one clear example of it. His father was earlier killed by Sipah-e-Sahaba and the case of this murder was registered against Maulana Azam Tariq the then chief of Sipah-e-Sahaba who had also been arrested in this connection. Then Riaz Pirzada woke up to the reality and won the elections of February 2008 by getting support from the extremist Deobandi outfit Jaish-e-Muhammad. It is significant that Jaish-e-Muhammad and Sipah-e-Sahaba are equally involved in ferocious attacks on people from the Shiite sect in South Punjab and both of these extremist outfits are equipped with thousands of trained jihadists originally prepared by secret agencies of the state for their warfare in Afghanistan and Kashmir. After the Mumbai attacks Riaz Pirzada showed his solidarity with Maulana Masood Azhar, chief of Jaish-e-Muhammad and issued a statement that any attempt to arrest Masood Azhar would be taken as an ugly attack on a son of the soil of the Saraiki Region.[201]

Multan, traditionally called a land of saints and Sufis, has its own significance in sectarian tussles and terrorist activities. Although the Prime Minister of Pakistan, Syed Yousaf Raza Gilani hails from a dynasty of caretakers of a shrine in Multan and his family is believed to be a mixture of Sunni-Shiite spirituality but still in his stint as prime minister he had to seek help from some powerful Deobandi organisations, especially an influential cleric of Wafaq-ul-Madaras (a powerful board of Deobandi seminaries), for the victory of his brother in the bye-election at Multan. The cleric forced the voters of this constituency to vote for Prime Minister's brother despite a strong opponent from the Muslim League (Nawaz). It was the same day that the Punjabi Taliban had launched a suicide attack on the Multan head office of I.S.I., killing several people and completely destroying the building.

In May 2010 the author of this book had a chance to access a report about Multan by the special branch of police in at the chief minister house in Lahore. According to that report Punjabi Taliban who are rapidly gathering in South Punjab had occupied 27 mosques in and around Multan where Barelvi imams were serving. Then the Federal Minister for Religious Affairs, Syed Hamid Saeed Kazmi – also a Barelvi cleric hailing from Multan – brought the complaint to the notice of the Governor of Punjab Salman Taseer, who in turn referred the complaint to the Home Secretary of Punjab. But he apologised for his inability to take any action as all. Affairs pertaining to South Punjab were taken care of by Mian Shahbaz Sharif Chief Minister of Punjab, and it was better to talk to him directly, he explained. Although the Governor did not take up the matter with the Chief Minister the very next day, during his talk with media representatives he alleged that Taliban were getting them assembled in South Punjab at a rapid pace and the government of Punjab was providing them with logistic support. In response, provincial Law Minister Rana Sanaullah opened a tirade of allegations against the Governor and emphatically denied any assembling of Taliban in South Punjab. Thus an issue of a highly sensitive nature was sidelined in this war of words between the Governor and Provincial Law Minister. Federal Minister for Religious Affairs took his complaint to Prime Minister but he also refused to interfere as he was afraid any action in this regard would enhance tensions between Federal and Provincial governments.[202]

As Multan due to the presence of Wafaq-ul-Madaris is considered a centre of Deobandis, hunter of incidents of sectarian killings is much higher here in comparison with other districts of South Punjab, for example Lashkar-e-Jhangvi murdered more than one hundred Shiite persons here beside the attacks on Iranian Consulate and Khana-e-

Farhang-e-Iran (Iranian Culture Center). A majority of cases against the chief of Lashkar-e-Jhangvi Malik Muhammad Ishaq pertain to Multan while Sipah-e-Sahaba is also considered very active with a considerable number of its mosques and seminaries here. Traditionally, there have been a considerable number of Shiite population, naturally Sipah-e-Muhammad and Mukhtar Force wield a remarkable support. However, these outfits have lost their effective centres here since the leadership of Sipah-e-Muhammad has been arrested.

The growing influence of Barelvi organisation 'Dawat-e-Islami' in the city is a matter of utmost concern for the Deobandi people and their organisations. Dawat-e-Islami arranges its biggest congregation (annual conference) in Multan and its vast headquarters are under construction in the outskirts of the city with a cost of billions of rupees. This is claimed to be the biggest headquarters of any religious organisation in Pakistan. There had been some attacks on activists of Dawat-e-Islami in Multan and an atmosphere of tensions between the two sects is clearly visible.

Districts of Dera Ghazi Khan, Layyah and Rajanpur are facing almost similar situation where the forest belt alongside river Indus is used by the Punjabi Taliban for a to and fro movement towards Waziristan. Rangers' troops were deployed here a short while ago to control that movement but they could not achieve any remarkable results due to shortage of manpower as well as non-cooperation from the Punjab Police. The ex-Chief Minister of Punjab, Dost Muhammad Khosa and his father are also hot targets for jihadist and sectarian outfits because they had refused to provide safe havens in Dera Ghazi Khan to some of the most wanted terrorist of Sipah-e-Sahaba and Lashkar-e-Jhangvi. Some people term this as one of the reasons for the strained relation between Chief Minister Shahbaz Sharif and the Khosa family because he wanted to help the sectarian elements through Rana Sanaullah but the Khosa family refused to do so. Thus they had to content themselves with strained relations with the Chief Minister. The suicide attack near their ancestral home in Dera Ghazi Khan is linked with this situation but no further information is available in this regard nor has group claimed responsibility for it.

However, in Faisalabad, there were clear signs of impending

conflicts between Deobandi jihadist and sectarian outfits and Barelvi organisations and after the firing on the Eid rally last year (birth day of Prophet Muhammad), serious differences between Sahibzada Fazal-e-Karim, an important ally of Muslim League (Nawaz) and the Provincial Law Minister, Rana Sanaullah, surfaced and Sahibzada held Rana Sanaullah responsible for this firing as well as for the suicide attacks on the shrine of Data Darbar Lahore and demanded his resignation. Barelvi organisations held protest rallies all over the province and tensions were at their peak in Faisalabad that is considered a stronghold of Sipah-e-Sahaba, Lashkar-e-Jhangvi and Punjabi Taliban.[203]

Although it is hard to predict when powerful and leading religious organisations and people affiliated with them in different parts especially big urban centres of Punjab would get out of control of any state institution, it is certain that even at present they have got support from innumerable members of law enforcement as well as legislative institutions. The clout and connections of extremist elements very cleverly arming themselves could be judged by the fact that scores of activists from Lashkar-e-Tayyba and Sipah-e-Sahaba are residing at the official lodging in Islamabad for members of the National Assembly and the Senate. They are there in a bid to get arms licences for their Lashkars (militant outfits). Thousands of 'Arms Licence Application Forms' were collected from Parliament Lodges Islamabad in the flat of a member National Assembly of Muslim League (Nawaz) from Lahore and even a photocopier was shifted there. A major portion of the hundreds of arms licences allotted to each member of parliament serves the purpose of Sipah-e-Sahaba, Lashkar-e-Jhangvi, Lashkar-e-Tayyba and Jaish-e-Muhammad. Although these militant outfits originally formed for combat at external sectors, do not require a huge quantity of arms or their licenses within the country, the quota of arms licences for members of parliament is utilised for imminent armed conflict(s) in the country. A number of officials from the Home Ministry and several sensitive agencies are playing an equally important role and provide full support to the outfits from their respective sects.

When this writer asked Abu Dajana (his jihadist name; it is nearly impossible to know his real name), the responsible person of Lashkar-e-Tayyba's "affairs of arms licences", about the types of arms licences he was striving for. He responded that they were for street fighting, while in the battlefield of jihad we fight face-to-face where conventional arms of smaller bore are more effective. When he was asked that for the real battlefield of Lashkar-e-Tayyba (jihad in Kashmir) they could get arms from various other sources, he responded that Pakistan was under enormous pressure then and the facilities extended during the peak of jihad in Kashmir were over. On enquiry as to whether these "national arms" are also being gathered for use within the country, he replied with his peculiar smile that those arms could be utilised whenever and wherever there was a need for jihad. Although the Federal Interior Minister has got enormous power due to his authority, still he is helpless in either prohibiting the issuance of arms licences to Lashkar-e-Tayyba and Jaish-e-Muhammad or to seek assistance from some intelligence agencies in this regard. When I asked that according to claims by Federal Interior Minister Lashkar-e-Jhangvi and Sipah-e-Sahaba are terrorist organisations and they have nothing to do with real Islam, (1) and Lashkar-e-Tayyba does not exist anymore, Then why does he not take any serious notice of issuance of arms licences in such a great number to activists of these outfits? He replied that Khalid Malik, the younger brother of Rahman Malik was the biggest 'commission agent' in the country and he got his share of commissions in everything from national identity cards and passports to arms licences while Rahman Malik is not unaware of this business of his younger brother and nothing in this country is out of his knowledge. At this response I had no further questions to ask this mujahidin.

Since the Peoples Party has formed the coalition government, the Interior ministry seems to have started a clearance sale of arms licences. Although under a special order there is a ban on the issuance of licences for certain arms of prohibited bore but these are still being issued on daily basis with effect from previous dates and major portion of them goes to extremist and jihadist outfits that get them sanctioned in the name of the local members of parliament. However, the issuance rate of these licenses during the Musharraf regime had been comparatively low; there were tough terms and conditions for these licences and allocations for parliament members had been very limited. According to sources, ten thousand arms licences were issued in one year only on the quota of members of parliament and a majority of them went to activists of jihadist and sectarian outfits as majority of politicians in Punjab were able to make it to parliament on the conditional support from armed jihadist and sectarian groups that they would be given allocation of arms licences after winning elections.

According to law-enforcement agencies, it has been observed that several arms were transferred illegally on a single licence and whenever the serial number of such arms was traced in any crime scene there were more than one arms under the same licence number and many of the most wanted accused were acquitted and cases against them dismissed due to this anomaly on the part of licensing authorities. This technique has provided many opportunities to extremist outfits as whenever any arms are seized by law enforcement agencies they are declared illegal under pressure from high-ups and the licence is saved from cancellation. It is also a common observation that police and other law enforcement agencies never check the licences from activists of armed religious outfits in the religious gatherings and congregations. Keeping many arms under the same licence number not only suits these organisations but they also take undue advantage of this strategy.

There is no tradition of checking valid licences of arms possessed by the activists of extremist organisations nor are they bound to periodically present their licensed arms in any police station. A suggestion in this regard was presented during the Musharraf era by the Ministry of Interior. But the powerful Chaudhry brothers of Gujrat hindered any progress on it because any action according to that suggestion could raise many questions on the arsenals of many influential political dynasties as well who keep them as a source of political superiority in their areas. For example, Chaudhry brothers had very close ties with a gangster family in Korla Arbab Khan and used to get their support in crushing their political adversaries. In return, a young person from the said family was allowed to deploy a Light Machine Gun on his Land Cruiser although he had been arrested in connection with the suicide attack on General Pervez Musharraf not a long time ago. This young man likes to be called "Salar-e-Qafla" (head of the caravan). Many murder cases had been registered against him but nobody dares to take any action against him. When, according to the results of the 2008 elections, Chaudhry brothers had to sit in opposition, this fellow took no time to change his political loyalties and started supporting Muslim League (Nawaz) so that Light Machine Gun remained installed on his Land Cruiser. He is said to have his connections with Sipah-e-Sahaba and alleged to be involved in many cases of sectarian violence and murder. Earlier, it was the Chaudhry brothers who performed the responsibilities of his leadership and now he is being patronised by Chief Minister of Punjab to terrorise the political opponents including Chaudhry brothers as well. It is also claimed that many of the sectarian killers take refuge at his place as a base camp before heading for their 'targets'. When rulers of the province take it upon them to safeguard him and when the Punjab Police gets special instructions not to register any case against him, it is but natural that he would continue the exhibition of his collection of murderous weapons and get a reward for his 'services' from the political elite.

The same 'Salar-e-Qafla' (real name Abid Raza), while addressing a political rally, warned Chaudhry Wajahat Hussein, brother of Chaudhry Shujaat Hussein to deprive him of the leadership of Gujrat and that he was not afraid of death as he had braved the prison of F.B.I. and many death cells. Its video clip is still available on YouTube while Malik Jamil Awan Member National Assembly of Muslim league (Nawaz) from that area could also be seen in the video where Salar-e-Qafla was challenging the district co-ordination officer that he could never arrest him no matter how large police force he brought along. In that address Salar-e-Qafla also threatened the Chaudhry family of dire consequences if they ever tried to play any dirty trick with him. The axis of his real power lies in Sipah-e-Sahaba and Lashkar-e-Jhangvi because hundreds of armed activists of both outfits always accompany him thus law enforcement agencies never think of conducting any raid at Kotla Arbab Khan. Hundreds of accused and most wanted criminal, have taken refuge at his place but police force cannot take the risk of entering his territory. It was not very long ago when his convoy was stopped at the police check post at Pabbi, the border area of Azad Kashmir and armed men in the convoy retaliated by opening gunfire at police officials killing two policemen on the spot, but it was still not possible to arrest Salar-e-Qafla or to register any case against him, so the lives of two policemen went in vain.[204]

Civil governments and law enforcement agencies in Punjab know very well about the influence and power bases of various jihadist and sectarian organisations in different areas of province as well as strategies adopted by them to achieve their goals. For example, there are huge centres of banned outfits like Lashkar-e-Tayyba, Sipah-e-Sahaba and Lashkar-e-Jhangvi in Faisalabad and Gujranwala and a large number of trained militants is available every time. Their sanctuaries could be found in scores of mosques and seminaries of the town but neither is police allowed to enter there nor can the officials of secret agencies have access to. A similar situation exists at Begum Kot in the outskirts of Lahore where militants of Sipah-e-Muhammad and Sipah-e-Sahaba are fully active but nobody dare venture into these safe havens. The Chief Minister of Punjab and a majority of his cohorts if fully aware of the power and clout wielded by these extremist groups and outfits as well as of the circles that provide them overt or covert support but many issues and a widespread fear have silenced them because any possible action by provincial government would not only be forcefully opposed on the floor of the Assembly but it would not be acceptable to some close aides of the Chief Minister either.

6

Dismal Situation of South Punjab

According to reports by important institutions of the state and intelligence agencies, Taliban are not only getting stronger in Southern Punjab but Punjabi Taliban has also joined the ranks of extremist elements in Waziristan. Latest reports state that Taliban of Tribal Areas have started supporting Punjabi Taliban in order to extend the arena of their influence. Five districts in South Punjab, including Dera Ghazi Khan have fallen under their complete control which poses yet another serious challenge to the solidarity of Pakistan. Taliban in South Punjab have already threatened barber saloons and CD shops while singing or playing instruments at marriages have also been banned by them; all these developments signify an increasing influence of extremist elements and the situation can go out of hand any time.[205]

Reports by local secret agencies also underpin the impression of a new alliance between Pashtun and Punjabi Taliban. Punjabi Taliban participating in the Jihad of Kashmir, went underground or took refuge in Tribal Areas during the Musharraf era. Now they have joined Pashtun Taliban and are providing them with logistical support against the U.S. drone attacks while Pashtun in return are arranging reinforcement in Punjab. Serious terrorist incidents like the suicide attack on Marriot Hotel, Islamabad or attack on convoy of Sri Lankan cricket team in Lahore were only possible due to availability of safe havens for Taliban in Punjab. On 5th February Taliban launched an attack with support from activists of a banned local militant outfit in Dera Ghazi Khan that killed 29 persons. All the people killed in drone attacks in Tribal Areas during 2010 included about 20 per cent Punjabi Taliban, while after including foreigner extremists the number of Punjabi Taliban in the Tribal areas is consistently on the rise. Tribal Taliban commit acts like suicide attacks, firing and other terrorist activities while Punjabi Taliban have the responsibility of providing them with logistic support or safe havens in Punjab when they run away from Tribal Area.

According to a report from the I.S.I. sent in March 2009 to the Chief Minister of Punjab, Taliban migrated from Wana and other parts of Waziristan, had grabbed government lands in Dera Ghazi Khan. The conservator of the Forest Department Ajmal Rahim said that a large number of people coming from Waziristan occupied some 4,500 acres of land of the Forest Department at 'Tarman' a belt situated between Punjab and Khyber Pakhtunkhwa. Although an operation against them was launched but only 1,500 acres could be recovered. According to the District Police Officer, most of the people from Wana have come to earn their living and they have no links with Taliban but still they are under strict surveillance. On the other hand, local people claim that the Tribal migrants pay bribe on a monthly basis to officials of the Forest Department for this occupation and they have a large quantity of arms as well. However, these reports have not been confirmed on the official level. The danger of any sectarian conflict in the area is increasing day by day two Federal Ministers also involves. Any analysis on South Punjab is not possible in isolation with Dera Ismail Khan as it serves as a crossroad not only for militants of Southern Punjab but for Sindh, Baluchistan and rest of the Punjab as well.[206]

Recently, the importance of Dera Ismail Khan has increased with young boys used for launching suicide attacks entering Dera Ismail Khan from Wana. Then routes to Punjab are chosen via Bhakkar, Darya Khan or Mianwali; for example the attacker on the building of Rescue 15 entered Punjab through Darya Khan and attackers of the Sri Lankan cricket team also took a similar route. So also the attackers on the Manawan Police Training School, Imam Bargah Dera Ghazi Khan and Imam Bargah Chakwal. According to the special branch of the Punjab Police, there are big centres of Taliban in Mianwali, Bhakkar and Darya Khan. Similarly their frequent movements in Muzaffar Garh, Dera

Ismail Khan and Rajanpur could not be denied. South Punjab has always been a victim of sectarian violence and most of the recruit of Lashkar-e-Jhangvi hail from the same region. Even the founder chief of Lashkar-e-Jhangvi Malik Ishaq belonged to the same city and the Chief Minister of Punjab got elected unopposed from Bhakkar, simply because of the overwhelming support from the group.

As these militants, involved in jihadist and sectarian activities, form a part of the Punjabi Taliban of FATA, their frequent movements in the region could hardly be denied. In fact South Punjab is providing shelter not only to the Punjabi Taliban but is also home to some elements from the Baluchistan Liberation Army (B.L.A.) as well. All of them are creating problems for local industrialists and traders. Most vulnerable districts of South Punjab include Dera Ghaza Khan and Rajanpur, where Taliban and sectarian outfits are more active in terrorist activities.

A report by the Punjab Police sent to the Inspector General of Punjab reveals that around fifty persons who were kidnapped from different areas of Punjab imprisoned in a compound at South Waziristan and a huge ransom has been demanded for their release. From January to June 2009. Seven persons were kidnapped from Multan alone, who were eventually released against payments of heavy ransoms. The abductees included Sheikh Aslam, ameer (head) of Jamaat-e-Islami Multan zone 10 who was kidnapped along with his son and a friend and later released on payment of rupees 2.7 million. He feels traumatised when asked to tell the details of his ordeal. However, he confided there were a number of other kidnapped persons where he was kept in confinement. Although he was unable to locate the place, he affirmed that the group that had kidnapped them was identified as one of the factions from the Punjabi Taliban.[207]

At present, the gangs that are at the forefront in criminal activities include Asmat Ullah Muavia, Qari Zafar, Rana Afzal and Qari Imran groups. Asmat Ullah is originally a residence of Kabir Wala and though his network is situated in Azad Kashmir still he is quite effective in his native town as well. Two terrorists from this group were arrested from Multan and Rahim Yar Khan who were planning a big criminal activity in Northern Punjab. One of them named Hashim had just returned after a recce of his target. They were to make a fatal suicide attack first through motor bike then an ammunition-laden truck.

Similarly, Qari Ismail and Ghulam Mustafa Qaisrani, the main facilitators of the suicide attack of 5th February 2009, on an Imam Bargah at Dera Ghazi Khan as well as attackers on Imam Bargah at Chakwal belonged to the same area. The supporters of different splinter groups Lashkar-e-Jhanvi include former activists of Sipah-e-Sahaba and present members of banned jihadist outfits like Harkat-ul-Mujahedeen, Jaish-e-Muhammad and Jihad-e-Islami. Many of them are absconders from police stations or prisons. Presently a nephew of former Inspector General of Punjab Police is quite famous in the ranks of Taliban in South Punjab.[208]

Some members of Deobandi seminaries and extremist organisations active in South Punjab especially in Multan and surrounding areas seem to complain that certain political leaders from Multan are trying to involve the Deobandi and Barelvi sects in a serious conflict and some mosques, seminaries as well as shrines of the Sunni majority, are being exploited for the purpose. It is highly possible that different Deobandi and Barelvi factions in South Punjab might be involved in some bloody feuds a la Karachi as there are reports of some neutral and tolerant Sunni organisations which are also engaged in arming their activists at a rapid pace and the possibility cannot be ruled out that they would launch a new type of battle for occupying different mosques and other place of religious significance.

Jaish-e-Muhammad is fortifying itself in Bahawalpur and its surrounding areas and there are reports that a vast training center comprising huge tracts of land is under construction at Cholistan. Funds for a proposed training facility are raised courtesy expatriate Pakistani businessmen, local feudallords and some very powerful institutions of the state. Jaish-e-Muhammad is also busy in constructing a modern office complex in Bahawalpur City on an area of five acres while chief of the organisation, Masood Azhar is present in the same city along with hundreds of his armed guards and companions. It is worthwhile to note that after Mumbai attacks a demand was made by the Indian government for the extradition of Masood Azhar, however Pakistani government had expressed unawareness about his whereabouts however it was claimed in the same breath that he was not present on Pakistani soil.[209]

A great number of seminaries from a specific sect were founded in order to churn out jihadist groups and the greatest number of them were located in comparatively backward areas of South Punjab like Bahwalpur, Bahwalnagar, Rahim Yar Khan and Dera Ghazi Khan. According to a 2008 report of the Intelligence Bureau, the number of such seminaries in Bahawalpur only reached 1,383 where around 84 thousand students were enrolled. In Bahawalnagar there were 310 and in Rahim Yar Khan 560 madrassas where number of enrolled students was 36 thousand. Apart from Khyber Pakhtunkhwa and Tribal Areas, there are nearly one million students in religious seminaries. It is estimated that at the time of 9/11 attacks a number of people having affiliations with extremist outfits reached 20 thousand but when General Pervez Musharraf banned jihadist outfits on American pressure the militants residing in these seminaries went back to their ancestral areas different regions of the country.[210]

A report in 2009 by Rangers on situation of South Punjab:

The semi-tribal areas of South Punjab have been a declared an epicentre of extremism by certain institutions of security forces which warned that if appropriate measures were not adopted in these areas adjacent to South Waziristan, neither, any military operation gain complete success nor would the networks of extremists in Punjab and other central regions of Pakistan. As Pakistan army was busy in operation against Taliban and other extremist outfits in South Waziristan, Rangers' force at this occasion had pointed out about possible security risks in South Punjab.

The report was initially compiled by Pakistan Rangers and sent to the Pak Army, Ministry of Interior Affairs and various security agencies. This document of seven pages include a two maps as well that specify the region in districts of Dera Ghazi Khan and Rajanpur that starts from South Waziristan and stretches to Kashmor in Sindh alongside border of Baluchistan. The whole area is located north of Indus and it is called Kacha (belt of forests alongside river bed). Report points out that extremists enter this area very comfortably from South Waziristan and their training centres are also located here. Report also identifies four seminaries that allegedly are engaged in proliferation of militancy the most.

The security forces that compiled the report mention that the number of registered seminaries in the area is 179 but four of them allegedly have strong ties with extremist groups. While certifying compilation of such reports, the spokesperson for Rangers Nadeem Raza affirmed that he also had performed his duties in the area for a considerable period and was aware of the fact that there was practically no writ of state in this vast region. Three names from the clerics are also mentioned in the report and one of them is a close relative to Maulana Abdul Aziz Ghazi the ex-imam of Lal Masjid in Islamabad. The second one is an administrator of a seminary that is situated in a remote area where there is no access to electricity but he has a 24/7 arrangement through a personal electric generator. Report claims that he gets donations in U.S. dollars and he had exchanged them for Pak rupees from local money changers for several times. The third personality, despite coming from a lower middle-class family, has become rich overnight and is allegedly involved in smuggling of arms.

The Director-General Pakistan Rangers affirmed reports that foreign diplomats freely and safely travel in such areas of the region where even the security agencies do not have adequate access and there are reports that these diplomats pay substantial amounts to local people. After becoming an ally of the U.S. in 'the war against terror' Pakistani officials had decided to give status of settled districts to these provincially administered tribal areas of Dera Ghazi Khan and Rajanpur and two police stations and 15 police posts were established there in Musharraf era but no police official had the courage to join duty in these areas.

D.G. Rangers said "It is quite true that extremists get safe shelters here, seminaries provide them with logistic support and adequate training and they have direct links with militants of tribal areas. Troops of Pak Rangers had been performing their duties at this tribal belt however they are deployed at Kashmir and Rojhan for a few years where they are deputed for security of gas pipeline of national grid". The control of five thousand square kilometers area of Koh-e-Suleman adjacent to this tribal belt was given to the Border Military Police but as mentioned in the report it is not a crime to possess latest and sophisticated arms accordance with the existing norms of the area. Hardened gangsters seek refuge here after committing serious crimes like murder, burglary, robbery and kidnap for ransom. Some 'Farari camps' (camps of insurgents or outlaw elements) are also located here that according to Rangers' official impart training of militancy as well. D.G. Rangers said they neither have the mandate nor the resources to make the area a safe place. However, the high-ups have been made aware of the existing situation.

7

Religious Minorities and Punjabi Taliban

Punjabi Taliban has targeted government installations and religious minorities the most, in the course of the last two years. Where Christian townships were targetted, members of Ahmadiyya community have also been killed in planned attacks. Although the laws of the country do not declare Shiites a separate religious minority but Punjabi Taliban consider them non-Muslims like Christians or Ahmadis rather in some of their sectarian literature and fiery sermons they are categorised worse than non-believers. Most of the public places in Punjab, local transport, trees in the park and even public toilets are 'adorned' with graffiti declaring them the worst Saracens in the whole universe. Similar kind of literature about the Ahmadiyya sect and their sacred personalities is abundantly available. In a sample survey of a modern township of Lahore only we were able to find a lot of signboards and banners that give a reflection of general (mis)perceptions and public sentiments (of hate) about this community. The most astonishing factor is that earlier this type of propaganda was made by Deobandi groups and organisations, but as the time passed Barelvi outfits and groups have also joined this fateful campaign, for example Anjuman Talba-e-Islam, a student wing of Jamiat Ulmae Pakistan has joined this campaigns and it is especially at the forefront against Ahmadiyya community.

The societal attitude towards religious minorities has increasingly became harsh as the Taliban have gained strength in Punjab and if the clerics and orators of Ahle-Hadith are targeting the beliefs of Christians and Ahmadis, the clerics of Deobandi and Barelvi sect have also become more rigid towards them. Even such people are being invited in TV talk shows that directly, hit the beliefs and ideologies of religious minorities and promote hatred against them, among ordinary Muslim citizens. For example, if we someone type 'Dr. Israr Ahmed death penalty for apostasy' on 'You Tube' the shameful rhetoric of this famous religious scholar starts thus: "So the Parliament concluded that they (Ahmadis) are non-Muslims; though it was a right decision but still it is awaited to be completed. I'm declaring it for the first time and it may be noted. It has done no harm to the fitna of Qadianiat (Ahmadiyya belief) and it is still creeping rather flourishing despite declaring them non-Muslims. It is still spreading in the society like a cancer. And now they have got mentorship at the international level and the Western World has become their greatest patron. However this fitna could have been eliminated at national scale had the logical and legal requisites of said decision were also fulfilled. That is to prosecute the apostates as Islam only suggests death penalty for them". The video uploaded on You Tube on 13th July 2009, was watched by thousands of people. Moreover, the thoughts of right honourable Dr. Aamir Liaqat Hussein and the genius of the age, Hamid Mir were heard by millions of people and Dr. Aamir Liaqat was lucky enough to get directly benefited by the blessing hereinafter (some fanatics killed two people of the Ahmadiyya community after getting inspired by his fiery sermon). There is a strong possibility that the spirit of Dr. Israr would be quite content in the heavens with the carnage of Ahmadis in Lahore while other great clerics would also feel victorious.[211]

There is little doubt that members of the Ahmadiyya community are the greatest target of religious hate-mongers and they are being persecuted soon after the country came into being. They are being used as a bull's eye, be it momentary political expediency or appeasement of religious parties. Fear among that community and hate against them have been promoted for so long that their social exclusion and helplessness after these tragic deaths of around a hundred Ahmadis could be judged by the fact that any political party even any group from civil society did not have the courage to condole aggrieved the families. Of course people are very scared of the media that have an overwhelming majority of right-wingers and the extremist religious parties among their ranks. They also fear the edicts of apostasy. When the present Federal Minister for Kashmir affairs Mian Manzoor Watto was the Chief Minister of Punjab, his father, a follower of Ahmadi creed expired. Mian Wattoo could not attend the funeral of his father for fear of public resentment. Similarly, the then President of Pakistan Farooq Ahmed Khan Leghari 'inadvertently' visited the family of deceased for condolence but immediately all representative of media were specially requested not to cover this visit because the President of Pakistan was well aware of the bitter reality that either he be declared a non-Muslim or edicts would be issued that his Nikah (wedlock in accordance with Islamic tenets) had become null and void. That is why no important personality, public office bearer or government official console. The Ahmadiyya community. Deeply scared the Ahmadiyya community also refused to a raise any voice of protest against these shameful brutalities as they were afraid that they would become further insecure and nobody would come forward to their support.

The massacre of Ahmadis in Lahore was an act by the Punjabi Taliban which is directly linked with Al-Qaeda while they enjoy support from Lashkar-e-Jhangvi and Jaish-e-Muhammad in districts of South Punjab. Initial investigations also mentioned the name of defunct Hakrat-ul-Mujahedeen with his supreme commander Maulana Fazal-ur-Rahman Khalil enjoying a peaceful and protected life in Islamabad and his lifelong connections with Osama Bin Laden, Al-Qaeda and Taliban are an open secret. Majority of the activists of Jaish-e-Muhammad come from Harkat-ul-Mujahedeen that had joined the new outfit after an internal tussle. Very carefully "official and political level mentorship" of Punjabi Taliban and sectarian groups was also pointed out and certain political characters in direct links with Punjabi Taliban kept trying for their face saving in the media.[212]

The Provincial Law Minister, who often used to lose his temper at the mention of the Punjabi Taliban and South Punjab, admitted that terrorists came from various towns of South Punjab. According to police reports, terrorists stayed at Tableeghi Markaz of Raiwind and headed towards Garhi Shahu and Model Town from the same base camp of

Raiwind. However, the investigation teams of Punjab police were not allowed to visit Raiwind as it was utterly in contrast with self-created 'sanctity' of Tableeghi Jamaat that any finger be pointed towards it. Like the name of Jamia Haqqania Akora Khattak was involved in the Benazir murder but nobody dared to go there. The Chief Minister of Punjab, with all his fame for orders of fake police encounters and humiliating suspensions of higher government officers is in the grip of fear because he is fully aware of the clout and might of terrorist and sectarian elements and that many of the leaders from his own political party are heavily dependent on the same elements for all their political ambitions. Earlier, he and his brother, the former Prime Minister of Pakistan had tried to control the terrorists and sectarian elements in Punjab but in turn both of them became the target of these elements, eventually they were forced to cede to their power. The circles which got present Chief Minister elected unopposed from Bhakkar are fully aware of the source of this success. The Chief Minister of Punjab (who has the portfolio of Provincial Home Ministry as well) is equally responsible for the failure to stop this bloodbath of Ahmadis.

Where these brutal attacks on the Ahmadiyya community in 2010, disclosed the defencelessness of religious minorities in the face of ever-increasing religious violence in the state, a totally new phenomenon also appeared very strongly that the media, while performing their responsibilities were engaged in competition of earning blessings for the life after. As everybody knew well that there is neither any space for Ahmadis in Pakistani society nor its laws nor were they in a position to lodge any considerable protest, everybody was engaged in issuing vague statements. A majority of them thought it an opportune moment to target beliefs and tenets of the Ahmadiyya creed, which could make them more insecure in society. We do not have any option but to admit that constitutional amendment of 1974 and the later legislations during Zia-ul-Haq era for bade the Ahmadiyya community to adopt Muslim symbolism or any resemblance with the Muslim community and according to the figures and facts issued from time to time by Human Rights organisations, hundreds of Ahmadis are still languishing in prisons just for uttering Muslim phrases like 'Bismillah' or 'Assalam-o-Eleikum'. No political leader dare call them brethren even metaphorically, while innumerable media 'analysts' have written that

Ahmadis are traitors to Islam and Pakistan as well. Now the only thing remains for them to point out the areas where Ahmadis are living, so that religious zealots do not have to face any difficulty in persecuting them. No wonder such an action could prove a source of salvation hereinafter for said media (pseudo) intellectuals.[213]

Is not sufficient that a parliament comprising an overwhelmingly single religion declared Ahmadis non-Muslims and afterwards the most tyrannical dictator of our history further tightened the noose around their necks? It looks quite weird that it was the only democratically elected parliament in the world that had the shameful distinction to isolate a minority community simply on the basis of its beliefs. Many of these 'great' intellectuals often quote Ahmadi Caliph Mirza Nasir Ahmed that he considered non-Ahmadis as non-believers (or non-Muslims). But was it only Mirza Nasir Ahmed to declare that? There are thousands of evidences in Pakistan that cleric of one sect declared followers of other creed as non-Muslims and this practice is still going on. Mirza Nasir Ahmed was also a cleric of a certain creed and like others he could also declare anything about the believers of the tenets different from him. During the last two decades more than 460 such religious books have been published in Pakistan only where some of the well respected clerics and religious from different sects had proved that people from the opposing sect are not only excluded from Islam due to their beliefs but their Nikahs have been annulled and to prosecute them through death penalty is the religious obligation of every 'true' Muslim.

These books not only severely criticise creeds of adversaries but also their highly-respected rather sacred personalities are subjugated to character assassination and accusations of the worst kind. Most of them have been banned by successive governments but it made the only difference that they have gone out of easy access to ordinary people otherwise they are still available in seminaries and other specific places and they are also used as reference books in order to 'punish' the adversaries. There are at least one thousand video clips on 'You Tube' where clerics from different sects are declaring each other 'Kafir' (non-believer) and demeaning the elders of opposing creeds. It is not wrong to ask that here how many books has already, community published since 1974 about other Muslims of Pakistan where they are declared non-believers or their elders are treated with disrespect? Whereas thousands of books and pamphlets could be cited that demonize Ahmadis and insult their respected personalities.

It was fully justified to expect from media outlets to condemn massacre of Ahmadis and demand stern actions against the responsible elements, had they were not dominated by right wing zealots. But the situation is totally contrary to that and efforts are made to hide all the inhuman treatments against Ahmadis behind the smoke screen of false allegations against them and demonizing their code of beliefs. It clearly indicates that preparations for their ethnic cleansing are underway. Some are proclaiming them agents of MI-16 and C.I.A. and other insist upon declaring the seditious to Islam and Constitution of Pakistan. But nobody calls the elements non-believers or subversives to Islam and Pakistan who are involved in butchering people from other Muslim sects for many decades now, engaged in worst kind of massacre in mosques and Imam Bargahs, declaring people from opponent creeds non-Muslims and publishing ads in national newspapers about killing their males, confiscating their properties and turning their females and children into slaves. In fact, it is the last warning for religious minorities living in Pakistan that the state has absolved itself of the responsibility to safeguard them and from now on they are at the mercy of madrassas, jihadist outfits, sectarian organisations, extremist political leaders and pro-violence elements that are dominant on the media. Anybody calling them 'brethren' in reference to them belonging to same country, he runs the risk of being declared non-Muslim. He would be considered excluded from Islam till he apologised unconditionally. All the information about the cases and investigation proceedings against the people arrested in connection with these attacks, was kept in strict secrecy and nobody can claim to be sure whether the real accused had been arrested or it was simply an eyewash and that the apprehended people would eventually be released for want of sufficient evidence.

8

Attacks on Data Darbar and Karbala Gamay Shah

O n 1st July a group of terrorists burst into Data Darbar, the shrine of Sufi Saint Gunj Bakhsh at Lahore and killed 43 people and seriously wounded 175 in two consecutive blasts. It was an evening of Thursday when the shrine has the maximum number of pilgrims. Tehreek-e-Taliban claimed responsibility for the attacks in a telephone call from some unknown place while one of the high-ups in the administration of Lahore emphasised that no Muslim could commit such an act and it was surely India that was behind these attacks. Organisations of Barelvi sect announced a mourning period of ten days. Sunni Tehreek and other prominent Barelvi outfits demanded the removal of the Provincial Law Minister Rana Sanaullah who according to them had special ties with Punjabi Taliban and other Deobandi extremist groups. Despite strict orders from the Chief Minister of Punjab neither were any suspects arrested nor was the Provincial Law minister dismissed from his post.[214]

If 'Raw' or 'MOSSAD' were not blamed for these blast in police investigations, it would be easier to know about the instigators of these attacks and those responsible for promoting an extremist and violent Islam in Punjab. The evidence so far available of the suicide bombings attacks in Islamabad and Punjab point towards local extremists and jihadists who are concentrated in safe havens in South Punjab and who are also provided with protection by the Government of Punjab. The Chief Minister of Punjab now look more than a Chief of these extremist outfit than a chief administrative of the province and many member of his cabinet are not only providing Punjabi Taliban with a complete protection but are also bound not to do any 'one-sided' operation under certain 'agreements' made between terrorist and extremist groups and Government of Punjab in Lahore, Rahim Yar Khan and Bahawalpur.

It is primarily the beginning of a new sectarian war in Pakistan that is going to be fought with comparatively new "targets" and against new enemies. Many people have started realising the new situation but still it is very hard to convince many of the media analysts that a totally new and extremely lethal war has begun in Pakistan and especially in Punjab. There is no doubt about it that according to the standpoint of highly-powerful religious extremists of Punjab and Islam of Taliban brand shrines and mausoleums are in fact the centres of 'shirk' (idolatry) and heresy and the greatest hurdle in the implementation of 'real and pure Islam'. Taliban have already targeted innumerable mausoleums and shrines in Swat and other Tribal Areas. Now they have headed towards Punjab where they are pitched against religious minorities and opponent sects and they have started targeting shrines and centres of Barelvi sect. They have already killed Dr. Allama Sarfraz Naeemi, a leading representative of that sect while a life attempt on another leader of same sect and Fedaral Minister for Religious Affairs Syed Hamid Saeed Kazmi was made in Islamabad. An administrator of an extremist madrassa in Faisalabad (who has direct links with a banned outfit) declared in an open rally at Lalazar Stadium Attock that the Federal minister for Religious Affairs is a mushrik (committer of idolatry) and deserves severe punishment. Provincial Law Minister has special relations with the said cleric and the main reason is the support from his banned outfit that has helped win many leaders of Muslim League (Nawaz) in elections and come into power. It is worth mentioning that the father of the said cleric was considered one of the founders of Sipah-e-Sahaba.[215]

Since the clarion call for jihad in Kashmir was made, the outfits championing the implementation of 'Pure Islam', apart from launching special recruitment campaigns, have also taken upon themselves the task of 'cleansing' to the beliefs of ordinary Muslims. It is the result of these special efforts that sectarian killing in Pakistan has reached its extremes and mausoleums of Sufi saint and shrines are being targeted. The intensity of provocation by these torch-bearers of an extremist Islam can easily be assessed if one listens to their speeches at special congregation and sermons during Friday prayers. In these sermons the pilgrims to shrines and mausoleum are declared 'mushriks' and perpetrators of the worst sin ever for whom the death penalty is even a 'lighter' punishment. At present there are more than one thousand books and pamphlets in circulation in Pakistan where the visitors to the mausoleums and shrines are condemned as 'mushriks' and non-believers; they are also declared worse than beasts. The situation is a clear indicator of increasing power and influence of extremists and violent religious outfits.

The Deobandi (mamati) and Ahle Hadith sects in Pakistan consider visits to the mausoleums and shrines as 'shirk' and worst of sins. On March 2010, a highly extremist Wahhabi cleric Maulana Altaf-ur-Rahman Shah while addressing at a big seminary in Gujrat declared that our Foreign Minister is a worshipper of graves (said foreign minister belonged to a dynasty of caretakers of a shrine in Multan) and in our parliament there are many people like him and all of them are 'mushriks' according to sharia law. Similarly another Ahle-Hadith cleric Maulana Chaudhry Manzoor Ahmed also known as "lion of Punjab" while addressing a rally at Sheikhupura in January 2010 used quite abusive language about the President of Pakistan and announced that it is the people of Ahle-Hadith sect who will safeguard Islam and Pakistan. It is not difficult to judge the gravity of the situation; how bluntly the extremist ideologies are being promoted and how the sentiments of utter hatred against sacred places of other sects are provoked among the jihadist elements.[216]

Whereas the extremist jihadist outfits and sectarian outfits in Punjab have constantly been enjoying unconditional support from a number of powerful institutions of state, they have also made a considerable advancement in enhancing their resources at the local level. If Deoabandi organisations remained victorious against the opponents on sectarian fronts, the jihadist Salafi circles of Ahle-Hadiths, made remarkable achievements in the jihad of Kashmir and other prospective jihads and certain 'hidden hands' connected them to rich sheikhs of the gulf states and local affluent businessmen and traders so that they would not have to face any difficulty regarding resources. All the seminaries that had been dependent upon paltry donations from local communities or meagre allocations from Bait-ul-Mal managed to deposit 'heaps of riches' within the span of a few years. Many jihadist and sectarian outfits constructed properties and commercial plazas worth billions of rupees in Lahore itself. As these groups had their affiliations with right-wing parties like the Muslim League (Nawaz) and Jamaat-e-Islami etc., they also built a strong rapport with rich trader communities and had an arrangement of local funding as well. Banned Lashkar-e-Tayyba and Jaish-e-Muhammad got monthly collections of hundreds of millions of rupees from the main gold market of Lahore only to get their jihadist caravans going. When a difficult phase of jihad in Kashmir commenced after attacks on the Indian Parliament and Pakistan had to face a severe international pressure because of his home grown jihadist outfits, many sources of aids and donations to these organisations were also jeopardised and they were advised to 'take a nap'.

Although the external jihad was interrupted for a while due to international pressure, especially from India, their power within the country and a free flow of resources obliged them to divert their attention towards preaching and dissemination of their extreme and inflexible ideologies among the masses and there was a rigorous campaign of jihadist pedagogy as well as promotion of sectarian hatred. If one reviews the books published from the Urdu Bazaar Lahore only, ninety percent of them comprise either jihadist titles or literature full of sectarian dogmas and arguments or condemnation and apostasy of other creeds and sects. That also gives a fair idea of the direction these powerful jihadist and sectarian groups are steering the whole nation towards.

The government of Punjab is repeating a fatal blunder; that investigations about almost every terrorist involved in serious crimes were not carried out in an impartial manner for the last two years and almost one hundred accused of very serious offence were released unconditionally. Many suspected persons arrested from Multan and

Dera Ghazi Khan confessed to having close ties with terrorists fighting in Tribal Areas. Some critical analysts blame some key officials of Punjab for this situation because they are directly providing support to these groups in exchange for political favours. The Attitude of leaving lacunae and loopholes by police and other law enforcement agencies during the investigation process against terrorists and sectarian killers is the second biggest cause as it becomes easier for them to get released on bail or acquitted by the courts of law. In such a case, law enforcement agencies generally rely on some weak witnesses or themselves assume the role of a witness which is eventually declared unreliable after initial arguments turns out to be useless. Moreover, in the cases of terrorism and sectarian killings witnesses are provided by the plaintiffs who are either killed later on or they become too afraid to present any forceful evidence because police generally fails to provide them adequate security. Cases against Malik Muhammad Ishaq, the chief of Lashkar-e-Jhangvi are a prominent example of this stark reality. Around three dozen murder cases were registered against him but most of the witnesses against him were killed while the witness in the last murder case (that is about murder of many members of a same family) is too afraid to appear before the courts. So these hardened criminals, involved in many serious crimes, are being released on bail or acquitted with much trouble and show off their power with great gusts.

Where the suicide attacks outside Karbala Gamay Shah at Lahore on 21st Ramadan in 2010, the eve of death anniversary of Hazrat Ali (the fourth caliph of Islam), have resulted in the loss of 40 innocent Shiite Muslims, they also have warned the government officials that unlike past, the sectarian violence now has gone beyond the deaths at specific targets and now terrorist groups trained with higher sophistication, have adopted new strategies of a bloodbath and they are at ease with collective carnage. Just like the other tragic incidents routinely official statements of 'stern actions with iron hands against the responsible' were issued but afterwards nobody bothered to have any follow-up of it. It is very hard to say whether intelligence agencies plus federal and provincial governments are fully aware of the might and access of sectarian terrorists or that they do not have any idea about the training camps and nerve centres of these groups.[217]

Why the police, law enforcement agencies and civilian governments are so reluctant to have any strict action against the elements involved in sectarian terrorism? It is very easy to answer this question while the details we get are as following:

1. The ruling party of Punjab is involved in reaping political benefits from sectarian religious parties and has full awareness of the clout enjoyed by them in South Punjab and that People's Party on the other hand is not in a position to "exploit" their influence, due to its peculiar image among the masses.

2. Countless activists and leaders from extremist and sectarian outfits that had been banned during Musharraf era have joined ranks of Muslim League (Nawaz) in Punjab in the elections of February 2008. Though they have their political loyalties with Muslim League (Nawaz) but still have their sectarian affiliations with those extremist outfits and they play a crucial role in preventing the ruling party to take any harsh action against these elements.

3. The efforts by the Federal Government and Pak Army to launch any operation in South Punjab had been hampered by Provincial Government due to its close ties with sectarian extremists and Taliban and providing them opportunities to strike all over Pakistan because in that case the provincial government could deprive itself of political support in South Punjab while its relations with federal government were already strained due to the support of movement for a new Saraiki province in South Punjab.

4. As the defence institutions of Pakistan and subordinate intelligence agencies are following a so-called policy of 'distinction' among various extremist elements they presume that hard liner outfits like Jaish-e-Muhammad and Lashkar-e-Tayyba are not involved in terrorist activities within the country therefore they should be treated in isolation with other sectarian and jihadist outfits and there is no need to have a strict surveillance of them. The fact is that their sectarian standpoints, aims as well as their traditions to implement these concepts could not ever be ignored. For example, neither any concession about Shiite and Ahmadis could be seen in the views of Jaish-

e-Muhammad nor could a soft corner be found in Lashkar-e-Tayyba about them. It is worth clarifying that the former is not willing to grant any allowance to Ahmadiyya community due to its doctrine of finality of Prophethood while the latter is desirous of getting popularity among common Muslims from the platform of "sanctity of Holy Prophet". Moreover Lashkar-e-Tayyba and other Ahle-Hadith organisations never miss any chance to criticise Shiite and other "Muqalid" (followers of any four schools of Islamic Jurisprudence) sects of Muslims due to their anti-heresy and anti-vice ideologies.

5. It has also been proven that all political parties active in the current scenario are always looking for effective electoral support from extremist jihadist and sectarian organisations wielding influence at local or community level and this factor makes it difficult to expect a harsh standpoint against these groups and organisations at the level of the masses, not to mention any real crackdown. While powerful military institutions are not willing to come out of their infamous concepts of 'strategic depth' and these groups and organisations exploit this situation to continue with their campaigns of ideological 'cleansing' within the country.

6. The Deobandi and Wahhabi sects and their subordinate jihadist outfits taking advantage of the ideological divergence of Shiites and Barelvis have not only been successful in getting their significance recognised in front of Pakistani establishment due to long-hauled (private sector) jihads in Afghanistan and Kashmir under official patronage but the number of their die hard supporters in several powerful institutions of state has also remarkably increased. They continue extending support to their respective outfits and vehemently oppose any proposed harsh action them. That is why extremist groups and organisations continue their activities without any hindrance and opposition.

On the other hand, it is nearly impossible for the people having a firm belief in conspiracy theories and always looking for an 'external hand' in every tragic incident of sectarianism and religious extremism, to accept that the actual causes for present circumstances of Pakistan especially for rapidly expanding religious violence, are purely local. In fact these are creations of local media outlets that have more interest in getting support from their readers/viewers than to make them aware of news and perspectives of important happenings and wrongly interpret this mass support as their institutional achievement. That is why most writers and speakers communicate in a style-based on utter verbosity and in they in a total contrast to a curious and objective demeanour their talk normally has a tone of finality like a preacher.

Moreover, there are people who think that sectarianism and extremism in Pakistan is linked with economic and social deterioration and the situation in Afghanistan and Iraq and as soon as these countries along with Pakistan will come out of the present crisis situation, there would be an ideal peace among all the Muslim sects and all the Islamists would give up violence. These thoughts could be considered quite positive and optimistic about the future but not realistic ones. The roots of extremism in religious demeanours and sectarian myopia are found not only in economic and social decline but it is getting considerable support from so many other quarters as well. And biggest source of this support is the mindset of Pakistani establishment that is eating rust and even some of the most serious and irreparable losses to the state did not succeed in breaking this stagnation of centuries. This mentality was never in favour of turning Pakistan into a modern democratic state and it always had its closest interaction with anti-democratic forces. It is sufficient to assess this mindset of perennial self-defeatism by the fact that it has been perpetually been dreaming of 'victory' no matter that it is gained against democracy, the advocates of provincial autonomy or the neighbouring countries. Now these flags of victory are marching towards religious minorities and different 'unwanted' sectarian Muslim groups that according to its perceptions, are not loyal with Pakistan and Islam.

As far as religious and sectarian violence is concerned it is going to be more intense with every passing day because the battlelines have been clearly drawn among various rival sects. The Barelvi and Ahle-Hadiths have also jumped into this traditional battleground of Deobandis and Shiites. As Deobandi and Shiites initially criticised the each other's creeds and then started attacking sacred personalities of the opposite sects, similarly Barelvis and Ahle-Hadiths are also bent upon condemning and apostacising the tenets of each other and similarly the sacrosanct personalities of each sect would be the next predictable target. It is interesting to note that the Barelvis have not only built this 'rapport' with Salafis but an unannounced war with both (Hayati and Mamati) sub-sects of Deobandis has also begun. On certain occasions they also have to compete with Shiites so presently the "busiest" army at the sectarian front of Pakistan belongs to the Barelvis pitched in a multi-pronged factional expedition. A glimpse of this engagement of Barelvi sect could be had from the example of a young Barelvi cleric Maulan Yousaf Rizvi, who almost every day addresses religious congregations and rallies in one city of Punjab or the other. Before starting his speech he fixes a huge hatchet on the table in front of him and announces "I'm going to axe the false belief and tenets of opposite creeds and if any cleric from the other sects manages to prove my premises and arguments wrong, he would be fully justified to behead me in front of this congregation with the same chopper. The excited rally adores his unique rhetoric and chants slogan "Lion of Sunni Sect: Yousaf Razvi hatchet-bearer". Some of his fans have even uploaded his videos with the title "Yousaf Rizvi Tokay Wali Sarkar" (Yousaf Rizvi a saint with a hatchet) that could be watched on Youtube. This would give idea of the 'heroic' manner in which the Barelvis are entering into this warfare.

As far as the Shiite-Deobandi conflicts in Pakistan are concerned, they have reached new heights of hatred and unique tactics are being employed to eliminate each other. In the very strong tradition of 'Majalis' in Shiites, the debater with best skills of 'Tabbara' and slandering and defaming the revered persons of the opposing sect is admired the most among audiences. The situation of Deobandi clerics is not much different and much accolades are showered on the cleric and scholar that has the ability to refute the beliefs of Shiites most forcefully and could skillfully denounce their sanctified persons. It is essential to understand the role played by congregation, religious rallies as well as that of a cleric (mis)using loud speakers of local mosques, if one is keen to have an objective view of the causes of sectarian onslaught in Pakistan. The standpoint adopted therein as well as the tactics used are also necessary to be understood. It is by all means possible that some of the sects had played some role in enhancing the violence and incidence of killing in sectarian conflicts due to external factors, ongoing tussle between different institutions within the country or under instruction by certain quarters of the establishment. However, the positions taken against the others' beliefs during the process of interpretation of ones' own, is the real bone of contention. It not only intensifies mutual animosity but also serves as a demarcation line between various warring sects. Written or "literary ammunition" is also being used abundantly to "destroy" the opponent factions. It is quite an old and time-tested tool and written material has been used to level allegations and slander each other to claims of 'apostasy' of opponent sects. However, earlier it was being used by clerics and theologians only and the general public was rarely affected by it directly by these tools of hate and frustration. Generally, the clerics used to read out the contents of arguments presented by their opponents in front of their followers and refuted them with their own argumentation. But if one listened to the audio records of these erstwhile fiery orators, one comes to know how they had relied upon clear deceit and exaggeration in order to enflame the emotions of their followers or to prove their conceited scholarship. No doubt, they gained a number of personal gains by this technique but it created misconception and feelings of hate about the opposite sects among their followers that aggravated as time passed and turned into sheer animosity.

If the speeches of the Shiite and Deobandi orators of the 1980s are heard, one finds a host of examples of mudslinging and quoting opponents utterly out of context. If the decade of the 1980s is recalled, the Shiites of Pakistan were very optimistic about the Iranian Revolution and deemed it a major source of the promotion of the Shiite ideology all over the world. They were told how Imam Khomeini defeated the U.S., the 'elder or senior Satan' and annihilated the enemy's war plane that had come to the rescue of the U.S. citizens made hostage by Pasdaran-e-Inqilan (Iranian Revolutionary Guards) merely by dint of his spiritual powers. Shiite clerics of Pakistan also brought the regional tussles between Saudi Arabia and Iran to Pakistani soil. Saudi rulers resembled Umayyad that had a special grudge against the descendants of Prophet Muhammad. The Deobandis, on the other hand, specially targeted Imam Ayatollah Khomeini and his Revolution. Maulana Manzoor Naumani, a famous Deobandi cleric, was a special critic of Khomeini and his ideology and issued an edict that he was a non-believer. The Shiite Iranian tenets were looked in isolation with historic context and their centuries' old rivalry with Arabs was declared as animosity and hate with the consecrated personalities of pioneer era of Islam. People, who were traditionally devotees of the first four caliphs of Islam, were told that Iranian Shiite scholars and religious leaders do not respect the sacrosanct persons of the pioneer era and Pakistani Shiite also follow similar beliefs while in actuality the Shiites of Pakistan and Iran differ greatly in so many significant affairs.

In these circumstances Shiite clerics and orators and Deobandi clerics and speakers joined their respective forefronts of sectarian jihad and took upon themselves to 'sharpen the edges' of the beliefs imparted to their followers. Till the end of the 1980s the situation of occasional violence and sporadic incidents of sectarian killing had been already created. All the factions had started fortifying themselves with conventional weapons and all of them were getting material aid and support required for the sacred jihad to be launched in the near future. Saudi Arabia and Iran, both played a crucial role in turning the soil of Pakistan into a Shiite-Sunni war front and provided their respective supporters with all the requisite material for this (un)holy warfare. The anti-shiite groups also had the full support of the military circles of Pakistan because these groups were also easily available for all militant activities aimed at getting their targets in Afghanistan and India. Due to the ideological proximity with Iran the Pakistani Shiite could never get closer to local militants and adventurist and that deprived them of "training and support" like that of their sectarian adversaries. That resulted in their humiliating defeat in the sectarian war going on in the country. However, the war fronts of 'majalis' and rallies remained active like before and all the factions kept themselves busy in harsh criticism of beliefs held by each other at also gave a sound justification their militant wings of killing of each other and the fatal onslaught of sectarian war kept intensifying with every coming day.

Now we are facing the horrible result of this warfare and it would not be wrong to declare that Shiite in Pakistan are far weaker than their sectarian adversaries and their backwardness from number to militant power and training is quite apparent. They had to sustain greater losses than others in this long war of many decades now, from Parachinar to Lahore and from Gilgit to Karachi. The movement to declare the Shiites non-Muslims had become quite strong in 1997 like the 'Anti-Qadiani Movement' of 1974 when the Ahmadiyya community was declared non-Muslims this move could not materialise into reality due to various factors like a timely intervention by Iran, clear rifts within 'Hayati' and 'Mamati' factions of the Deobandis themselves in this regard and lack of 'courage' on the part of the then Prime Minister Mian Muhammad Nawaz Sharif. Sipah-e-Sahaba had prepared the draft of this piece of legislation so cleverly that had the bill been considered for discussion in the parliament, the majority decision would have resulted in its adoption. It is quite another thing that the clerics, specially the Deobandis ones, had succeeded in chalking the walls all over the countries with edicts announcing proselytisation of Shiites and still this graffiti could be seen in different cities and towns, announcing that Shiite are excluded from the Muslim community.[218]

The war on terror once again diverted the attention of the Taliban and other anti-Shiite groups towards the Shiite community and a new wave of sectarian violence was unleashed from Tribal Areas to the settled districts of Pakistan. Once again the Shiite places of worship and their congregation and rallies became the hot target of suicide attacks. An all-out sectarian war has started in Pakistan especially in Punjab and unlike the past, it is a multi-faceted one. The intentions and aims of the Barelvi organisations have also become clear and it is generally presumed that they are getting themselves better equipped at a quicker pace in the "armed struggle" which sometimes seems to be an effort to catch up with opposite sectarian outfits and groups. Still it would be premature to predict that like other sectarian outfits they would also manage to get the aid and support from those mighty institutions of the state that have assumed the role of 'patron saint' for such outfits. However, if they offer their "services" like other traditional jihadist outfits there is a possibility of them being fostered and tried at any potential internal or external front. There is no doubt that people with a background of sentimental affiliations with the majority Barelvi sect are serving at some highest offices of the state and also have their adequate representation in military institutions. Obviously they would not miss any chance to provide support and aid to organisations and groups from their own sect if they were given opportunities to 'earn the blessings for hereinafter'. Intensifying sectarian tensions in Punjab are a clear indicator of the fact that in time near future, Barelvi organisations and groups would follow the same path that was adopted by the opponent outfits and groups who managed to wield enormous strength within no time.[219]

9

Murder of Shahbaz Bhatti and Height of Uncertainty

In order to assess the number, force and influence enjoyed by extremist elements in Pakistan it is worth underliving the fact that majority of countrymen there are apologists and the remaining small number is highly afraid of them. No such discernible force is visible in society that could be called impartial or detached in the milieu of this rapidly advancing religious extremism, thus the people are forced to agree with this monster or they are highly terrified of it. The intellectuals, who try to avoid the issue or to give it some space in their analyses, could be counted among the ranks of scared ones. On the other hand the experts presenting some vague analyses and backgrounds are in fact trying to deceive the people so that they do not lose the sympathies of the masses while they could also save them from being pinpointed. Nothing can depict the atmosphere of utter dread more than the Federal Interior Minister declaring himself on to be top of the hitlist of extremists instead of initiating any solid action against these elements as well as keeping silent till they strike another serious blow the very next day. This silence on the part of Interior Minister would have made him countable among the accomplices had there been any thing like governance in Pakistan and surely he would have been removed from his office. In reality, it is the forceful nexus among the extremists that nobody is even left now who could at least promise a stern action against them. There is another sad example of insecurity among the prominent leadership that TV anchorpersons in their programmes humbly request the Federal Ministers to not to be too harsh on exremists and to "run for their life".

No doubt, the political culture in Pakistan has now drastically changed and in this atmosphere of uncertainty, political parties are fast turning towards extremist religious forces that there are serious doubt about the political identity of their own. Everybody is running after an armed support and situation has reached to the point that the Chief Minister of Punjab has to assume extra responsibility of a spokesperson for extremist religious groups and he is furious as to why after the gruesome assassination of Shahbaz Bhatti, the Federal Minister for Minorities Affairs, the Federal Interior Minister was pointing towards 'Punjabi Taliban'. The most striking fact is that the Punjabi Taliban are not only distributing pamphlets with their names printed on them but also called themselves 'Tahreek-e-Taliban Punjab', while addressing their local adversaries verbally or in written from their centres that are stretched from South Punjab to Waziristan. They also claim responsibility for every act of terrorism in the province under the same title but the Chief Minister of Punjab declares that using this term is a conspiracy to a incite provincial bias.

Basically, the Chief Minister of Punjab is very scared and cannot forget the bitter incidents of the past, including that of his elder brother Mian Nawaz Sharif, the former Prime Minister and now they had to face humiliation in Punjab by Lashkar-e-Jhangvi and eventually the issue was resolved in the shape of an agreement. As an extension of the same agreement he was also provided with full support in getting elected 'unopposed' to the provincial assembly from a district crushed by sectarian tensions. After the said victory, he provided the key activists of that banned outfit with a number of special concessions and privileges. At present this group has gone beyond his control but in case the Chief Minister of Punjab requests the federal government for any intervention in the province for a crackdown against this outfit and its supporters, not only the said 'agreement' would lapse but there could be serious life threats to the Sharif Brothers as well. Moreover, his party, perennially at odds with Pakistan People's Party and Tehreek-e-Insaf in the province, could also deprive itself of the armed support it enjoys under the aforementioned agreement and which had also helped it to gain a clear majority in the elections.

On the other hand, the leadership of the Muslim League (Nawaz) is also caught up in the dilemma that its ties with extremist and terrorist elements in Punjab are alienating the Pak Army presently very forcefully engaged in a 'war on terror' and the Western powers while both are presumed to play a vital and supportive role in the race for coming to power at the Centre. The Muslim League (Nawaz) apparently seems quite happy because of the hardships faced by the People's Party and is ready to offer its 'services' for assuming powers of the central government. But in fact it is hung between a number of apprehensions and reservations and as a last resort do not want to risk losing its power-base in Punjab. In a bid to "conserve" the power of Punjab, it is badly in need of support from local militants, and is paying a very heavy price for it.

What would be the condition of the state after such circumstances; there is no doubt it and situation could be easily judged by the killing of important functionaries of the state every other day. We have two extremely tragic and quite recent examples of Salman Taseer and Shahbaz Bhatti in front of us. Anybody with a trace of scepticism in him would be murdered in cold blood be it federal or provincial, no government would dare support him openly. The Pakistani society, embedded in multi-layered extremism and sectarianism is sending out some very clear signals to the international community, while the state is also faced with serious challenges on the diplomatic front and it is increasingly being pushed into isolation. Many people are looking forward to another dictator in uniforms who would introduce the concepts of better governance in Pakistan, whereas a number of very important state institutions are heading towards renewed adventurism and perceive that better leadership could be brought forward were the incumbent government sent home. It is another thing to have the concept of 'better' of ones' own while there is a dearth of any broad-based consensus among different state institutions.

Investigative reporting about religious extremist and sectarian elements of Punjab is such a job that could annoy many. The Punjabi elite, having an overwhelming control over power and resources of the state, are not willing to admit that at present Punjab is hostage to armed religious militants. Many of the office-bearers of the ruling party in Punjab are involved in the help to extremists, the proof of which has been provided by the media time and again. The high-handedness of extremist and sectarian elements in most of the districts in Punjab has turned the local administration utterly ineffective while the police provide them with all possible facilities. Political leaders seek support from them for their electoral victories and provide them with protection from law after being voted into parliament. The situation in South Punjab is worst because there is a greater influx of militants from Tribal Areas that are provided shelter in this region and extended full support for their terrorist attacks against state institution, opposite sects and religious minorities in Punjab. Many religious extremists could be seen from Dera Ghazi Khan to Gujrat who had once been leaders of many sectarian or jihadist outfits banned during the Musharraf regime but now have joined ranks of a powerful political party of Punjab and securing protection is the main cause for this apparent change of loyalties. It is very hard to predict whether Punjab would manage to come out of this whirlpool because as long as the Punjabi elite do not give up supporting the extremists, there would not be any improvement in the circumstances and weaker sect as well as religious minorities would still remain vulnerable. No one in public office thinks himself/herself to be safe after the murder of Shahbaz Bhatti. At the same time, while nobody is willing to utter a single word about these religious organisations and groups as nobody likes to be butchered so ruthlessly while they also know that it might not be possible to apprehend the killer and take them to task.

10

Beginning of Terrorist Attacks
in Punjab

The Al-Qaeda, along with the local Taliban has now targeted Punjab for in highly lethal terrorist attacks. Some elements from Punjabi Taliban had launched an attack on the General Headquarters of the army in Rawalpindi and killed one brigadier, one lieutenant colonel and many troopers. This attack was quite astonishing for the army as there was a general perception that the GHQ premises have been made quite safer by stringent security measures. Many facts and evidence relating to this attack were kept secret from the general public and the media as it was thought by the army's higher officials if this information were made public it would not intensify panic about the might of terrorists, their resources and the level of their reach but the facts about their previous connection as well as material support and training imparted to them would create much misunderstanding about army and its intelligence institutions. The name of a prominent militant Ilyas Kashmiri was also frequently mentioned in connection with attacks on the GHQ. However, as the army had never shared details of these attacks with any other institution, these ideas were merely based on speculation.[220]

The attacks on the GHQ, were in fact the act of those jihadists, sectarian and extremist elements of Punjab, who has been fostered by Al-Qaeda now. Although the popularity and linkages with Al-Qaeda in South Punjab are on the rise, most of the terrorist elements in South

Punjab have their main contacts through Waziristan and those old time companions of terrorists (who were attached with local criminal gangs not a long time ago) are its main source who have been providing them with safe havens when they used to run away after committing sectarian killings in Punjab. These elements are not ordinary criminals anymore as they have expanded their militant links and have become a part of the groups who are increasingly posing various threats to the whole region.

For example, it was hard to predict in two past that an extremist and purely sectarian outfit like Lashkar-e-Jhangvi would become so strong as to challenge the Pak Army at its headquarters. At present, Amjad Farooqi group of Lashkar-e-Jhangvi that enjoys of considerable support by various militants and donors in Punjab pose the greatest threat to army installations as well as to other security agencies in Punjab. Apart from a commando style strike on the GHQ, this group has launched attacks on the offices of F.I.A., the Police Academy and P.A.F. Base Kamra. Amjad Farooqi group is expanding its power base in Punjab and it seems its activists have Punjab in their mind as their prime target.

When this group pounced on the Police Training School Manawan, intelligence agencies guessed that attackers belonging to the Bait-Ullah Mehsood group and Ministry of Internal Affairs also held Bait-Ullah group responsible for that but the suspects apprehended later on hailed from Punjab and were identified as Amjad Forroqi group. Some of the suspect attackers at Manawan Training School apprehended later also included companions of Amjad group belonging from Tribal areas. They admitted that these attacks were planned at Dera Ghazi Khan while maps of Training school and other requisite information were provided by Punjabi youths.[221]

The real identity of the attacker on the GHQ has been concealed from the media and general public while some preliminary information only about the main accused, Dr. Usman had been issued. He was a an official in the Pak Army before joining the terrorist outfit. There were also reports that the terrorists had also worked as labourers at some under-construction buildings inside GHQ some weeks before launching this operation and had deployed landmines at the premises. There was a serious threat of huge losses to GHQ buildings in case these landmines exploded. However, they were later defused by the Pak Army as their locations were pointed out by arrested terrorists.

The connections of terrorists currently active in Punjab with Bait-Ullah Mehsood group can turn out to be quite troublesome as for the time being it is not possible for the state of Pakistan to dismantle his network. It was not long ago when Islamabad had been engaged in long-drawn "negotiations" with Maulvi Fazal Ullah of Swat, a close ally of Bait-Ullah Mehsood. It was busy granting special concessions to this group provided it did not attack Pakistani security forces. The arrested militants of Bait Ullah Mehsood and Maulvi Fazal Ullah were released after the "Swat Peace Agreement" and both these warlords had authorised Maulana Sufi Muhammad, the father-in-law of Maulvi Fazal Ullah to strike a deal with the authorities on their behalf. Even after the killing of Bait Ullah Mehsood in a drone attack, his cronies are still in touch with some highly skilled 'experts' of suicide attacks, including Qari Hussein and Maulvi Akbar who not only have a vast experience in such attacks but have trained suicide bombers in these tactics as well.[222]

The seeds of this prolonged spate of terrorism have been sown by security and intelligence agencies of Pakistan. For example, Maulana Sufi Muhammad agreed to strike this lop-sided "peace agreement" after getting heavy allowances and 'allowed' security forces regular patrolling in the valley of Swat with the 'permission' of the Taliban. Islamabad had provided misleading information about this highly disputed agreement to the people of Pakistan as well as the Western World and had tried to create an image that the state machinery had controlled the advancement by Taliban in the area and it would soon be cleared of terrorist elements.

The terrorist groups about whom tall claims had been made that they have been pushed away from their traditional sanctuaries in the rugged mountainous areas, have found some easy targets in the plains of Punjab and they are busy in launching, fatal attacks in urban areas of Punjab where they have an easy access on anytime, anywhere basis. The situation has beyond "official assumptions" and at present the terrorists from Tribal Areas and different regions of Afghanistan enjoy every possible support of local religious extremists in each and every corner of Pakistan. They are not only facilitating them with safer lodgings before such attacks but also providing them with information and opportunities to access their targets. It is generally estimated that at present there are more than one hundred and fifty thousand adequately trained religious extremists in certain big urban centres of Punjab and they have full capability of making any type of terrorist operation, a complete success. The mighty and powerful institutions of the state have specially imparted these militants with training of the latest commando techniques under their "specific agenda" at different points of time.

According to reliable reports, thousands of trained jihadists of banned outfit, like Lashkar-e-Jhangvi and Jaish-e-Muhammad, are not only fighting alongside Taliban occupying vast areas in the Tribal Belt but in every incident of terrorism outside Tribal Areas as well while the Pak Army and other law enforcement agencies are their foremost target. Moreover, they are engaged in eliminating their sectarian adversaries and never miss any chance to target the political opponents. The attack in Lahore on cricket team of Sri Lanka was also made by Punjabi extremists of Lashkar-e-Jhangvi and Jaish-e-Muhammad with the support from those Tribal militants who did not have any difficulty in disappearing in the city after completing that vicious operation. Sources claim that the same elements were responsible for attack on the Manawan Police Training School and it is highly possible that the arrested terrorists could provide some very important information about attacks on the Sri Lankan team as well.

Like Iraq and Afghanistan, Pakistan is also facing the crisis of maintaining the administrative structure of its state and symptoms of its disintegration are becoming increasingly imminent. The state machinery looks utterly incapable in fully comprehending the gravity of the dangers to its existence and to steer it towards a path of improvement while its political elite are badly divided and at odds with each other. Provincial governments are heavily dependent upon central government on a host of administrative affairs which look awfully perplexed, rather frustrated and exhausted. The Federal Ministry of Foreign Affairs is under siege by powerful institutions of the military that have a world view of their own. This way of looking at things is quite weird and in sharp contrast to existing norms of international community as it determines its external affiliations on the basis of so called 'honour' and 'enmity' instead of safeguarding one's economic interests. An overwhelming majority of populace is cursed to pass a life of material as well as emotional deprivation while a very small minority is living a luxurious life and they also from time to time, get a considerable share in the pie called governance and resources of the state by dint of their existing affluence, tribal clout and their shared material interests with high-ups of state institutions.

Attacks on Punjab in fact signify the fanatic whims of turning Pakistan into a fractured state structure like Iraq and they have a clear aim of dissolving the existing dispensation of civilian rule however weak or strong it is. Like Iraq, there is a prolonged radical sectarian warfare in Pakistan and religious minorities are caught up in an inferno of continuous fatal attacks. Terrorists have launched a well determined onslaught in each and every sector of society and the institution of the state, from sports to culture to every walk of life, is a target of extremist elements. For about one year the people engaged in the business of video CDs as well as working women in certain districts of South Punjab are receiving threats and being forced by some seminaries and sectarian outfit to leave their occupations in order to 'mould' their lives according to the dictates of sharia. Naturally the situation in these districts is becoming increasingly tense.

The government is unable to launch any effective crackdown against them or their local supporters and mentors. The abundance of these terrorists in Khyber Pakhtunkhwa is such that there is no city or town in the province where they are not present in thousands. They routinely cut off supplies of NATO forces to Afghanistan and in order to save its life, the leadership of the ruling Awami National Party prefers to spend most of its time in Islamabad instead of the provincial capital of Peshawar. After the terrorist activities had intensified in Punjab, the feelings are intensifying that neither is any place safe anymore in this Land of Pure nor is it now within the might of the state machinery to control the terrorists.

As far as wanton activities of these terrorists in Punjab are concerned, it is beyond doubt the next destination of all extremist elements where they enjoy full support by local terrorists and provincial administration do not have the capacity to control them. Thousands of activists of a banned extremist outfit have started returning back to Punjab who had migrated towards Tribal Areas a few years ago. In the course of operations in Punjab by the security agencies during the Musharraf era, a great number of terrorists had been detained while the remaining had sought refuge in Tribal Areas. Some reliable sources claim that a majority of the cohorts of Maulvi Fazal Ullah in Swat comprises former activists from various banned outfits of Punjab who had special training for jihad in Afghanistan and Kashmir.

Details of Suicide Attacks in Punjab
(From end of 2003 till March 2011)

2003

25th December

Fourteen people were killed and 46 injured on a second time suicide attack on the convoy of President General Pervez Musharraf. General Musharraf remained safe and it is highly probable that the suicide attackers were also killed in the blast.

2004

28th February

The suicide attacker was killed and four people were severely injured in a suicide attack on a mosque in Satellite Town Rawalpindi.

30th July

In an attack on the motorcade of the Prime Minister designate and serving Finance Minister Shaukat Aziz at the village Jaffer, Fatah Jang, district Attock seven people were killed including the attacker.

1st October

At least 31 persons were killed while 75 were injured in a suicide attack during the Friday congregation in an Imam Bargah at Silakot. Lashkar-e-Jhangvi claimed responsibility for this attack.

10th October

In the Mochi Gate area of Lahore a suicide attacker targeted an Imam Bargah killing five persons including two children while six people were injured.

2007

4th September

Thirty persons were killed and 70 injured in two simultaneous attacks at Qasim Market and R.A. Bazar in Garrison city of Rawalpindi. The suicide attacker first targeted a bus of defence forces near Qasim Market. Twenty of the 35 passengers were killed while a second blast occurred a few minutes later near police station of R.A. Bazar that killed 10 people.

30th October

A suicide bomber attacked a police post in the cantonment area, resulting in the death of eight persons including three police officials and injuring eighteen persons including 14 policemen. President General Pervez Musharraf was holding a meeting with Chief Ministers of four provinces in his camp office hardly a kilometre from the venue. Blood stains were even seen on army check points outside the residence of General Tariq Majeed Chairman Joint Chiefs of Staff Committee.

1st November

A suicide bomber hit a bus of Pakistan Airforce with his motorbike at Faisalabad Road Sargodha that resulted in the death of seven air force officers and three civilians, 28 persons were also injured in this attack. The Air Force bus was taking the crew from Mus'haf Air Base to Karana ammunition depot when the attacker crashed his motor bike at 6:45 a.m.

24th November

Two suicide attackers targeted army officials and installations at Rawalpindi one after another killing 32 persons and injuring 55. The first blast occurred at 7:55 a.m. when a suicide bomber tried to enter the district central office of I.S.I. (Hamza Camp) and hit himself to a vehicle of an intelligence agency only two hundred metres from Faizabad square that resulted in the death of 30 persons including troops on guard duty at main gate. In the meantime, suicide attacker's vehicle hit an army checkpost in the high-security zone not far from the GHQ and killed two persons and injured one.

10th December

A suicide attack on a school bus with children of officials of Kamra Aeronautical Complex, 50 km north of Islamabad, injured eight persons including five children. According to the officials of Air Force, a suicide attacker in a white car, hit his vehicle with the bus of Pakistan Aeronautical Complex School at 7:30. The bus was taking the children to Attock city and the suicide attacker died on the spot.

27th December

The Chairperson of the Pakistan Peoples Party and twice elected Prime Minister of Pakistan, Benazir Bhutto was assassinated in a firing incident at Liaqat Bagh Rawalpindi. At that time Benazir Bhutto was returning after addressing a rally of supporters. She was waving back at her workers and fans from the roof of her vehicle when she was fired at. At the same time a suicide bomber riding a motor bike blew himself, killing 30 persons and injuring more than 100. Some eyewitnesses say that three terrorists were seen aiming at the bullet proof SUV of Benazir Bhutto moments before the suicide attack.

2008

10th January

A suicide attack was made on the outer wall of the Lahore High Court a few moments before an anti-Musharraf demonstration by lawyers was going to start. The blast occurred at the G.P.O. square where around 60 policemen were present to disperse anti-Musharraf lawyers while a suicide attacker blew himself. At that time around two hundred lawyers were standing near the outer walls of Lahore High Court while some were marching from the district courts.

4th February

A suicide attacker hit his motorbike against a bus of the Army Medical College Rawalpindi near the GHQ taking students and staff to Medical College. Ten persons were killed and ten were injured. An eyewitness said that the attackers hit his motor bike against the bus of the Army Medical College in front of the office of the National Logistic Cell that blew the ceiling, windows and doors of the bus while many surrounding vehicles were also badly smashed.

A passing school bus was also damaged however school children remained safe.

25ᵗʰ February

Eight persons were killed, including Army Surgeon General, Lieutenant General Mushtaq Baig, in a suicide attack in Rawalpindi. He was the most senior army officer killed in an incident of terrorism since Pakistan joined the U.S. 'war against terrorism'. A young suicide bomber suddenly came in front of the convoy of the Director General of Army Medical Services at a busy road of Rawalpindi and blew him up. According to Pak Army sources five civilians were also killed and 25 were injured in the incident.

4ᵗʰ March

Eight people were killed and 24 injured in a suicide attack in the parking area of Pakistan Navy War College. The blast occurred at around 1:10 p.m. and classes at Navy War College were going on at that time. According to eyewitnesses and police officials, five army men and two suicide bombers were killed on the spot while one official succumbed to injuries in hospital.

11ᵗʰ March

At least 30 people were killed and 200 seriously injured, in a series of suicide attacks at Federal Investigation Authority (F.I.A.) Lahore headquarters at Temple Road and the premises of an advertising agency in Model Town Lahore. The eight-storied complex of F.I.A. was completely shattered to and nearby buildings seriously damaged. An American trained anti-terrorism unit was also located in the same premises. In the incident of Model Town, a gardener and two children died while 12 persons were seriously injured. The location of this advertising agency was not far from Balawal House, the office of Pakistan People's Party while a 'Safe House' was also situated just behind the advertising agency where some high-value accused of terrorism were under investigation.

2ⁿᵈ June

A suspected suicide bomber smashed his car into the Danish Embassy in Islamabad and killed at least eight people and injured 30. The Foreign Ministry of Denmark declared that five persons, including a Pakistani cleaner at the Embassy and a Danish citizen were killed while four embassy staff remained safe.

6th July

A suicide attack at Melody Market, a thickly-populated area of Islamabad killed 20 people including 15 policemen and injured 40. The main targets of attack were policemen who were deputed for the security of participants of the protest rally on the first anniversary of Lal Masjid operation.

13th August

At least nine people were killed and 35 were injured in an attack at Dubai Chowk Allama Iqbal Town, a busy marketplace at Lahore. Again the policemen were the main target who were on security duty on the eve of Independence Day. People were coming back from the Independence Day celebrations and the dead included two police officials and a woman.

21st August

Two suicide bombers blew themselves in a very high security zone of Wah Cantonment at the front gate of Pakistan Ordnance Factories and killed 30 persons while more than 70 were severely injured. It was the first ever attack by any terrorist group on an installations of the Pak Army. Tahreek-e-Taliban Pakistan claimed responsibility for the attack. Pakistan Ordnance Factories is a complex of about 20 different industrial units where artillery, tanks and anti-aircraft ammunition for Pak army are manufactured. The number of employees in this complex ranges from 25 to 30 thousand.

20th September

A suicide attacker hit a truckload of explosive material going to Marriot Hotel, the biggest five star hotel in the federal capital of Islamabad. This attack killed 60 people and 200 people, including a central leader of Pakistan People's Party were seriously injured. The said leader was scorched in flames when the gas pipeline burst. A U.S. official died in the attack while many foreigners were seriously injured. A comparatively unknown group, Fidayeed-e-Islam claimed responsibility for the attack.

6th October

A suicide bomber blew himself up at a big gathering of people at the residence of Rashid Akbar Nawani, a local Shiite leader and Member National Assembly of Muslim League (Nawaz) from district Bhakkar, some 260 km south-west of Islamabad. Twenty five people were killed in this incident while 60 including Rashid Akbar Nawani were injured.

9th October

A suspected attacker hit his car with the office of Anti-Terrorist Squad at Islamabad and six policemen were wounded as a result.

2009

5th February

A suicide attacker rushed into an Imam Bargah in Dera Ghazi Khan and blew himself. Thirty two were killed and 48 severely injured. Police sources stated that people were going back after a congregation at Al-Husseinia mosque. No responsibility was claimed by any known or unknown extremist outfit. Police declared it was 100 percent a suicide attack launched by religious extremists. Inspector General Punjab Police Shaukat Javed stated that the blast occurred just fifty feet from the mosque and it aimed to harass the Shiite community.

16th March

A suicide attacker blew himself at highly-congested bus stand of Pir Wadhai at Rawalpindi and killed 15 persons injured 25. Some sources claim that the main target were the participants of the Long March led by former Prime Minister and chief of Muslim League (Nawaz), that was due to pass from the same route after some time. Regional Police Officer Nasir Durrani told the media that the blast occurred a few minutes before the stipulated time. However the target were the participants of the long march. He said a suicide bomber riding a motor bike suddenly appeared who was already hiding in the parking of a nearby restaurant.

23th March

A suicide attacker blew himself near the entrance door of the "special branch" of an intelligence wing of the federal police, Islamabad. The suicide attackers died on the spot while two policemen were severely injured. According to the officials of special branch, about 120 policemen were residing at the headquarters and a majority of them was present in their barracks at the time. An official said he wanted to target the residential area. Police constable Faisal Khan was deputed at the main gate of the special branch. As he saw the suspected suicide attacker coming he grabbed him. The attacker blew himself, so both died at the spot.

4th April

A suicide bomber entered the check post of Frontier Constabulary (F.C.) on Margalla Road Islamabad and blew himself. Eight F.C. officials were killed while seven were wounded. The blast occurred at around 7:35 p.m. during an exchange of firing between F.C. constables and an unknown suicide attacker. An eyewitness said that the exchange of firing continued for about 20 minutes however police refuted the claim by saying that F.C. officials started aerial firing in order to ward off the attackers and avoid any further casualty.

5th April

A suicide attacker barged into Imam Bargah Sarpak in district Chakkwal that resulted in killing of 24 people including three children and injuring around 140. At the time a Majlis-e-Aaza was going on in the Imam Bargah and more than eight hundred people including women and children were participating in it. The majlis had finished at around 12:15 and people were preparing to go back when a boy of about 15 years apparently having Afghan features rushed into the congregation and blew himself up despite all efforts by the private security guard to stop him. Inspector General Punjab Shaukat Javed confirmed that the attack was a part of the ongoing wave of terrorism in the country and that the mutilated limbs and head of the 15-year old attacker were recovered from the spot.

27th May

A suicide attacker slammed his vehicle, laden with at least 100 kilogram of explosives into the building of Rescue 15 near the offices of City Capital Police Officer (C.C.P.O.) and I.S.I. at Queens Road

Lahore and killed 27 people while 326 were injured while two-storied building of Rescue 15 was completely demolished. The dead included a colonel of I.S.I. and 15 policemen. Eyewitnesses shared that two armed persons suddenly appeared in the street located between the offices of police and I.S.I. and opened fire on officials of security forces deputed as guards outside the building of Rescue 15. They also hurled grenades over security personnel while the driver of explosives laden vehicle tried to smash the concrete barriers to enter into the building but failed. Superintendent Police Sohail Sukhera said that three armed persons tried to target offices of C.C.P.O. and I.S.I. but only settled to hit their vehicle against the building of Rescue 15 about 100 feet away due to hard resistance by the security forces.

6th June

Two policemen were killed and four were seriously wounded in another suicide attack on the office of Rescue 15 at Sector F-8, Islamabad. According to an eyewitness there was a huge blast and innumerable shards were landing in front of his eyes. The spokesperson for police Muhammad Naeem said that many suspects had been arrested and legs of the suicide attackers have been found while police officials are still looking for his head.

12th June

A suicide attacker entered in the famous seminary of Jamia Naeemia, Garhi Shahu Lahore just after Friday prayers and blew himself up as a result the renowned Barelvi cleric and the administrator of the seminary Dr. Sarfraz Naeemi were killed along with six more people. The terrorists were already in Dr. Naeemi's Hujra (room adjacent to mosque) and waiting for his arrival. Muhammad Faisal a student at the seminary said that the terrorist posed as a student of the same seminary. District Officer Civil Defense Mazhar Hussein said that the suicide attacker used 20 kilograms of explosives. According to the police the attacker looked around 16 to 17 years old and was clean shaven with an attractive personality.

2nd July

A young suicide bomber hit his motorbike against the vehicle of

Heavy Mechanical Complex a subsidiary of the Pak Army and 36 persons were severely wounded as a result. Initially there were reports of six deaths. However, later the security forces confirmed only the death of the suicide attacker. Additional Inspector General Police Nasir Khan said it was a suicide attack and limbs of the assailant had been collected along with other evidence. Eight nearby vehicles were completely destroyed while many shops and buildings in a radius of half kilometre were damaged also.

5th October

A suicide bomber attacked on the office of U.N. World Food Programme in Islamabad and killed five people including a U.N. official and two Pakistani female staff members and injured six. According to an official of the investigation agency, the attackers clad in Frontier Corps' uniform entered through the side door of the office and blew themselves up of the reception. The office of World Food Programme is located in a very high security zone in Islamabad. The dead included a U.N. diplomat, an Iraqi citizen Bothan Ali, In-charge Reception Gul Rukh, Assistant In-charge Reception Farzana Barkat and staff members Abdul Wahab and Abid Rahman.

10th October

Eight terrorists wearing army uniforms tried to enter into the GHQ premises through gate number 1 and meanwhile opened fire on the army officials at the check post. After killing the security men they entered into the GHQ compound and took several people hostage after killing a brigadier and a colonel. Most of the terrorist, were eliminated after a long-drawn operation lasting sixteen hours while a few of them were captured alive. The terrorists killed eight army men in all.

20th October

Two suicide attackers blew themselves up in the International Islamic University Islamabad and killed six people including two female students. In fact the female students were the main targets, who were present in a cafeteria. All educational institutions of the country were temporarily closed after the incident.

23rd October

A suicide bomber attacked a check post of the Kamra Aeronautical complex on G.T. Road. Eight persons were killed and 17 injured. The attacker wanted to enter into the Complex building but the security personnel managed to stop him at the checkpost while he blew himself up.

24th October

A suicide attacker travelling by car on the motorway blew himself up while the car was being checked by security staff at Bhera Interchange and a police officer was killed on the spot. An accomplice of the attacker was arrested who confided that they intended to launch an attack on the red light area of Lahore.

2nd November

Thirty four persons were killed and 50 seriously wounded in a bomb blast at Mall Road Rawalpindi. The blast occurred in front of a bank where there was a big crowd of people drawing their salaries. The terrorists had selected the date for their attack because a large number of serving and retired army personnel as well as other supporting army staff were present there to draw their pay or pensions and were killed in the flash of an eye. The later investigations showed that members of the same group were involved in this blast that had attacked the GHQ.

2nd November

Two suicide attackers blew themselves at Motorway Babu Sabu interchange of Lahore. One other person was killed and 19 were seriously wounded.

4th December

Five attackers unleashed a reign of terror on the faithful engaged in Friday prayers at Bilal Mosque in a high-security zone of Rawalpindi Cantonment and killed more than 40 persons and severely injured 85 people in indiscriminate firing by automatic rifles and attacks of hand grenades. Nine army officers including one major general, one brigadier, two colonel and two majors were killed. Terrorists had entered this highly sensitive area by foot and were eventually killed in an encounter with army commandos. The sources of Pak Army declared that it was the most fatal attack in the course of the 'war on terror' while they held Al-Qaeda, Taliban and their allied terrorist outfits responsible for it. Wali-ur-Rahman, a commander of Tehreek-e-Taliban Pakistan through telephone calls to various newspapers claimed responsibility for the attack and declared it a repercussion of military operations in Swat and Waziristan and a revenge for the people killed there. After the assassination of Major General Mushtaq Baig, it was the second incident where most senior army officers were killed by terrorists. Many serving officers including some senior officers of I.S.I. were also seriously wounded in this attack. Seventeen young children who had come for Friday prayers with their elders were killed. Country-wide mourning was announced and the Chief of Army Staff announced that they were pitched in battle against such an enemy that is cowardly and barbarous and involved in the cold-blooded killings of innocent people engaged in prayers.

7th December

Around 50 people were killed and more than one hundred injured in two consecutive bomb blasts in the busy Moon Market at Allama Iqbal Town Lahore. Initially no terrorist group claimed responsibility for the blasts and senior police officials claimed to have arrested terrorists involved in these bomb attacks but later on no information or follow-up was available about the blasts or the people responsible for them. Although groups of terrorists apprehended from South Waziristan during investigations admitted to have committed these blasts but as usual no information was made public about this horrendous incident nor were the killers of dozens of innocent people taken to task. A big portion of the moon Market was destroyed in the attacks and people were afraid to go to markets, bazaars and other the public places. Though Chief Minister and other officials announced financial assistance of the affected people but eventually no practical step was taken.

8th December

Three terrorists, equipped with machine guns, grenades and explosive materials attacked the central office of I.S.I. in Multan and according to official sources, 15 people including officials of I.S.I.

There were cues of attacks on I.S.I. offices all over the country while such incidents had already occurred in Rawalpindi and Lahore. Contradictory figures about the number of deaths were presented while according to one report all the dead were officials of I.S.I. whereas the Multan office of the said intelligence agency was investigating from a group of Punjabi Taliban arrested from South Punjab. It was also heard that certain elements that had participated in the jihad of Kashmir through this office and had access to some very sensitive information about the office, were among the planners of this attack. Although the leadership of Taliban in Waziristan claimed responsibility for the attack, no information was provided to the Pakistani media as to whether those responsible for these attacks had been traced or whether they had apprehended. Like so many other suicide attacks, nothing was heard about the follow up of this fatal attack on a sensitive intelligence agency. Thus another important incident was trashed in the dustbin of the past. Later, the Qari Hussein group of the Tehreek-e-Taliban calimed responsibility for the attacks, and at the same time blamed the said office of I.S.I. for a majority of the arrests in South Punjab.

15th December

A market in Dera Ghazi Khan completely collapsed as a result of a number of violent blasts. These blasts occurred near the house of Sardar Zulfiqar Khosa, the central leader of Muslim League (Nawaz) and killed 34 people and injured more than 60. Some sources maintained that terrorists tried to kill Sardar Khosa and his family. The responsibility of these blasts was also claimed by Qari Hussein group and it threatened to launch further attacks in Punjab. These blasts in Dera Ghazi Khan intensified the impression that Taliban had enhanced the speed of advancement towards their targets in Punjab.

24th December

Two people were killed and two were injured in a suicide attack on an Imam Bargah at Kurri Road Rawalpindi. Had the attacker succeeded in entering the Imam Bargah the death toll would have been even higher. Usman Punjabi, the spokesperson of Punjabi Taliban, claimed responsibility for this attack. Punjabi Taliban on the one hand were engaged in targeting vital installations in a bid to launch a perpetual war against security forces and were attacking people from the Shiite sect and their places of worship on the other.

2010

8th March

The first suicide attack of 2010 in Punjab occurred in March on the office of an intelligence agency in Model Town Lahore that killed 14 people and seriously wounded more than 80. The federal government had warned the administration of Punjab about an eminent attack on this highly sensitive center of a secret wing of the Punjab Police and there were also reports that the Punjabi Taliban are planning to attack this investigation cell. Some sources claim that some very dangerous terrorist arrested from district Dera Ghazi Khan of South Punjab were under investigation there and one of them had confessed to attacking the Sri Lankan cricket team. The centre that became a target of terrorist attack was located in the middle of the residential area of Model Town and local people had requested the administration several times to shift it elsewhere because of its sensitive nature but it could not be shifted till its complete destruction in a suicide attack. The responsibility of this attack was also claimed by the Punjabi Taliban living in Tribal Areas who had threatened to launch further attacks of this type.

12th March

After attacks on the GHQ, extremists lodged another major offensive against the Pak Army in R.A. Bazaar Lahore that killed 63 people, including eight serving armed personnel, and injured about 100 people. In a series of suicide attacks of short intervals, terrorists targeted the cantonment area and killed scores of innocent people and due to heavy loss to human lives it is considered one of the biggest suicide attacks in Pakistan. According to media reports, terrorists were trying to enter garrison areas but failed due to tight security measures and set off the blasts in a busy marketplace. The responsibility for this gruesome act was also accepted by Taliban concentrated in Tribal Areas through a suspected phone call to newspapers and declared it a reaction of operations by the Pak Army in Tribal Areas. That spate of suicide attacks was clearly an indication that terrorists mere mounting pressure on the Pak Army to give up any possibility of further operations in Waziristan by launching an all-out onslaught against security forces.

28th May

On 28th May, highly-trained groups of terrorists barged into places of worship of the Ahmadiyya community at Model Town and Garhi Shahu areas of Lahore and remained involved in well planned and cold-blooded carnage of worshippers of the said community. Altogether 97 persons from the Ahmadiyya sect were killed in both incidents while all the terrorists were also eliminated during the operation by the police and law-enforcement agencies. About one hundred Ahmadis were injured in these incidents however local and provincial administration could not even condole with the affected families for the loss of lives merely for the fear of a harsh reaction by the right-winged extremists. In the process of live coverage of these incidents media representatives kept themselves busy in issues of 'more significance' than the loss of lives, like what should be the proper name for the places of worships of Ahmadiyya community? When a reporter inadvertently called them 'mosques', there was an outcry of condemnation through live calls for this 'unpardonable' blunder on the part of the said reporter and why any action has not been taken against the 'blasphemous' reporter who had called the place of worship of those non-Muslim Ahmadis a mosque. The TV channel was obliged to stop its emergency transmissions to extend its 'heartfelt' apologies and promised to take strict action against the said reporter. After that instruction were passed to all media outlets that the killed people should be called Qadianis instead of the Ahmadis and the place where they had been attacked should be simply called 'their places of worship'. As they were engaged in performing their Friday prayers like ordinary Muslims, all the reporters were instructed to call these Friday congregations simply a 'Qadiani worship' so till that evening they kept telling their viewers how these Qadianis were mercilessly murdered by the terrorists while they were busy in their worship.

It was later revealed that terrorists had headed towards Lahore from

Southern Punjab and first of all they had collected all relevant information about both the places of worship. In the meantime, they had stayed at the famous Markaz of Raiwind where they took sufficient time to plan the attacks while they were fully-equipped with all their grenades and sophisticated guns. When former Prime Minister Mian Muhammad Nawaz Sharif while condoling with the Ahmidis called them his brethren there was such a hue and cry against the former Prime Minister in all media outlets that he had to re-issue his statement with the amendment that Ahmdis were their compatriot brethren but still he remained a target of edicts of 'blasphemy' for many days. Neither could the elements responsible for these heinous attacks be traced nor could their locally influential cohorts be apprehended. The responsibility for these attacks was again accepted by the Punjabi Taliban but the Ahmadiyya community could not lodge any forceful protest for fear of further prosecutions by the religious zealots.

1st July

After about one month the terrorist burst into Data Darbar, the shrine of Sufi Saint Gunj Bakhsh at Lahore and the suicide attackers killed 43 people and seriously wounded 175 in two consecutive blasts on the evening of Thursday when the shrine has the maximum number of pilgrims. Tehreek-e-Taliban claimed responsibility for the attacks in a telephone call from some unknown place while one of the high-ups in the administration of Lahore emphasised as usual that no Muslim could commit such an act and it was surely India that was behind such attacks. Organisations of the Barelvi sect announced a mourning period of ten days and there were clear signs of eminent Barelvi-Deobandi confrontations all over the country. Sunni Tehreek and other prominent Barelvi outfits once again demanded the dismissal of Provincial Law Minister Rana Sanaullah who, according to them had special ties with the Punjabi Taliban and other Deobandi extremist groups. Although the Chief Minister of Punjab under such an extreme pressure, issued special orders for an immediate arrest of the accused of these suicide attacks, neither any suspect was apprehended nor was the Provincial Law minister removed from his post. Taliban were held responsible for these attacks and there was a harsh reaction all over the country. Even MQM arranged a massive protest rally and demanded stern actions against those responsible for attacks on shrines and mausoleums. The suicide attacks on Data Darbar were a sort of peak point of the campaign by Taliban against mausoleums started from Swat. This dreadful attack proved that extremist element went bent upon demolishing every place where there people had different tenets than their own, no matter they are mosques or shrines.

18th July

A suicide attacker succeeded in entering the gate of an Imam Bargah at Sargodha and causing a blast that killed four people and seriously wounding more than 20. Luckily, he could not manage to enter the main congregation hall and was stopped at the hall entrance by a security guard. At this he pulled the button of his suicide jacket. The responsibility of this attack was claimed by Lashkar Jhangvi Al-Aalami a group of Punjabi Taliban and a subsidiary of Al-Qaeda while it also threatened more attacks on the Shiite worship place in Punjab.

1st September

On the eve of the death anniversary of Hazrat Ali the fourth caliph of Prophet Muhammad, two suicide attacks and a bomb blast were made on the mourning procession at Karbala Gamay Shah Lahore that killed 45 persons and injured more than 250. The provincial government claimed that there were threats of such attacks and it was feared that terrorists would target the mourning procession. Tahreek-e-Taliban and Lashkar Jhangvi Al-Aalami jointly claimed responsibility for these attacks. It is worthwhile to note that Lashkar Jhangvi Al Aalami comprises Punjabi Taliban that were formerly a part of Sipah-e-Sahaba and Lashkar-e-Jhangvi and were involved in target killing of Shiites all over Pakistan. Lashkar Jhangvi Al-Aalami telephoned newspaper offices to claim responsibility. Shiite groups called it an utter failure on the part of the provincial government as it had the main responsibility of providing security to the congregation. Once again the removal of Provincial Law Minister Rana Sanaullah was demanded and allegations were also repeated that he had 'special relations' with extremist outfits and knew where the assassins of people from the Shiite community had taken refuge before and after their atrocious acts. The agitated Shiite demonstrators as a reaction to this dreadful attack on the procession of mourners, attacked a local office of the Punjab Police and damaged the building as well as vehicles parked there. It also revived the oft-repeated allegations and counter allegation about the presence of sectarian outfits and groups in Punjab and they never missed any chance to launch an attack on worship places and congregations of rival sects.

25th October

Seven people, including three women, were killed and 25 were seriously wounded in a bomb blast outside the shrine of Sufi Saint Baba Fareed Ganj Shakar. The terrible blast occurred at the break of dawn when the faithful were just coming out from the mosque in the premises of the shrine after Fajar prayers and there was panic everywhere. According to police sources terrorists had installed ten kg explosive material in a milk drum on the motorbike of a milkman and it was detonated through an improvised remote control device and killed innocent faithful and pilgrims. Sunni Tehreek and the members of the committee formed for the security of mausoleums and shrines, accused Deobandi outfits in Punjab and their patrons for creating an environment of fierce sectarian conflicts by targeting shrines of saints. The demand of sacking the Provincial Law Minister again surfaced. It is worthy to mention that there was a devastating suicide attack on the shrine of the famous Sufi Saint Abdullah Shah Ghazi in Karachi and many shrines have been targeted in Punjab as well while the provincial government had been making special and strict security measures for the shrines. These attacks are an indication that sectarian conflicts could intensify while outfits of majority Barelvi sect are also in the process of preparing themselves for a terse reaction and this could lead to further deterioration of situation.

2011

8th March

An explosive material laden car, exploded in a blast at a petrol station near the office of I.S.I. in Faisalabad. According to official figures,

35 people were killed in the blast whereas independent sources claim that the death toll exceeded 40 people. Later on Ehsan Ullah Ehsan the spokesperson for Tehreek-e-Taliban Pakistan telephoned newspaper offices from an unknown place and claimed responsibility for the blast and the office of the I.S.I. was the target of this attack as the Intelligence agency in collaboration with the local police had killed several of their activists in 2009. On the other hand, a Member of the National Assembly of the Muslim League (Nawaz) from Faisalabad told a TV channel that the attack had directly been made on the office of the I.S.I. and terrorist threw two grenades on security guards and then a car blast occurred.

Notes

1. *Daily Jang* Lahore, 'Attacks on Ahmedi Mosques in Lahore', 29 May 2010.
2. *Daily Jang* Lahore, 30 Feb 2010.
3. *The Nation*, 'Murder of Raja Asad Hameed Reporter' 27 March 2009.
4. Tanveer Qaiser Shahid, Editor *Daily Express* Islamabad, 26th Fab 2011.
5. Salman Taseer's murder in Islamabad: 4th Jan, 2011.
6. Interview Mufti Naeem: BBC Urdu 15 Jan, 2011.
7. Inhrafaat, *Daily Aajkal* Lahore: Jan 20, 2010.
8. Wajahat Masood, *Niwa-a-Insan* Lahore, June 2010.
9. Monthly *Herald*, June 2010.
10. Khaled Ahmed: *Nawa-e-Insan*, July 2010.
11. Majalah Dawa 15th May 1996.
12. Khaled Ahmed: *Nawa-a-Insan*, July 2010.
13. Riasat Ka Buhran by Hamza Alvi: Fiction House Lahore, 2002.
14. Monthly *Herald*, August, 1992.
15. Inharaffat by Khaled Ahmed, Takhleqaat Publishers, 1998.
16. Dehshat Gard ya Jihadi by Maqbool Arshad; Mashal Books, 2005.
17. *Militancy in Pakistan* by Khaled Ahmed; DCHD Report, June 2006.
18. Ibid.
19. Mumbai attacks 2008.
20. Militancy in Pakistan by Khaled Ahmed, DCHD report. April 2006
21. Majalah Dawa: June 1996 Lahore.
22. Pakistan aik Nikam Raiasat by Mujahid Hussain: Nigarshat Publisher Lahore, 2009.
23. Sectarianism in Pakistan by Khaled Ahmed: Aurat Foundation Lahore, June 1996.
24. Murder of Arif Al Hussaini, *Daily Jang*, 6th August 1988, Peshawar.
25. Sectarianism in Pakistan by Maryam Abu Zahab.2001
26. Sectarian war episode 3: Weekly *Aajkal* Lahore Oct, 1995.
27. Murder of Shia Doctors: Imran Abbas, monthly Araf Aug 2007.
28. Report Pakistan Institute of Policy Studies: Jan 2010.
29. Pakistan aik Nikam Riasat: by Mujahid Hussain, Nigarshat Publishers Lahore, 2009.

30. Ibid.
31. *Daily Jang*, Rawalpindi, 11th Oct 2010, GHQ attack.
32. Fanish Maseeh's death in Sialkot Prison: *Daily Jang*, Lahore, 15th Sep, 2009.
33. Human Rights Commission of Pakistan, Report, 2009.
34. Human Rights Commission's report published in *Daily Times* Lahore: 5th Aug 2009.
35. Minorities in Pakistan, report published in *Daily Aajkal* Lahore on 25th May 2009.
36. Aslam Maseeh blasphemy case Faisalabad, Special Report published in Daily Aajkal 10th Sep 2006.
37. First information report (FIR) Police Station Sumandri, Faisalabad. 15th June 1995.
38. Hindu girl converts to Islam, daily Jang May 3rd 2003.
39. Hindu sister's story of conversion: Nawa-a-Shamal Sailkot May 2003.
40. *Daily Khabrain* Multan, 28th Jan 2009.
41. Jamaat-a-Ahmdia, monthly report: Feb 2009.
42. Jamaat-a-Ahmdiyya, monthly report: Feb 2009.
43. Sectarian war in Pakistan: by Maryam Abu Zahab, 2001.
44. Facts report: by Maqbool Arshad Lahore,5th Dec 2008.
45. Markaz Dawat wal Irshad: weekly Aajkal Lahore, 15th April 1996.
46. Lashkar-a-Tayyba, Special Report by Zaigham Khan: monthly Herald Karachi, June 1997.
47. Militancy in Pakistan by Khaled Ahmed, DCHD Lahore May 2010.
48. Sectarian war in Pakistan by Adnan Adil: TFT Lahore 10th March,1997.
49. Attack on Christian's houses in Qasur District, 1st July 2009: Daily Jnag Lahore.
50. Women undressed by a Mullah in Bazar in Phool Nagar City near Lahore, Daily Jang 28th September, 2009.
51. Sectarian groups in South Punjab by Mujahid Hussain published in Nawa-a-Insan Lahore, June 2010.
52. Special report on Bahawalpur by Syed Qamar Abbas published in monthly Mustaqbil Lahore, June 2008.
53. Dehshat Gard ya Jihadi by Arshad Maqbool: Mashal Books Lahore, 2005.
54. Ibid.
55. Arrests of Al Qaeda fighters from Pakistan: The News Lahore,15th March 2005.
56. *Daily Jang*, Lahore, 13th July 2009.
57. Mumbai attacks, 2008.
58. Kamran Maichal Minister for minorities Punjab: *Daily Jang*, Lahore, 20th August 2007.
59. Fighters of Jaish-e-Muhammad: Daily Aajkal Lahore 5th December 2009.
60. Sectarian war in Punjab. Fact Lahore Special report by Zakria Khan June 2009.
61. Asianews, IT 12th November 2006.
62. Special report on Gojra incident: by Human Rights Commission Pakistan, 2007.
63. *Daily Jang*, Lahore, 2nd August 2009.

64. *Daily Jang*, Lahore, 1st August 2009.
65. Kamran Maichal Minister for minorities Punjab: *Daily Jang*, Lahore 20th August 2007.
66. Kamran Maichal Minister for minorities Punjab: *Daily Jang*, Lahore 20th August 2007.
67. The News Lahore, 27th March 2002.
68. *Daily Dawn*, Lahore, 28th March 2002.
69. Dehshat Gard ya Jihadi by Arshad Maqbool: Mashal Books Lahore, 2005.
70. Dehshat Gard ya Jihadi by Arshad Maqbool: Mashal Books Lahore, 2005.
71. Report special branch Punjab police Lahore, 2005.
72. Ibid.
73. Wave of militancy in Punjab: by Imran Saqib, monthly Mustaqbil Lahore, March 2009.
74. *Daily Jang*, Lahore, 30th Feb 2010.
75. *The News*, Lahore, 2nd July 2010.
76. Election 2008 and sectarian groups by Muhammad Asim: monthly Mustaqbil Brussels, March, 2008.
77. *Daily Dawn Lahore*, 7th May 1997.
78. *The Nation*, Lahore, 21st Feb, 2007.
79. *Daily Dawn Lahore*, 26th July 2004.
80. *Daily News*, Lahore, 27th July 2004.
81. Al Qaeda leadership in Pakistan by Maqbool Arshad: Fact Lahore, 2008.
82. Ibid.
83. *Daily Jang*, Lahore, 30th July 2004.
84. Special report: Nawa-a-Shamal Sialkot 2006.
85. *Daily Jang*, Lahore, 2nd Oct 2004.
86. *Daily News*, Lahore, 15th Sep 2009.
87. Ibid.
88. *Daily Jang*, Lahore, 16th Sep, 2009.
89. Militancy in South Punjab by Mujahid Hussain: monthly Mustaqbil Brussles, March 2007.
90. Special report on Multan by Muhammad Tanveer: monthly Mustaqbil Brussles, May 2008.
91. History of terrorism in Pakistan by Sarfraz Ahmad: monthly Mustaqbil Brussels, June 2008.
92. *Daily Jang*, Multan, 18th Jan 1997.
93. Religious schools and South Punjab by Mujahid Hussain: Nawa-a-Insan Lahore, Dec 2009.
94. *Daily Khabrain*, Multan, 31st July 2009.
95. Sectarianism in South Punjab by Zakria Khan: Fact report Lahore, June 2010.
96. *The News*, Lahore, 14th July 2009.
97. *Daily Dawn*, Lahore, 15th July 2009.
98. *Daily Khabrain*, Multan, 17th July 2009.
99. Special report by Punjab Police, Lahore 2009.

100. Sectarian killings in Punjab by Muhammad Ali, Fact Lahore, 2009.
101. *Daily Khabrain* Multan, 24th Dec 2006.
102. *Daily Express* and *Daily Jang Lahore*, 6th Feb 2009.
103. Dera Ghazi Khan, Police report on suicide attack in city, 10th March 2008.
104. *Daily Khabrain* Multan, 10th March 2008.
105. *Rise of Taliban in Punjab* by Sarfraz Ahmed monthly Mustaqbil April 2010.
106. *The News* Lahore, 2nd Nov 2007.
107. Ibid.
108. Dehshat Gard ya Jihadi by Maqbool Arshad: Mashal Books Lahore, 2005.
109. Sectarianism in Punjab by Zaigham Khan: Monthly Mustaqbil Lahore Dec 2009.
110. Sectarian gropus and their networks in Punjab: by Maryam Abu Zahab, 2007.
111. *Daily Dawn Lahore*, 4th Jan 1999.
112. *The News* Karachi, 3rd May 2002.
113. *Daily Dawn* Karachi, 15th June 2002.
114. Murder of Commissioner Sargodha Syed Tajmal Abbas by Adnan Adil TFT, 15 August 1995.
115. Maolana Muhammad Akram Awan and his group, report by Muhammad Abbas, monthlay Almurshid Chakwal, June 2000.
116. Maolana Muhammad Akram Awan and his group, report by Muhammad Abbas, monthlay Almurshid Chakwal, June 2000.
117. *Monthly Al Murshid* Lahore, April 2000.
118. *Monthly Al Murshid* Lahore, August 2000.
119. Interview Maolana Muhammad Akram Awan, Daily Pakistan Lahore magazine 10th August 2000.
120. *Monthly Al Murshid* Lahore, Jan 2000.
121. *Daily Jang* Rawalpindi, 24th Dec 2000.
122. Khaled Sheikh Muhammad's arrest in Rawalpindi: 1st March 2003.
123. Ibid.
124. Militancy in South Punjab by Muhammad Zakria Khan: Monthly Mustaqabil Lahore, March 2010.
125. Forest Department Report Dera Ghazi Khan, 2009.
126. Ameer Jamaat-a-Islami, Multan Zone 10.
127. *Daily Khabrain Multan*, 6th Feb, 2009.
128. Jaish-e-Muhammad Centre, Bahawalpur by Muhammad Kamran Fact report Lahore, 2010.
129. Religious Schools in Bahawalpur Special Police report, 2008.
130. Diretor General Rangers's report, 2009.
131. *Daily Jang* Rawalpindi, 2nd March 2003.
132. Report on Lashkar-a-Tayyba by Mujahid Hussain weekly Aajkal 15th June 1995.
133. DIG Police Dr Shaoib Saddal's press conference in Rawalpindi, Daily Jang, 5th March, 1996.
134. Sectarianism in Pakistan by Mujahid Hussain, *Weekly Aajkal* monthly Mustaqbil July 2009.

135. Lashkar-a-Tayaba by Mujahid Hussain, *Weekly Aajkal* June 15th 1995.
136. Fatwa about Afghan Jihad by Maulana Mufti Mehmood, 1979.
137. Lashkar-a-Tayaba by Mujahid Hussain, *Weekly Aajkal* June 15th 1995.
138. Sectarianism in Pakistan: by Mujahid Hussain, *Monthly Mustaqbil* July 2009.
139. Lashkar-a-Tayaba by Mujahid Hussain, *Weekly Aajkal* June 15th 1995.
140. Murder of Irani Counslate Sadiq Ganji in Lahore 19th Dec, 1990.
141. Ibid.
142. Lashkar-a-Tayaba by Mujahid Hussain, *Weekly Aajkal* June 15th 1995.
143. Abu Jihad Lashkar-a-Tayyba: ex militant. Fact report 16th June, 1997.
144. Mumbai Attack, 26th November 2008.
145. Militancy and Sectarian war in Pakistan by Zaigham Khan Jan 1999: Monthly Hearld.
146. Ibid.
147. Abu Abdullah Shaheed Majalh al Dawa, Dec, 1997.
148. Ibid.
149. Muhammad Sarwar, father Shaheed Azhar Sarwar, Majalah al Dawa, Dec 1997.
150. Abu Alhaibat Shaheed: Majalah al Dawa, Dec 1997.
151. Special report Majaha al Dawa, Dec 1997.
152. Net work of Lashkar-a-Tayab in India, Majalah al Dawa, Dec 1997.
153. Fadai Hamlay (suicide attacks) by Lashkar-a-Tayyba in Kashmir from 1999 to 2002
154. Attack on Indian Parliament, 17th Dec 2001.
155. State Department Report on Jamaat-a-Dawa: 2008.
156. Mumbai blast: 11th July 2006.
157. Lashkar-a-Tayyba and Earth Quike 2005
158. Special report BBC News: 3rd March 2009.
159. Interior Ministry of Pakistan, Special report, 15th July 2009.
160. Highjacking of Indian Airliner from Khatmandu: 1999.
161. Jihadi culture and Jaish-e-Muhammad in Punjab by Muhammad Sarfraz: monthly Mustaqbil Lahore, July 2010.
162. Jihadi culture and Jaish-e-Muhammad in Punjab by Muhammad Sarfraz: monthly Mustaqbil Lahore, July 2010.
163. First suiside attack in Sirinagar by Jaish-e-Muhammad, 19th April 2000.
164. Masood Azhar, *Daily Jang Lahore* 15th December 2002.
165. Special report about attacks on Musharraf: IB Rawalpindi.June 2005.
166. Highjacking of an Indian plane, 1999.
167. Second ban on Jaish-e-Muhammad in 2003.
168. Ibid.
169. Asad Hameed's special report on Jihad Fund: Fact Lahore Oct 2009.
170. London attack, 7th July 2005.
171. Rashid Raouf's arrest from Bahawalpur: *Daily Jang*, 10th August 2002.
172. Rashid Raouf was released, *Daily Jang* Lahore 13th December 2006.
173. Rashid Raouf's death in Drone Attack: *Daily Jang* Lahore, 23rd Nov. 2008.
174. England's demand in 20th April 2009. *Daily Mail* London.

175. *Weekly Alqalam* Lahore 2nd December 2008.
176. *The News* 23rd June 2008.
177. *The News* Lahore23rd June 2008.
178. Agreement between CBI (India) and FIA (Pakistan) 1989.
179. Interior Minister Rehman Malik, 14th Jan 2009.
180. *Daily Dawn* Lahore 8th May 2009.
181. *Daily Times* Lahore, 18th June 2009.
182. Sectarianism in Pakistan: by Maryam Abu Zahab, 2001.
183. Ibid.
184. *Daily Jang* Lahore 20th Jan, 1997.
185. Sectarianism and Jhang by Salim Ilahi, 2002.
186. Murder of Maolana Azam Tariq, *Daily Jang Lahore*, 5th Oct 2003.
187. *Daily Jang* Lahore, 8th April 2006.
188. Ban on Sipah-a-Sahaba, 12th Jan, 2002.
189. *The News* Lahore special report, 27th March 1995.
190. Taliban's Afghanistan by Raheem Ullah Yousafzai: The News Rawalpindi, 26th December 1996.
191. Murder of a Polish by Taliban, the News Lahore 8th Feb 2009.
192. Human Rights Pakistan Report: 2009.
193. Terrorist or Jihadi by Maqbol Arshad: Mashal Books Lahore, 2005.
194. Asian Development Bank report on Pakistan: 2009.
195. Punjabi Taliban and Rana Sana Ullah by Mujahid Hussain, Monthly Mustaqbil Brussels, April 2010.
196. Sectarian war in Punjab by Sarfraz Ahmed: Monthly Mustaqbil Brussels, June 2010.
197. Mumbai attacks, 26th Nov 2008.
198. Muhammad Ahmed Ludhianvi, ARY TV interview 20th June, 2010.
199. Ibid.
200. Ibid.
201. Riaz Hussain Pirzada Member National Assembly, *Daliy Jnag* Lahore, 13th June 2007.
202. Report by Special Branch Police Punjab, May 2010.
203. Sectarian War in Faisalabad by Khaled Mehmood Monthly Mustaqbil Brusels, Nov 2010.
204. Militancy in Gujrat: by Muhammad Abbas, http//www.gujratlink.com,27th Aug 2010.
205. Militancy in South Punjab by Zakria Khan: Fact Report 2010.
206. Forest Department report Punjab, 2010.
207. Amir Jamat-a-Islami, Multan zone 10.
208. *Daily Khabrain* Multan, 6th Feb, 2009.
209. Jaish-e-Muhammad in Bahawalpur by Muhammad Kamran: Fact report, June 2010.
210. Religiuos Schools in Bhawalpur: Special Report by Punjab Police, June 2010.
211. Youtube vedio by Dr Israr Ahmed: uploaded on 13th July, 2009.

212. Attacks on Ahmadies in Lahore, 28th May 2010.

213. Ibid.

214. *Daily Jang Lahore*, 2nd July 210.

215. Maolana Zahid Qasmi's Khutba in Atock, 10th May 2010.

216. Maolana Altaf Reham Shah's Khutba in Gujrat, 5th March 2010.

217. Attack on Karbla Gamay Shah Lahore, 1st September 2010.

218. Namos-a- Sahaba bill: Tareekhi Dastawaiz, 1997.

219. New Sectarian war in Punjab by Khaled Mehmood: Fact report May 2010.

220. *Daily Jang* Rawalpindi: 10th October 2009.

221. *Daily Jang* Lahore, 30th March 2009.

222. Swat peace agreement: 16th February 2009.

Index

Council of Islamic Ideology (CII), 8

D

Daily Dawn, 128
Daily Times, 120
Darkhwasti, Maulana, 45
Data Darbar and Karbala Gamay Shah
　Attacks on, 171-83
'Dawat-e-Islami', 152
'days of ignorance', 50
'decisive declaration', 17
Deputy Inspector General (D.I.G.), 52
Dr. Fazal-ur-Rehman, 8

E

Elahi, Chaudhry Pervez, 64

F

F.B.I., 66
Faisalabad, 38
Farooqi, Amjad, 57
FATA, 95
'fatwa', 14
Federal Investigation Authority (F.I.A.),
　142, 189

G

General Zia-ul-Haq, 6, 8, 9, 13, 14, 15,
　29, 37, 42
　era, 101, 143
'geo-political', 6
George Tenet the chief of C.I.A., 54
'Ghazvi-e-hind', 100
Gilani, Ahmed, 66
Gilani, Syed Yousaf Raza, 150
Gojra, 27
　incident of, 24
Gul, Lt Gen (r) Hameed, 2, 42, 102
Gulbadin Hikmatyar, 7
Gunj Bakhsh, Sufi Saint, 171

H

Harkat-ul-Ansar, 58, 88
Harkat-ul-Jihad-ul-Islami, 78
Harkat-ul-Mujahedeen, 64, 88
Hassan, Munawar, 2

Hayden, Michael, director of C.I.A.,, 115
'hidden hands', 174
Holy Koran, 24, 27, 72
　damaged copy of the, 51
Holy Prophet Muhammad, 28, 43
Husain, Abdullah, 66
Hussain, Mufti Jaffer, 13-14

I

'Idara Khidmat-e-Khalq', 113
Imamia Student Organisation (I.S.O.),
　14, 97
'impartial and dauntless media', 31
'important personality', 54
Indian Central Bureau of Investigation
　(C.B.I.), 127
Indian National Congress, 44
'inside story', 18
Inter-Services Intelligence (ISI), 7, 10, 11,
　15, 17, 18, 20, 42, 45, 98, 99, 101,
　102, 113
　expertise from, 12
Iran, revolution in, 37
Iraq, 3
Ishaq, Malik Muhammad, 46, 73
Islamabad, attack on a church at, 57

J

Jacobabad airport
　Attempt to hit, 57
Jaish-e-Muhammad (J-e-M), 44, 45, 47,
　60, 61, 76, 78, 79, 84, 88, 93, 118,
　119, 120-125, 146, 148, 153, 161,
　167, 174, 176, 191
Jamaat-e-Islami, 2, 3, 6, 7, 10, 91
Jamaat-ud-Dawa (J-u-D), 11-13, 40,
　103, 112, 114, 145
'Jamia Al-muntazir', 40
Jamiat Ahle Hadith, 40
Jamiat Ghurba-e-Ahle-Hadith, 11
Jamiat-ul-Mujahedeen, 74, 106
Jatt-Rajput tug-of-war, 61
Jhang, District of, 49
Jhangvi, 191
Jhangvi, Haq Nawaz, murdered, 129